BEETHOVEN'S CRITICS

Contents

List of Abbreviations	*page* vi
Preface	vii
Introduction	1
1 The Leipzig *Allgemeine Musikalische Zeitung*	5
2 Berlin and A. B. Marx	45
3 Other German sources: the controversy over the late music	65
4 French Beethoven criticism	105
5 The Fifth Symphony	126
Conclusion	144
Appendix A Index of reviews cited	153
Appendix B Originals of quotes given in translation	157
Notes	166
Bibliography	175
Index	181

Abbreviations

AMZ	*Allgemeine Musikalische Zeitung*
BAMZ	*Berliner Allgemeine Musikalische Zeitung*
Caec.	*Caecilia: eine Zeitschrift für die Musikalische Welt*
WAMZ	*Wiener Allgemeine Musikalische Zeitung*

BEETHOVEN'S CRITICS

Aesthetic dilemmas and resolutions during the composer's lifetime

ROBIN WALLACE

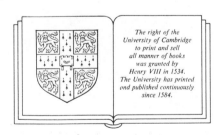

The right of the
University of Cambridge
to print and sell
all manner of books
was granted by
Henry VIII in 1534.
The University has printed
and published continuously
since 1584.

CAMBRIDGE UNIVERSITY PRESS

Cambridge
London   New York   New Rochelle
Melbourne   Sydney

Published by the Press Syndicate of the University of Cambridge
The Pitt Building, Trumpington Street, Cambridge CB2 1RP
32 East 57th Street, New York, NY 10022, USA
10 Stamford Road, Oakleigh, Melbourne 3166, Australia

First published 1986

Printed in Great Britain at
the University Press, Cambridge

British Library cataloguing in publication data
Wallace, Robin
Beethoven's critics : aesthetic dilemmas and
resolutions during the composer's lifetime.
1. Beethoven, Ludwig van — Criticism and
interpretation
I. Title
780'.92'4   ML410.B4

Library of Congress cataloguing in publication data
Wallace, Robin.
Beethoven's critics.
Bibliography.
Includes index.
1. Beethoven, Ludwig van, 1770–1827 — Criticism and
interpretation. 2. Beethoven, Ludwig van, 1770–1827 —
Appreciation. I. Title.
ML410.B4W24   1986   780'.92'4   86-8250

ISBN 0 521 30662 0

WS

Preface

This book has been many years in the making. Along the way, it has had the assistance of some extraordinary people. First among them was my piano teacher, Pat Carter, who bought for me the scores of the Beethoven string quartets when I was 15 years old. Since that time, I have been convinced that the supposedly impenetrable late quartets represent the summit of human creativity. My decision to make a career in teaching and writing about music also dates from this comparatively early age. During my undergraduate years at Oberlin, my thesis adviser, Sylvan Suskin, was particularly encouraging. Without his inspiration, I might not have braved the whims of an unstable job market and gone on to do graduate work in musicology.

It should be no secret that this book bears a distinct resemblance to the doctoral dissertation which I wrote at Yale. For his help on that *magnum opus*, I must particularly thank Leon Plantinga, who trimmed away mercilessly at my ambitious prospectus and kept me from putting my foot in my mouth too often. His wide knowledge both of nineteenth-century music and of philosophy were a constant inspiration to me, yet he left me with the satisfying feeling that what I had written was my own work from start to finish.

My wife, Lara, was unfailingly supportive. Particularly during the final years of work, she spent many thankless hours listening to my ideas take shape, and made me feel that what I was writing about was important enough to lose sleep over. She also proofread and typed the final manuscript.

Claude Palisca, Reinhard Strohm, Jane Stevens and Owen Jander also gave much valuable help along the way. I owe a special debt of gratitude to my colleague at California State University at Long Beach, William Weber, who contributed from his special expertise in the field of history to many of the ideas which helped transform this work from a doctoral thesis into a book.

Music historians, beware: this is not primarily a book about Beethoven's music. It is a book about how people reacted to that music during its first crucial years, and as such I hope that it will be helpful not only to

Preface

Beethoven specialists but to all critics, theorists and historians of music who continue to define the reception of music, both past and present, in the late twentieth century.

Robin Wallace

Long Beach, California
July, 1985

Introduction

This book will present the history of Beethoven's reception in the musical press of his time. Few writings about music can have been as little read or as widely misused as the reviews whose first published history appears in the following pages. Only one critic – E. T. A. Hoffmann – is known to most historians, even though he is in many ways the least representative of all the authors we shall examine. This rather limited view has not prevented some scholars from repeating time-honored clichés about Beethoven's critical reception.

No myth can have been so obstinately preserved as the claim that Beethoven's music was not well received by the press. Anyone who has read Nicolas Slonimsky's *Lexicon of Musical Invective* can quote the Leipzig *Zeitung für die Elegante Welt*, which described the second symphony as 'a hideously writhing wounded dragon that refuses to expire and, though bleeding in the finale, furiously beats about with its tail erect',[1] or Alexander Oulibicheff, who found in the Fifth Symphony 'discords to shatter the least sensitive ear'.[2] Slonimsky deliberately gives the impression that these quotes are typical. They are not. Beethoven was almost at once, and universally, recognized as a composer of genius, and this recognition is reflected in practically everything that was written about him during his lifetime.

Even more surprising, perhaps, is the fact that these reviews, with the exception of those by Hoffmann, provide no evidence that Beethoven's contemporaries accepted the views of early Romantic philosophers on musical aesthetics, even though the contrary opinion has been almost universally maintained by modern writers on the subject. In his otherwise much maligned book *Music in the Romantic Era*, Alfred Einstein presents what has since become the canonical view of music theory in the first half of the nineteenth century. Quoting the Danish philosopher Hans Christian Oersted, whom he juxtaposes with Schelling, Hegel and Schopenhauer, Einstein finds that one of the central characteristics of this epoch was its rejection of an earlier preference for vocal and imitative music in favor of the pure instrumental music represented by Beethoven's symphonies. 'A Romantic feature of (Oersted's) philosophy,' Einstein writes, 'is the assertion that the inner agitation occasioned by hearing a good piece of

1

music does not arise from conscious reflection, but from obscure depths of consciousnesss.'[3]

A few years earlier, in 1944, Paul Henry Lang presented an equally familiar characterization of German musical thought during this time. 'French musical genius,' Lang wrote in a review of Leo Schrade's *Beethoven in France*, 'has a definite affinity with literature, just as the essence of German music is in the abstract instrumental ... How then could the symbol of this German symphony, Beethoven, become the idol and spiritual savior of the country least receptive to abstract symphonic thought?'[4]

Einstein and Lang both imply that the attitude of early nineteenth-century Germans, at least, toward instrumental music was simple and easy to grasp. This new music was superior to vocal and 'representative' music precisely because it was accessible to the inmost depths of the soul, and was hence the most spiritual of all the arts. In this view, music's expressive character could only be vaguely defined, but this was seen as a strength, not a weakness.

Such theories, however, are drawn entirely from the writings of philosophers and poets, who, with the exception of Hoffmann, were not practicing musicians. Much of their aesthetic theory is foreshadowed by Kant, who is known to have rather disliked the music of his time. Their preference for so-called 'absolute' music is highly attractive because it forms a unified, linear progression away from eighteenth-century Aristotelian theories which traced all art, including music, to the imitation of nature. Music's special role was considered by eighteenth-century theorists to be the arousal of the passions. The final demise of this attitude is supposedly found in Eduard Hanslick's 1854 treatise, *Vom Musikalisch-Schönen*, which for the first time rejected entirely the concept of expression as a key to understanding music.

Not all twentieth-century writers endorse this view. Carl Dahlhaus, for example, takes E. T. A. Hoffmann as the most representative critic of his time, and traces his glorification of the sublime, spiritual aspects of Beethoven's Fifth Symphony to the late eighteenth-century poet-philosophers Ludwig Tieck and Wilhelm Wackenroder. Unlike the writers just cited, Dahlhaus does not ignore the fact that many distinguished nineteenth-century musicians wrote representative and programmatic music as well as abstract symphonies, and were influenced by literature. He finds the key to this apparent contradiction in Wagner's characterization of his later music dramas as 'ersichtlich gewordene Taten der Musik' — 'deeds of music become visible'. In Dahlhaus' view, nineteenth-century musical programs differ from their eighteenth-century predecessors in that they do not attempt to paint events and feelings, but to illuminate the mysteries of the musical processes which they describe.[5] Other modern writers have proposed less radical interpretations,[6] but to the majority of musicians today, there exists an unbridgeable gap in the musical aesthetics of Beethoven's time, symbolized by the emphasis placed by the eighteenth century on expression and by the nineteenth on formal analysis.

The critics whose work is the subject of this book provide a link between these two explanations of music. Most of them were familiar with the aesthetic theories of the German idealists, from Kant through Schopenhauer, who ultimately saw music as the key to the transcendental world of absolute ideas. With few exceptions, though, they were little interested in these theories, which have been taken by modern writers as representative of the Romantic attitude toward music. Ironically, these same writers may only have emphasized what was seen by early nineteenth-century critics as a significant break between musical aesthetics and Romantic epistemology – the theories of knowledge which were crucial to early nineteenth-century philosophy.

In a recent book, James Engell provides support for the idea that diverse thought processes were synthesized within Romantic epistemology. Engell finds that the concept of the active imagination as a central element in human thought has its roots in the early eighteenth century, and is thus by itself hardly characteristic of Romanticism. However, in those writers who were most Romantic, imagination tended to become a force for reconciling opposing points of view. In Schelling's system, for example – a system which has been used to support musical 'absolutism' – it is only through imagination that 'perception and reality, the ideal and the real, work through each other and become one'.[7]

It is precisely this sort of synthesis, formulated in musical terms, which is found among the critics who wrote about Beethoven during his lifetime, Hoffmann not excepted. If there is a unifying principle in their writings, it is that of an assumed identity between approaches to music which may at first seem antithetical: specifically, those of analysis and extra-musical interpretation. Their reviews, although they differ drastically from one another, all combine abstract, idealistic views of Beethoven's works with sincere attempts to anchor these views in the everyday world of sense perception.

These critics, then, bridge the gap between Enlightenment theories about music and the 'absolute' ideal of later nineteenth-century writers. In their attempt to unify opposing viewpoints in a single approach, however, they are more than simply transitional figures; they are characteristically Romantic, just as they believed Beethoven to be the most Romantic of all composers.

3

It is these assertions which I will seek to document in the following pages. I will examine French as well as German sources, since the similarities between the two suggest a common set of priorities which transcends national boundaries, and is therefore more universally valid than any viewpoint which can be traced to German writers alone. This is not, however, a comprehensive study of Beethoven's reception by the press. I have limited myself, with few exceptions, to those articles published in musical journals in Germany before 1830, and in France between 1825 and 1840. I have not even attempted to examine the countless newspaper reports of Beethoven performances which appeared during this time, many of which are no longer than a few lines long. To do so would be the work of a lifetime, and a thankless lifetime at that. This study is devoted to specialized music journalism, which began in Germany, and whose spread to France is nearly coincidental with the course followed by Beethoven's music. It is also shortly after the first appearance of works by Beethoven in Germany that serious music critics gained their first permanent forum, earlier, unsuccessful attempts to start a lasting journal notwithstanding.

Let us, then, begin at the beginning, in Leipzig at the close of the eighteenth century.

1

The Leipzig *Allgemeine Musikalische Zeitung*

The *Allgemeine Musikalische Zeitung* was a weekly magazine published at Leipzig from 1798 to 1848 by the firm of Breitkopf und Härtel and devoted to reviews of recent music and books, theoretical articles and reports by correspondents on the musical life of Europe's major cities. During its first 20 years it was edited by Friedrich Rochlitz, a prolific writer and amateur composer who had studied theology and, like his acquaintance Goethe, dabbled in science.[1] Rochlitz was only 29 when he assumed the position which quickly made him one of the most familiar figures in the German musical world, and it was presumably due to his integrity and his skill in managing an exceptionally large staff that the *AMZ* enjoyed the pre-eminence which it could safely claim during his tenure and for many years thereafter.[2]

So much has already been written about the *AMZ* that further description would be superfluous. The early period is particularly well documented in secondary sources. Marthe Bigenwald's *Die Anfänge der Leipziger Allgemeinen Musikalischen Zeitung* and Hans Ehinger's *E. T. A. Hoffmann als Musiker und Musikschriftsteller*[3] are considered authoritative, and Peter Schnaus' *E. T. A. Hoffmann als Beethoven-Resenzent der Allgemeinen Musikalischen Zeitung*[4] deals at length with some of the material of the present chapter in its historical context as *AMZ* journalism.[5]

The attitude of the *AMZ* toward Beethoven neatly parallels Rochlitz' own: awed but skeptical, and becoming more so with the passage of time. The tenor of the reviews printed during Beethoven's lifetime reflects, on the whole, neither condemnation nor outright acceptance, and this was as true in the later years as it had been from the beginning. What they do show is an acutely tuned sensitivity to musical fashion, broken in rare instances by genuine insight and sympathetic understanding. There are, of course, dangers involved in equating insight with sympathy; if all the critics who understood Beethoven's music were sympathetic, then that music must have been predestined to succeed. Sympathy, however, means in this context not the awe of the disciple but rather that state of intellectual preparedness which makes advanced criticism possible. A review of a new serialist work which showed only the vaguest awareness of the nature of the style and its historical antecedents, and took no stand on the aesthetic problems it has created, would be unsatisfactory regardless of the ultimate verdict it expressed; but in truth many of the *AMZ*'s critics seem to have been no more prepared than the hypothetical author of such a review to evaluate the progressive music of their own day. Their writing is predictably bland, interesting from an historical standpoint for the opinions it contains, but frustrating and pedestrian nevertheless. In this chapter, such articles will be considered only to the extent that their historical interest justifies, extended treatment being reserved for those which really have something to say. It will quickly become clear just what this difference involves.

Two critics in particular stand apart from their contemporaries for the level of intellectual integrity with which they approached their task. It is unusually fortunate that both of their names are known since the majority of articles in the *AMZ* were printed anonymously. E. T. A. Hoffmann needs no introduction; he was one of the most influential figures in the entire Romantic generation, and the partial eclipse he has since suffered is probably due to the same factors which made him outstanding in his own time: unbridled, often bizarre fantasy, and a quite unprofessional reluctance to let himself be tied down to any one field of artistic endeavor. Amadeus Wendt, by contrast, is known only to specialists, but, like Hoffmann, he contributed lengthy and profound articles on Beethoven which attracted the composer's attention. These writers will be discussed in a separate section of this chapter, since their work provides as convenient a framework as any around which to structure the entire subject of Beethoven criticism in the *AMZ*.

I will begin, therefore, with a survey of those articles printed before Hoffmann's monumental review of the Fifth Symphony in July, 1810, and conclude with an overview of the last period, when Beethoven's works began to meet with widespread incomprehension for the first time in his life. Neither of these surveys will very much deal with aesthetic or philosophical issues, since these issues did not really become current until the last decade of Beethoven's life, and they tended to arise in other sources than the conservative *AMZ*. This chapter, therefore, is primarily a documentary one, and as such should help to fill a significant gap in current knowledge of Beethoven's career: the story of his reception by Germany's most influential music journal.

The early reviews

In the 12 years before Hoffmann reviewed the Fifth Symphony, Beethoven's name appeared continually in the pages of the *AMZ*. Not a single volume passed without mention of the composer, and most contain five or more.

The Leipzig Allgemeine Musikalische Zeitung

There are 29 reviews, as compared with 2 for Haydn, 11 for Peter Winter, 9 for Jan Vanhal, and only 4 for the prolific Pleyel. These statistics are misleading, however. During the last 16 years of his life, Beethoven received only 37 reviews in the *AMZ*. Since this was the time during which he achieved almost legendary status in the eyes of the musical public, it is surprising to find that the numerical average of reviews per volume is actually lower than it was in the early years of the journal. The reviews themselves tell a different story. The early ones rarely cover more than a single column of print, and many are limited to a few inches, often under the rubric 'Kurze Anzeigen'. Even the important set of violin sonatas, Op. 12, was slighted in this manner. From 1810 on, however, there was no significant publication of Beethoven's music reviewed in the *AMZ* which was not treated at length, regardless of the critic's opinion. Hoffmann's review of the Fifth Symphony covers 18 columns, and had to be serialized in two successive issues, while the enormous review of the last three piano sonatas covers 13 columns in a single issue. The true measure of the journal's regard for a composer was not the number of reviews printed, but the amount of space which the reviewer was allowed.

In this respect, then, Beethoven's standing with the editorship of the *AMZ* can be seen to have increased beginning with the fourth volume, and to have risen dramatically with volume 6, after which it remained at a fairly constant level during the period now under discussion. I should emphasize once again that this was a measure of the esteem in which Beethoven was held and does not reflect the actual opinions of the reviewers, which tended to be unpredictable throughout the composer's lifetime. Only during the first six years can a general improvement in opinion be traced, counterbalancing the decline which took place more than 20 years later.

Little justice is done to Beethoven in the first volume of the *AMZ*. There are four reviews, three of them totally unfavorable and two of them extremely short. Two sets of variations, on Mozart's 'Ein Mädchen oder Weibchen' for piano and cello and Grétry's 'Une fièvre brûlante' ('Mich brennt' ein heisses Fieber') for piano solo, leave no doubt that Beethoven is an accomplished keyboard player, but 'whether he is equally fortunate as a composer ... is more difficult to affirm' (*AMZ* I, col. 366). The piano variations on Salieri's 'La stessa, la stessissima' provoke the same comment in more forceful terms: 'Hr. v. B. may be able to improvise, but he does not understand how to write variations' (*AMZ* I, col. 607). The diatribe against the violin sonatas, Op. 12 (*AMZ* I, col. 570) needs to be read in full, preferably aloud, to be appreciated as the lyrical peroration that it is.[6] Only the Piano Trio, Op. 11, receives a favorable nod (*AMZ* I, col. 541).

Taken together, these reviews demonstrate either a maddening non-chalance or a forceful consistency of opinion, depending on one's point of view. Why, at a time when seven piano sonatas and some important chamber music were already in print, should Rochlitz have settled upon such generally insignificant works, giving the greatest priority to variations? These works may have been more likely to interest the amateurs among his readers, but it is also possible that newly published music at first found its way into the hands of the *AMZ*'s reviewing staff in a rather arbitrary manner. At least two critics must have been assigned to Beethoven, since the author of the Op. 12 review states his agreement with opinions already expressed on the composer in the same pages. His own attitudes, however, are revealing. He begins by disclaiming any prior knowledge of Beethoven's keyboard music. This and other remarks of a similar nature indicate that these early critics felt no need to be generally familiar with the music of a composer whose individual publications they had been assigned to review. Since the editorial policy of a well-managed journal is reflected in the attitudes of its writers, Rochlitz, too, must have had other priorities in this inaugural year.

There is nothing arbitrary, however, about the musical judgments expressed in these reviews. Beethoven is recognized as an important composer, and the first critic does not hesitate to compare the 'Mich brennt ein heisses Fieber' Variations favorably to a (spurious) work by Mozart on the same theme,[7] while reserving his criticism for the other, more audacious, set. The intensity of the violin sonata critique also needs to be seen in context; the reviewer had expected the music to be ingenious ('genial'), and had found it only learned ('gelehrt'). The implications of this contrast are clear: if Beethoven could make his music more accessible, he would be a composer of the first rank. This is precisely what is said, in so many words, in the review of the Piano Trio, Op. 11, a piece which the critic finds wholly acceptable because of its flowing ('fliessend') style and its avoidance of affected ('gesucht') mannerisms.

Exactly the same criteria are applied in the reviews of Beethoven printed in the second volume of the *AMZ*, even though these may seem dramatically more favorable than those of the previous year. The difference is not one of kind; a review of the piano sonatas, Op. 10, still features the by now familiar appraisal of Beethoven's works to date:

His abundance of ideas . . . still leads Beethoven too often to pile one thought wildly upon another, and, in a rather bizarre manner, to group them in such a way that not infrequently an obscure artificiality ('dunkle Künstlichkeit') or an artificial obscurity ('künstliche Dunkelheit') is produced. *AMZ* II, col. 25

8

The critic continues, however, by affirming that Op. 10 is well above Beethoven's average, and he singles out one passage which he particularly admires: the famous syncopated chord progression toward the end of the rondo of Op. 10, no. 3. For the rest, Beethoven is still advised to practice greater economy.

In the extraordinarily favorable review of the 'Pathétique' Sonata which appeared four months later (*AMZ* II, col. 373), there is only the slightest hint of criticism, but there is an implicit thesis which explains why this sonata was so well received. The clear return to the mood of the first movement in the finale, after the lyrical interlude of the Adagio, gives the work a binding aesthetic unity which, one is led to conclude, transcends the 'künstliche Dunkelheit' and the 'gelehrte Masse ohne gute Methode' of Beethoven's earlier works.

In the third volume of the *AMZ* there are no reviews of Beethoven's music, but those in the next few volumes show, for the first time, a marked shift in attitude. It is tempting to speculate that this was the result, at least in part, of a letter written by Beethoven to Breitkopf und Härtel on April 22, 1801. The composer begins by apologizing for not having written earlier. He then states that at present he is unable to satisfy a request for new music, although he would be glad to accede in the future. Mollo, he says, is bringing out eight new works, Hofmeister, another Viennese publisher, four. Then he gets down to business:

I may just mention that Hofmeister is publishing *one of my first concertos*, and Mollo, one actually composed later, but neither *do I reckon among my best of the kind*. This is just a hint for your *Musikalische Zeitung* with regard to the reviews of these works, though they can be best judged if one can hear them well performed. Musical policy necessitates the keeping to one's self for a time the best concertos. Advise your critics to exercise more care and good sense with regard to the productions of young authors, for many a one may thereby become dispirited, who otherwise might have risen to higher things; for myself, though I am indeed far from considering myself to have attained such a degree of perfection as to be beyond censure, the outcry of your critics against me was so humiliating, that when I began to compare myself to others, I could scarcely blame them; I remained quite quiet, and thought they do not understand it. And I had all the more reason for being quite quiet when I saw how men were praised to the skies who here are held of little account.[8]

Gottfried Christoph Härtel, the *AMZ*'s publisher, could certainly be forgiven if he read into this passage a less than veiled threat, and advised Rochlitz that if the *AMZ* reviewers were not kept at bay, lapses in Beethoven's correspondence, during which his new works would be given to other publishers, might become more and more frequent. There is no way to tell whether Rochlitz was so advised, but there is no question whatsoever that Beethoven had been following closely the first volumes of the *AMZ* and that he felt, quite apart from his resentment of the stinging criticisms, that his true merits were not represented in the music chosen for review. Rochlitz may have begun about this time to look for a critic who could write thoroughly sympathetic, analytical articles on Beethoven's major works.

Such a critic did not appear until 1804, but in the meantime the *AMZ*'s attitude toward Beethoven was almost completely transformed. In May, 1802 (*AMZ* IV, col. 569) the two violin sonatas, Opp. 23 and 24, brought forth the following re-evaluation of their creator:

> The original, fiery, and intrepid spirit of this composer, which even in his early works could not escape the attention of astute observers, but which did not always find the most cordial reception, probably because it sometimes sprang forth in a manner that was ungracious, impetuous, dismal and opaque ('unfreundlich, wild, düster und trübe'), is now becoming ever clearer, ever more disdainful of all obstacles, and without losing its character, ever more pleasing. *AMZ* IV, col. 569

In this ponderous sentence the author concedes, for the first time in the 4½-year-old journal, that Beethoven is entitled to write music noticeably different from the stylistic vernacular of his time. The review reads almost as an atonement for the harsh words elicited by the previous set of violin sonatas. The critic praises the scherzos in particular, and mentions that the first sonata is more accessible since it is easier to perform. A few years earlier, however, these would have been backhanded criticisms of the other works under review; now the tone has changed completely. Never again (with a few notable exceptions) will Beethoven be advised in these pages to abandon his natural inclination and write in a more accessible manner. He is now recognized, not only as a gifted composer, but as a creative personality whose idiosyncrasies are valued in their own right, for the pleasure which they can afford to discriminating listeners.

In the review of the piano sonatas, Opp. 26 and 27, which appeared the following month (*AMZ* IV, col. 650), these sentiments are codified: 'Less educated musicians, and those who expect nothing more from music than a facile entertainment, will take up these works in vain.' The critic feels that some elements of the music are too intricately worked out ('allzukünstlich'), but he once again praises the unity of the three-movement cycle in the 'Moonlight' Sonata, and despite some minor criticisms he is able to understand the entire group of sonatas by virtue of what must have been a newly awakened sympathy for the style of the music. He points, in what seems to be the customary manner, to previous unspecified articles which express the same opinion on Beethoven's newest works. He was mistaken, however, if he believed that anything approaching his own nearly complete acceptance of the composer had appeared in earlier volumes. 'The class of musicians for whom Beethoven writes', and whom this critic mentions with respect, had been described three years before as a 'fringe' group 'who love excessive difficulty in invention and composition; that which one might call perverse'. A great deal must have changed in a relatively brief time.

Furthermore, the change was to be a permanent one, as even Beethoven's detractors realized. A critic who is evidently disenchanted with the 'Pastoral' Sonata, Op. 28 and the variations on Mozart's 'Bei Männern welche Liebe fühlen' says simply that Beethoven's personal style, being already widely known, requires no further description; none is forthcoming (*AMZ* V, col. 188). Even more to the point: when the Violin Sonata, Op. 30, no. 1, is reviewed in volume 6 (col. 77), it is described as unworthy of its composer. Formerly, that composer had been warned to keep his imagination in check; now he is mildly chastised when one of his works, though 'by no means mediocre', fails to live up to his usual standard of inventiveness.

No less a person than the editor called attention to the novelty of the review of the 'Eroica' Variations, Op. 35, which takes up most of the issue of February 22, 1804, by the unprecedented device of placing Beethoven's portrait at the front of the issue. Prior to this time, composers' portraits had been used only for the frontispiece to an entire volume. Composers so honored included J.S. Bach, I.A.P. Schulze, C.P.E. Bach, Handel, Gluck, and J.A. Hiller; one for each year of the journal's history to date. Joseph Haydn, the most famous of all living composers, did not appear until the following year.

Internal evidence also distinguishes this review from its predecessors; it is not only longer, but more perceptive as well. It is, in fact, the first review which makes an honest attempt to come to terms with the nature and significance of Beethoven's musical style. As a model of clarity and forceful presentation of opinion, it leaves little to be desired. Although it is fully as long as some of the later reviews of Beethoven's later works (though not as long as those by Hoffmann), it does not adopt the casual, narrative-like manner which was soon to become all too common, and which makes some of those later reviews read like travel guides for musical connoisseurs. Instead, after a few introductory paragraphs dealing with the composer and the work as a whole, the author begins a threefold critique, each part of which is designed ostensibly for a different group of readers. He is thus able to present his favorite examples to all of Beethoven's admirers, while reserving his criticism for a personal apostrophe to the composer. Finally, for pianists only, he discusses the technical interpretation of the work -- the only instance that I know of this in an *AMZ* review.

The first of these sections is certain to strike the modern reader as the most perceptive. It is almost frightening to contemplate what the critic who denounced Op. 12 as 'a mass of learning without good method' would have made of the cross-grained fugue with which these variations conclude. His successor does not hesitate to meet Beethoven on his own terms, proclaiming that 'it is here the connoisseur, and also the educated amateur, will receive the most satisfaction'. He goes on to praise the ingenuity with which the theme and countersubject are exchanged among the voices, climaxing with the appearance of the main subject *al rovescio* just before the final dominant pedal. This is not a very complex or learned analysis, and the author admits that his main motive is to stimulate the reader's curiosity.

Here, as elsewhere, what is most remarkable is the lack of any obvious prejudice. Most, if not all, of the previous critics had found certain chord progressions and modulations unacceptable *a priori*, because they could not possibly produce a good effect. Here the only criterion is the appropriateness of each passage within the context of the piece. The enormous ingenuity of the final fugue thus meets with his approval despite unprepared dissonances and (by traditional standards) some abysmal voice leading, while the relatively inoffensive canon of the seventh variation is dismissed as a 'Künsteley'; an intellectual exercise too systematic for inclusion in a work of this sort. The author's other judgments are on a par with these. He singles out for praise precisely those variations – nos. 3, 10 and 12 – which contain the most original keyboard writing, passing over in silence the more traditional virtuosity of variation 2. Even his criticisms in the second section show an inherent sympathy with the composer's aesthetic goals. For example, having already praised the Largo variation (no. 15) in extravagant terms, he writes that:

If the second to last 16th in the second measure of the Largo were based upon the F minor triad, it would be more correct, and would sound better in this slow tempo. The strict analogy between this and the fourth measure, where the upper voices move similarly in thirds, cannot compensate for the harsh effect.

AMZ VI, col. 388

Beethoven had already been mildly chided for not making the bass of the second part of the theme more interesting in its unadorned appearance at the beginning of the piece. It was conceded, however, that he might have wanted the theme to be recognized in its familiar form. These are both minor points of no great consequence, but they reveal a critic with an instinctive sympathy for his subject, even when his personal taste is momentarily offended. More than anything else, it is this combination of sympathy and objectivity which distinguishes a truly important critic from a merely competent one. By this standard, then, the review of Op. 35 is the first important piece of Beethoven criticism to appear in the *AMZ*: the first that might actually help an amateur musician who knew little of the composer to reach an informed, personal decision on the merits of one of his most recent works.

Two reviews of equal size, and perhaps even greater significance, followed during the next three years. They deal, in turn, with the Third Piano Concerto (*AMZ* VII, col. 445) and the 'Eroica' Symphony (*AMZ* IX, col. 321): both works which had already been widely performed.[9] Unlike their predecessor, these reviews contain evidence of a nascent sense of purpose; the authors seem to feel that they will lose their readers unless they explain what they are doing and why, and they do so in definitive terms:

With regard to both spirit and effect [the Third Piano Concerto] is one of the most outstanding ever written, and I will try to clarify, with reference to the work itself, where this effect originates, to the extent that this can be determined from the materials and their construction.

The individuality and rich content [of the 'Eroica'] would seem to require that we now direct our attention to matters of compositional technique and of mechanical execution, following the composer closely, step by step. The thoroughness with which this work was composed calls for this procedure; if further justification is needed, it may be found in the profit the young composer may derive from such analyses and in the increased pleasure the educated amateur may afterwards derive from listening to it. Perhaps someone may then combine all of this and bring it into focus; if this doesn't happen, we have at least progressed to the point where one's feeling about it is no longer vague and doubtful but can lead to a satisfactory judgment. This will gradually become general opinion, thus determining the position of the work of art, its general influence, and fate.[10]

The last sentence quoted above is not merely presumption on the part of an anonymous critic; in an age which was beginning to think seriously about historical process, statements like this had a philosophical tinge, and carried a conviction that helps to explain the conscientiousness with which all three of these reviews were carried out.

Were they, then, written by the same person? I believe they were, for several reasons. All three refer to the 'Kenner'/'Liebhaber' dichotomy (see the last quotation above) which was widely used in the eighteenth century, but was not characteristic of *AMZ* reviews. It is, to make an only partially facetious analogy, like a formula from an epic tradition, which once called forth a set of associations, but is now repeated simply out of habit on the part of an individual author.

These reviews also have in common a concern for musical unity: not the superficial unity that had been observed in the 'Pathétique' Sonata but, to an unprecedented extent, unity of structure within each movement. Earlier reviewers, both for and against Beethoven, had found his music to be 'fantastic', in the literal sense; it was considered wild and unconstrained, with flights of imagination following one another as in an improvisation (German 'Phantasie'). This attitude, which conflicts dramatically with our modern view of Beethoven, was to determine the canonical image of the composer, as I will often have occasion to observe, throughout his lifetime and beyond. It is thus enormously significant that the reviews of the Third Piano Concerto and the 'Eroica' both emphasize the unity of these works, and document it with musical examples. These comments on the concerto would not be out of place in a modern theory textbook:

The first movement, an Allegro con brio, begins with an idea which is played in unison by the string instruments, and repeated on the dominant by oboes, bassoons, and horns. In the course of the movement, this idea and its rhythm, sometimes complete and sometimes in part, lie behind the different sections and are themselves developed. Beethoven was especially fortunate in his treatment of the third measure, whose five notes appear throughout the movement, often very unexpectedly, and support, hold together and unify the most heterogeneous material.

The 'Eroica', which the *AMZ*'s Viennese correspondent had found to be 'almost totally lacking in unity' (*AMZ* VII, col. 321), is now described in statements like the following:

During the course of the second section [of the first movement], at the point where the development of the original ideas begins to be almost excessive, a completely new melody is taken up by the winds and treated episodically ... Not only does this increase the total charm and variety, but it also refreshes the listener so that he is once again happy to follow the composer when he returns to the principal ideas, adorning and developing them ever more richly ... This Allegro, in spite of its length, was composed with a concern for unity which we can only admire.

All three reviews also contain passages which show that they were written not for the 'Mittelmässigkeit', but for the musical intelligentsia of the time. The review of the Third Piano Concerto is intended 'only for those who think as well as enjoy, or who wish to study the work themselves'. In other words, it is a technical analysis, to be read, if possible, with score in hand. The 'Eroica', too, 'presupposes an audience which can get beyond a mere string of variations which ripple along pleasantly and are over in a moment. In order to produce its effect, this symphony must have an audience that is capable of giving and sustaining serious attention to it.' In the review of the Variations, comments like these are directed to the would-be performer, who must belong 'to the first rank of keyboard players'. The last third of the article is written only for this select group.

The affinity among the three articles is, however, more complex than any of these points suggests. An instinctive sympathy with the composer, seen already in the review of the 'Eroica' Variations, is evinced even more strongly in the two later reviews. The critic of the Third Piano Concerto, for example, is able to present the psychological essence of the finale with remarkable acuity in technical terms:

The presentation of the first complete cadence in the dominant is drawn out with ever-growing intensity over 32 measures, and grips the listener irresistibly. Beethoven produces a similar effect in the places where, traversing one or more octaves, usually in chromatic scales, he arrives again at the minor 7th or 9th with which the main theme begins, without, however, letting the listener come to rest, but holding him in tension until the theme is stated in its entirety.

Confident recognition of the truly original was one of the hallmarks of the first long review, and the 'Eroica' Symphony is treated with as much discernment as are the Variations of the same name:

The reviewer would without any hesitation declare [the funeral march] to be Beethoven's triumph, at least in terms of invention and design. It is conceivable that a talented composer after a great deal of study and tireless effort might produce a work that could equal the first movement. But only a true genius could conceive a work such as this second movement, give birth to it and bring it to fruition so perfectly.

The 'perfection' of the second movement, like the unity of the first, was probably clearer to the critic than to his readers, since neither concept is adequately explained. He should, however, be given benefit of doubt for recognizing the integrity of a movement which seems to have struck even sympathetic audiences at the time as cumbersome and overlong.[11] Few admirers of Beethoven, either then or now, would fault the first movement of the 'Eroica' for invention and design, but only one seems to have accepted the challenge of a movement-by-movement critique when the symphony was still new and obscure,[12] or to have made judgments of quality transcending his own visceral reactions of like and dislike.

It has already been suggested that the limitations of this review are as striking as its accomplishments, but these may stem in part from a semantic tradition in the *AMZ* which only an outsider and experienced author like E.T.A. Hoffmann could successfully avoid. Peter Schnaus, in a monograph on Hoffmann's Beethoven criticism which will be discussed in more detail below, has studied the vocabulary of the early *AMZ* reviews with Teutonic thoroughness, and found that it fits neatly into a polarized system with little room for fine distinctions.

Positive terms, mostly nouns like 'Kunst', 'Kraft', 'Tiefe', or 'Originalität', are balanced by censorial adjectives: 'wild', 'bizarr', 'seltsam', 'künstlich', 'gesucht', 'schwierig'.[13] Each of these occurs so frequently that it was probably both unnecessary and impossible for *AMZ* readers to absorb their meanings in any but the most superficial sense. Often, in fact, the same word, by a subtle metamorphosis into adjectival form, alters its meaning completely: positive 'Kunst' becomes negative 'allzukünstlich'; positive 'Gelehrsamkeit' becomes negative 'gelehrt'.[14]

When he began writing for the *AMZ* in 1810, Hoffmann introduced some new words with a personal touch; 'Besonnenheit' became one of the positive attributes, and the roster of adjectives was expanded to include the equally positive 'unermesslich', 'unnennbar', 'unaussprechlich', and a host of others which increased the range and subtlety of his opinions.[15] If the present critic is not so rich terminologically, some of his inarticulateness may result, like Hoffmann's 'un-' vocabulary, from a characteristically Romantic awe before the great works of art. He has certainly perceived qualities in the second movement of the 'Eroica' which transcend the 'Kunst' and 'Originalität' of other composers and beggar description in the terms to which he still felt confined.

All three long reviews thus show a forward-looking concern for originality which, in context, is highly unusual. It is hardly likely that after six years of printing lukewarm praise mingled with occasionally damning criticism, Rochlitz should have found three critics, or even two, equally capable of such discernment. Today, after nearly 200 years of Beethoven research, it is easy to treat these reviews with condescension; they are often sketchy and unsystematic analytically, and beyond the few traits observed above they show little awareness of the aesthetic problems which obsessed Hoffmann and many others of his generation. When they first appeared, however, they were probably the three most perceptive Beethoven reviews ever printed: the first, certainly, to meet the composer on his own ground with something like Hoffmann's intellectual integrity. They are, in short, an important landmark in the history of Beethoven's reception by the press, and this alone implies that a single critic was behind them all.

It would certainly be gratifying to modern curiosity to know the identity of Beethoven's first ardent champion in the press. Unfortunately, there is no documentary evidence to work with, and what follows must therefore be taken as pure conjecture and valued accordingly. I have already suggested that Rochlitz began looking for a critic capable of doing full justice to Beethoven's major works by 1801, and possibly earlier. At least two and a half years must have passed, therefore, before a suitable person was found. It is not unreasonable to suppose that this delay was deliberate — an ostentatious reversal of opinion is less embarrassing if taken in small steps — and that Rochlitz knew, at least from 1801, who the most appropriate critic would be.

Bearing in mind that this critic seems to have disappeared from the scene after 1807, we can at least make an educated guess as to who he was. Friedrich August Kanne, a native of Saxony, was born in 1778 and came to Leipzig to study medicine. He also studied theology at Wittenberg, but his main ambitions were musical, and in 1801 (the pivotal year) he scored a success at Leipzig with his cantata *An die Tonkunst*. He lived in Leipzig until 1808, when he moved to Vienna to begin a career as a music teacher and journalist. Before his death in 1833, his sympathetic reviews of Beethoven's music appeared regularly in Viennese newspapers and in the *Wiener Allgemeine Musikalische Zeitung*, which he helped to found in 1817.[16] He is credited with being one of the most astute critics of his time, and he is one of the few who seem to have fully understood Beethoven's late works.[17] Could this be the same person who, in 1804, praised the unorthodox fugue from Op. 35 as a triumph of musical art? The question is best answered by posing another: who else, at that time, had such a strong, inherent understanding of Beethoven's musical idiom, together with the ability to express himself convincingly in writing? No other critic before Hoffmann, and few since, combined these assets to such a degree. Kanne's move to Vienna in 1808 need not have put him out of the picture completely; many of Rochlitz' most prominent writers were in fact correspondents. He seems to have wished, however, to begin a new career in the Viennese press. This evidence, too, thus points strongly in his direction. Kanne's later reviews, it is true, are somewhat more fanciful in tone than these, and seem at first glance to stem from a different pen. In the meantime, however, as will be seen, he had become familiar with the aesthetics of German idealism, which may still have been unfamiliar to him during his years in Leipzig. Thus there is no reason to doubt that Kanne is the author of the reviews we have been discussing.

Apart from these three reviews, there is very little new or unusual in the *AMZ*'s Beethoven criticism between 1804 and 1810. Even after the advent of Hoffmann, outright apostles of Beethoven are rare, making up in column inches for what they lack in absolute numbers. The general tone of the shorter reviews changes little after the fourth volume; although favorably disposed, they continue to be suspicious of innovation, and if anything in the music comes into conflict with the critic's *a priori* principles of judgment, the battle is invariably decided in favor of the latter. Since these principles are fairly consistent, the only distinguishing feature is the extent of the critic's self-importance. In a review of the 'Appassionata' Sonata, printed in April of 1807 (*AMZ* IX, col. 433), the author recognizes the powerful effect of the outer movements, finding them more successful than some of Beethoven's earlier works in the same manner, but he admits, almost apologetically, that he prefers the variations of the second movement. When the 'Harp' Quartet, Op. 74, is reviewed four years later (*AMZ* XIII, col. 349), there is nothing even vaguely timorous about the critic's advice to the composer: he should write more quartets in the manner of Op. 18, and give up the obscurities of his new style. This review seems once again to have aroused Beethoven's ire,[18] and indeed it is the exception. Most critics had long since stopped advising Beethoven on how to write, preferring to concentrate on more specific matters. What seemed insightful after the tirades of the *AMZ*'s first volume, however, seems less so when compared to Hoffmann and Kanne. To take just one example: the critic who reviewed the two piano sonatas, Op. 27, in 1802, criticized the ending of the first sonata because it resembled a comic opera finale; he apparently felt that this was inappropriate in a piano composition. This was written in the context of an otherwise favorable review, and as an opinion it is certainly supportable. The author, however, made no attempt to support it, treating it instead as observed fact. Kanne would have tried to determine Beethoven's motive for writing such a passage before judging the result, thus raising himself above the common level of German music criticism in the early nineteenth century.

Three other reviews do rise above this level, and deserve to be considered briefly before the subject of Hoffmann is formally introduced. In the issue of June 6, 1804, the six *Gellert-Lieder* are given a sympathetic critique (*AMZ* VI, col. 608) which shows some awareness of the complexities of text–music relationship, even in conservative strophic settings like these. The third song is valued more highly than the second, for example, because its powerful harmonies, inappropriate for some of the later stanzas, graphically illustrate the opening text. Its less adventurous predecessor is based on a text of no real expressive quality which the critic feels should not have been set at all. Here, as in few other *AMZ* reviews, both the critic's opinions and the criteria which lie behind them are clearly set forth, leaving the reader free to compare his own ideas and accept or reject the review accordingly.

The same is true of a review of the 32 Variations in C minor, WoO 80, in the issue of November 4, 1807 (*AMZ* X, col. 94), which is also marked by historical sensitivity. Beethoven returned, in this work, to the antiquated bass-variation, and the critic judges it accordingly, ignoring the currently fashionable variation style. In view of the *AMZ*'s frequent and unimaginative adherence to musical fashion, this short review must be considered a major landmark on the road to more solidly grounded criticism.

Finally, in 1810, a few months before Hoffmann's first Beethoven review, Rochlitz himself wrote a lengthy and analytical review of the 'Pastoral' Symphony (*AMZ* XII, col. 241). This review confirms Rochlitz' reputation as a benevolent, even warm, admirer of Beethoven's more accessible works. It is doubtless significant that Rochlitz chose to review this work himself, while giving the Fifth Symphony to Hoffmann.

On the whole, the tone of the formal reviews during the *AMZ*'s early years is marked by deepening understanding of Beethoven's music, together with a few pockets of determined resistance. This picture is broadened, but not substantially changed, by the correspondence reports published throughout the same period. It is worth pausing here for emphasis, because quotes from these reports have more than once been given out of context so as to appear more negative than they actually are.[19]

The *AMZ*'s correspondence section, a regular feature from the earliest volume on, provides an invaluable record of the musical life in most of Europe's major cities for half a century. Recorded here are not only the programs of concerts, public and private, but also, in many cases, the response of the audience to the pieces performed. The correspondents' own opinions, usually given in a few laconic sentences, tend to reflect audience reactions, and could hardly have been ventured in the same spirit as a lengthy analytical review.[20]

During the period under discussion, Beethoven performances are reported in five cities: Vienna, Leipzig, Berlin, Mannheim and Prague.[21] The first three symphonies, the Septet, Op. 20, *Christus am Oelberge*, and the Third Piano Concerto are each mentioned several times. Also cited are the Fifth Symphony, the Fourth Piano Concerto, the Triple Concerto, the Horn Sonata, Op. 17, two sets of variations, WoO 78 and 79, the concert aria 'Ah perfido', Op. 65, the string quartets, Op. 18, the Coriolan Overture, one of the Leonora Overtures and *Fidelio*, each only once. (In the case of *Fidelio*, we know that it received only one short run of perform-ances in 1805, and another in 1806, before being scrapped for nearly a decade.) Of these, all but the Second and Third Symphonies, *Fidelio*, *Christus am Oelberge* and the Triple Concerto are either mentioned only in passing ('Ah perfido') or praised virtually without reservation.[22] The 'cantata' *Christus am Oelberge* was admired by the Viennese correspondent after what may have been the first performance (*AMZ* V, col. 498), but it was criticized, apparently by another writer, after a later performance in Vienna which did not succeed (*AMZ* V, col. 590). *Fidelio* and the Triple Concerto were criticized, respectively, by the correspondents from Vienna (*AMZ* VIII, col. 238) and Leipzig (*AMZ* X, col. 490) for the same reason: they were considered dull. (In the latter case, at least, modern opinion has tended to concur). The Second Symphony was found by the correspondent in Leipzig to be 'bizarre, harsh, and undisciplined'. However:

This impression is so far overcome by the powerful, fiery spirit which is felt in this colossal work, by the wealth of new ideas and the almost total originality of their treatment, and by the profound knowledge of the principles of art that [this symphony] ... will be heard with ever-increasing pleasure when a thousand celebrated, fashionable pieces of today have long since gone to their graves.

AMZ VII, col. 215

Only the 'Eroica' met with anything like determined resistance to change, and that only from the Viennese correspondent, who continually described himself as a staunch admirer of Beethoven, despite his disapproval of particular works. In Prague, this symphony was more successful (*AMZ* IX, col. 610), and in Leipzig it scored a triumph which was seconded in an extraordinary page-long statement (*AMZ* IX, col. 497).

It seems to me literally impossible for an unbiased reader to conclude from these reports that Beethoven was treated with anything but the most scrupulous fairness and objectivity.

E. T. A. Hoffmann and Amadeus Wendt

Although Hoffmann achieved success during his lifetime as a writer, composer, theater director and lawyer, it is probably as a music critic that the most extravagant claims have been made on his behalf by posterity. Charles Rosen calls him the finest among Beethoven's contemporaries,[23] and the *New Grove Dictionary* credits him with ending 'the old-fashioned doctrine of the affections in musical aesthetics'.[24] Ironically, out of 58 articles on music printed in the new edition of Hoffmann's collected works,[25] only the review of Beethoven's Fifth Symphony, which first appeared in the *AMZ* in July, 1810, is at all widely known, and few non-specialists are aware that two-thirds of this review consist of rigorous technical analysis.

Like most ironies, however, this one is easily explained. Hoffmann clearly regarded the review of the Fifth Symphony — the first of five he was to write on works by Beethoven — as a challenge to his ingenuity, and he used the occasion to set forth a theory of art which can easily stand out of context, and to which the later reviews constantly refer. Much of this material was incorporated verbatim into his article on Beethoven's instrumental music, which is not included in the collected works but is widely available in English.[26] The original review has only recently been translated.[27]

Hoffmann also has a reputation, owing partly to his portrayal in Offenbach's opera, as an irrational conjurer whose dream fantasies were generously abetted by alcohol.[28] It is hard to imagine such a man placing himself in the pedantic role of the formal analyst, especially after having penned phrases like these:

Now Beethoven's instrumental music opens to us the realm of the colossal and the immeasurable. Glowing beams of light shoot through the deep night of this realm and we perceive shadows surging back and forth, closer and closer around us, destroying everything in us except the pain of that endless longing in which each joy that had risen in jubilant tones sinks back and perishes; and it is in this pain which confuses love, hope, and happiness without destroying them, in this pain which seeks to break our breast with the chords of all the passions that we live on and become enchanted visionaries![29]

Thus, even if it is true, as Gerhard Allroggen has claimed, that Hoffmann 'distinguished between analysis of compositional technique and interpretation of the musical content',[30] most English-speaking readers have had neither curiosity nor opportunity to find out how he did this, or even that he did it. In England and America, at least, Hoffmann lives in the popular imagination through his fantasies alone.

In the pages which follow, I will try to show that, far from having distinguished between analysis and interpretation, Hoffmann synthesized these two elements to an extent that no critic before or after him has ever achieved. I am not the first to suggest this; the idea apparently originated with Peter Schnaus, whose monograph on Hoffmann, cited above in another context, is and will probably remain the definitive study of these five reviews. In this chapter, I will be constantly in Schnaus' debt; I will reserve a more original approach for Chapter 5, where Hoffmann and his contemporaries will be compared and contrasted.

Hoffmann reviewed five works by Beethoven for the *AMZ*: the Fifth Symphony (*AMZ* XII, cols. 630, 652), the 'Coriolan' Overture (*AMZ* XIV, col. 519), the piano trios, Op. 70 (*AMZ* XV, col. 141), the C major Mass (*AMZ* XV, cols. 389, 409), and the incidental music to Goethe's *Egmont* (*AMZ* XV, col. 473). Formally, these reviews resemble 'ausführliche Beurtheilungen' by other authors; they begin with general remarks on the composer, his style and the nature of the work, and proceed to more specific analysis.[31] The novelty of Hoffmann's approach lies in the significance he gave to the introduction. The opening pages of the Fifth Symphony review are nothing less than a treatise on musical aesthetics. Haydn and Mozart are discussed as well as Beethoven, and instrumental music is put forward as the most Romantic of all the arts, since it leaves behind feelings determined by means of concepts ('durch Begriffe bestimmbaren Gefühle') and embodies the unspeakable. Hoffmann was fully conscious that he had overstepped the limits set by his predecessors; the reviewer, he said, was 'overwhelmed by the material which he is to discuss, and no-one may begrudge him if ... he strives to put into words everything which this composition impressed upon his spirit'.

In so doing, Hoffmann faced an enormous contradiction, of his own making, and solved it with equanimity; he unblushingly invoked a 'wonderful, infinite spirit-kingdom' ('der wunderbare Geisterreich des Unendlichen') whose total independence from terrestrial experience made it the perfect metaphor for instrumental music's ineffable nature. The specific feelings which Hoffmann describes are inseparably bound up with this spirit-kingdom, and hence with the nature of Romantic music itself. Awe ('Schauer'), fear ('Furcht'), horror ('Entsetzen'), pain ('Schmerz') and endless longing ('unendliche Sehnsucht') are its attributes, and Beethoven does not express them; he makes them accessible. In this way, music was freed from the obligation to refer to anything outside itself, but a verbal point of reference was maintained.[32]

As a result of this system, it became impossible to characterize individual works. Old-fashioned critics could still refer to a wide range of affections and choose those most appropriate to the piece under review. Hoffmann maintained that all of Beethoven's instrumental music referred to the same spirit-kingdom, with its small, self-contained emotional world. He was later to modify this rather extreme position, but in the Fifth Symphony review everything is carefully ordered around it. The character sketches of Haydn, Mozart and Beethoven, given at the beginning, become increasingly austere; Haydn is described as childlike ('kindlich') and happy ('heiter') belonging strictly to the here and now; Mozart leads us into the spiritual world, but only Beethoven makes it possible to find transcendental pleasure in emotions of pain, fear and longing. No writer before Hoffmann had so forcefully applied the idea of character to an individual composer, and in his enthusiasm he treated his discovery with an almost religious fervor.[33]

It was hardly likely, therefore, that Hoffmann would choose to write an extended analysis that said nothing of this noumenal dimension in Beethoven's art. What he did write, in place of the loosely organized commentary, richly adorned with critical judgments, which an *AMZ* reader might expect, was a minute description of the manner in which the Fifth Symphony, 'more than any other work of Beethoven, reveals his romanticism in a climactic unfolding which mounts until the end ("in einem bis zum Ende fortsteigendem Klimax''), and draws the listener irresistibly into the wonderful, infinite spirit-kingdom'. Here is what he says about the opening measures:

The first Allegro — 2/4 meter in C minor — begins with a principal idea only two measures long, which reappears in many different guises in the course of the movement. In the second measure there is a fermata, followed by a repetition of the principal idea a tone lower, and by another fermata; both times only strings and clarinets [are heard]. Not even the tonality is yet established; the listener expects E-flat major. The second violin begins again with the principal idea, and in the following measure C, the fundamental note, is played by the cellos and bassoons, while the viola and first violin, entering in imitation, establish C minor. Finally, these same instruments build the opening idea into a two-measure cell which, repeated three times (the last time with full orchestra) imparts a foreboding of the unknown and the mysterious to the listener's spirit ('des Zuhörers Gemüte das Unbekannte, Geheimnisvolle ahnen lassen').

After quoting this passage in full score, Hoffmann continues:

Violin and viola imitate the principal idea in the tonic, while the bass plays a similar idea; an increasingly powerful ('immer steigender') transposition, making the foreboding ('Ahnung') even more forceful and impulsive, leads into a tutti whose theme repeats the rhythm of the opening idea and is intimately related to it. A sixth chord on D prepares the new major tonality of E-flat, where the horn once again recalls the opening idea. The first violin now plays a second theme which, though melodious, remains true to the character of anxious, restless longing which the whole movement expresses.

I have quoted at such length because it is important to understand that Hoffmann's analysis, thorough and technical though it is, would be gratuitous were it not for the extra-musical allusions which crop up constantly and bind it together. If these were removed, they would leave behind a blow-by-blow description, such as any reasonably competent musician equipped with a score could provide for himself. Hoffmann, however, had too much scope and imagination, and was too polemical in intent, simply to fill up space in this manner. What he did can best be judged in perspective. If we recall the difficulties faced (and only partially surmounted) by Kanne because of the limits in the *AMZ*'s standard vocabulary, we will be better prepared to appreciate the semantic feats accomplished in this review.

Hoffmann did not simply insert fantastic references into a self-contained analysis; he chose his material on the basis of its relevance to the spirit-kingdom which he felt the symphony proclaimed. For example, after explaining the relationship of the second theme to the principal idea, he glossed over the remainder of the exposition, having nothing of moment to say about this music. As can be seen from the samples of the original

German included in the quotes above, Hoffmann managed to incorporate elements of his fantastic vocabulary into the technical analysis itself. It is characteristic of him that he had considerably less to say about the second movement than about any of the other three; this was the movement in which the symphony emerged from its 'storm-clouds' into the everyday world, providing a vision of the 'friendly faces which surround and reassure us'. Everything works together to demonstrate the central thesis, which is driven home with an almost irrational consistency. Even the finale, which every other analyst has seen as a point of release, is forced by Hoffmann into the model of the previous movements, so that the symphony may conclude with a renewed expression of fear and longing.[34]

For Hoffmann, as for many of his generation, the Fifth Symphony had been the epiphany of a new era in musical history. It is understandable, therefore, that the later reviews cannot quite match this one in force or conviction. To some extent, they are all dependent on it. The review of the 'Coriolan' Overture begins by noting the disparity between Beethoven's impetuous music and the introspective drama by Collin for which it was written, but as soon as the music itself becomes the center of attention, the drama is forgotten and the spirit-kingdom of the Fifth Symphony reappears:

The ... principal theme of the Allegro has a character of irresistible restlessness, of unquenchable longing ... The transposition of this theme a tone lower is unexpected, and increases the tension ('steigert die Spannung') which was already felt in the opening measures ... Everything combines ... [to create] the highest pitch of expectation for that which the rise of the mysterious curtain will reveal.

Hoffmann is obviously not speaking here of Collin's drama; the curtain hides the same mounting, irresistible fantasy to which even the Fifth Symphony was more prelude than fulfillment. The review of the piano trios also mentions 'formless longing' ('unbestimmte Sehnen') in an introductory paragraph which plainly summarizes Hoffmann's earlier position. The C major Mass, however, is described as 'the expression of a childlike, happy spirit': exactly the same words which had earlier been used to characterize Haydn.[35] The review of the *Egmont* music is perhaps less derivative than any of the others; but by this time, as will shortly be seen, Hoffmann's view of Beethoven had undergone considerable development.

The decisive change took place in the piano trio review. Here, for the first time, Hoffmann was faced with works by Beethoven which could not possibly be fitted into the emotional world of the Fifth Symphony, and he responded not by backtracking (as he would do soon after with the Mass), but by enlarging his field of vision. The descriptive phrases became more

24

varied, dealing with individual movements and themes.[36] To some extent, this meant a reversion to more traditional metaphoric language: a tendency which had already been foreshadowed in the previous review.[37] Here, for example, are Hoffmann's comments on the beginning of the finale of the first trio:

Just as when a stormwind drives away the clouds, with light and shadow alternating within a single moment, as, in the restless pursuit which follows, images take shape, are swept away, and form themselves once more, so, after the second fermata, this movement rushes unceasingly forward.

Much of this imagery recalls the spirit-world of the Fifth Symphony, but the central theme of clouds and stormwinds is, in itself, hardly worthy of Hoffmann. To apply it in the way that Hoffmann did to this particular piece, however, was a stroke of inspiration, symbolizing the change in priorities that had led the critic away from his earlier self-contained and exclusive musical universe.

Hoffmann's priorities for analysis also changed. The lack of a guiding concept in this review led him to attach greater importance to musical technique, and he set out to explore the questions of form and style which his earlier metaphysics had obscured. In the introduction, for example, he allowed his opinions on the nature of the medium to come to the fore; he stated that he considered the piano to be a poor vehicle for melody, though ideally suited for harmony, and that he disliked piano concertos, because the contrast between the solo instrument and the full orchestra seemed to him only to underscore its weaknesses. It is not entirely clear how he intended to vindicate Beethoven's trios, which also combine the piano with more lyrical instruments, from the same charge. His idea seems to have been that only a virtuoso of Beethoven's stature, having fully explored 'the secrets of harmony' at the keyboard, could have developed the lyrical themes which abound in these works into unified movements, expressing not only the pain and sadness so dear to Hoffmann but their antitheses as well. In the first movement of the 'Ghost' Trio, Op. 70, no. 1, he found only 'a cheerful good nature; a happy, proud consciousness of strength and abundance', but he pointed with unfailing acumen to the contrapuntal 'development', making this the focal point of his analysis.

This review is certainly less doctrinaire than its predecessors, but it is also the only one in which Hoffmann enhanced the music with a fervor akin to that inspired by the Fifth Symphony, and penetrated its secrets as deeply. By comparison, the review of the C major Mass is thorough and systematic, but a little cold — Hoffmann had already said on two separate occasions (in the reviews of the Fifth Symphony and the piano trios) that

Beethoven's vocal music was inferior to his instrumental music — while that of the *Egmont* music is somewhat perfunctory, due to the large number of pieces involved. In the first case, Hoffmann nearly abandoned extra-musical associations, and appropriately so in view of the liturgical nature of the text. In the second, he made a very specific association between the 'Egmont' Overture and Goethe's play, which he evidently admired (more, at any rate, than Collin's *Coriolan*). The love story of Egmont and Clärchen was for Hoffmann the subject of the Overture, being more suited than any other part of the play for musical development. Except for their lengthy philosophical introductions, neither of these reviews would have seemed unusual or innovative to the readers of the *AMZ*.

The first three reviews, however, and especially the review of the Fifth Symphony, were unlike anything that had been read before, and they remain striking even today. Hoffmann's special talent was his ability to use non-musical associations in a way that enriched the music he was interpreting rather than demeaning it. It was in the nature of his accomplishment, however, that it could not be repeated often or with much success. The conceptual world which Hoffmann created was especially designed to explain the effect brought about by the Fifth Symphony; to explain how music of an unprecedented power and almost painful intensity could be more worthwhile than the pleasant, melodious works of more traditional composers. The result seems today to be highly unorthodox; it has already been mentioned that even the jubilant finale was suborned to Hoffmann's purpose. Technically, these reviews are in many ways one-sided and inadequate. As a critic, however, the creator of the *Phantasiestücke* was not a technician, but a theorist, in the boldest sense of the word. His foremost aim was always to explain how the music worked upon his emotions, and he chose to do so as directly as possible, even when that meant overlooking important passages in favor of those which suited him best.

Like other Romantics, Hoffmann believed that he had a mission to fulfill, and his success in accomplishing that mission surely earns him the accolades which our century has so generously granted him. Hoffmann's accomplishment can best be gauged by the fact that he fulfilled the goals of his own era, yet has remained, in the eyes of posterity, the first true music critic, the forerunner of a new generation in Beethoven criticism.

'Thoughts on contemporary music, and on van Beethoven, specifically his *Fidelio*' was the ambitious title of an article printed in six weekly installments in the *AMZ*, beginning with the issue of May 24, 1815. Formally, this was not a review at all, but an examination of certain problems in musical aesthetics followed by a commentary on the newly revised opera which had just appeared for the third time on the Viennese stage.[38] Like many other *AMZ* articles, it seems to have attracted 'van Beethoven's' attention; in a letter from the year 1815, the composer asked his friend Tobias Haslinger to send him 'what Rochlitz has written about what B. has written'.[39] The author, however, was not Rochlitz but Amadeus Wendt, professor of philosophy at Leipzig. Wendt was a philosopher, aesthetician, author of books on music, amateur composer, and one of the founders, with Robert Schumann, of the *Neue Zeitschrift für Musik*, which was to be the *AMZ*'s principal rival in later years. Over the next few decades, Wendt was to contribute several more articles of a speculative nature to the *AMZ*, some of which may have had a deep influence on the musical thought of his generation.[40] It is in Wendt's writing that one senses for the first time the pervasive Hegelianism that was to become a hallmark of A. B. Marx and the Berlin school of Beethoven criticism.

Wendt, however, was not a mere forerunner of Marx; he had a highly personal view of Beethoven's place in music history. Nor was he a disciple of Hoffmann, whose ideas he often recalls, only to transform them in a way of which their author probably did not approve. Wendt is unique among *AMZ* critics in that he can be counted neither as an admirer nor a detractor of Beethoven. His opinions are given with a detachment which, in the highly partisan atmosphere of early nineteenth-century criticism, could probably have come only from an amateur musician with an academic background in another field. Beethoven, he says, is the musical Shakespeare, but this seems not to have been a term of unqualified praise. It points to the composer's ability to mix contrasting feelings with no apparent rhyme or reason beyond the sweep of his own fantasy. As if to emphasize the weakness of such a style, Wendt also draws a parallel between Beethoven and Jean Paul, a thoroughly original writer who also seemed to neglect the traditional unities in his search for new modes of expression.

For Wendt, awareness of form was an indispensable stage in the development of music; once achieved, it could not be transcended, even by an artist of Beethoven's stature. Mozart was his ideal. Like many of his contemporaries, Wendt had a limited view of music history perfectly suited to his own opinions: all early music was based solely on form; Haydn brought formalism to its highest peak of development while at the same time pointing the way to a new era; but only Mozart was able to combine form and expression to the fullest degree. It was for this reason that Wendt later described Mozart's music as 'classic', and he may have been the first to apply the term to a composer of the later eighteenth century.[41] Mozart's works, he wrote, are the product of a deeply sensitive spirit, but nothing betrays their origin; surrendering to them, we live in a unique, imperceptible world, and only the return of our thoughts to reality after the sounds have faded reminds us of the artist and his work. If in Haydn's compositions fantasy often seems subordinate to the power of reason, in Mozart's music both are inseparably bound together; hardly ever do they appear distinct from one another.

For Beethoven, on the other hand, reason seemed to have lost its constraint. Wendt was careful to draw a distinction between empty formlessness, arising from a facile striving after effect, and the inspired, other-worldly vision which he found in Beethoven's music. It is clear, though, that he thought the composer guilty of gross errors ('grosse Verirrungen') which personality alone could not excuse. All of Beethoven's instrumental works seemed to Wendt to have a manner appropriate only to one very specific genre: that of the fantasy. They lacked unity, and had no specific character of their own. Wendt recognized in Beethoven an inspired ('geistvoll') musician, but he clearly regretted that other composers with less talent had begun to follow the example of formlessness. Beethoven, it may be surmised, seemed to Wendt likely to be remembered as a great composer with a disastrous influence on music history.

Wendt's affinity with Hoffmann is most apparent in his first few paragraphs. Of all the arts, he writes, only music originates in the 'paradise of ideas' ('Elysium der Ideen'), and speaks a 'magical language' ('Wundersprache') which everyone can hear, but few can understand. Hoffmann, speaking specifically of Beethoven, had also emphasized the recondite nature of pure instrumental music. Wendt adds a few terms of his own to Hoffmann's already extensive list of negatives: for example, he says that the communications of music are invisible ('unsichtbar'), since they deal with the secrets of the heart, into which no mortal eye can see.

Although Wendt, as a regular contributor to the *AMZ*, had probably read Hoffmann's articles, it is doubtful whether he borrowed from them directly. He was certainly familiar with the aesthetic theories of the German Romantics: particularly Friedrich Wilhelm Joseph von Schelling and August Wilhelm Schlegel, to whom both he and Hoffmann are clearly indebted. Echoing ideas expressed a few years earlier by Chateaubriand,[42] Schlegel in his lectures on dramatic art and literature, given in Vienna in the spring of 1808, had defined Romantic art as the embodiment of Christian transcendentalism: the antithesis of classical self-sufficiency and worldliness. In Christianity, he said, 'everything finite and mortal is lost in the contemplation of infinity ... Hence the poetry of the ancients was the poetry of enjoyment, and ours is that of desire: the former has its foundation in the scene which is present, while the latter hovers betwixt recollection and hope.' In Romantic poetry, 'the impressions of the soul are to be hallowed, as it were, by a mysterious connection with higher feelings, and the soul, on the other hand, embodies its foreboding, or indescribable intuitions of infinity, in types and symbols borrowed from the visible world'.[43]

Schlegel was concerned primarily with poetry, but Schelling, six years earlier, had said unequivocally that 'the form of art in which the unity of existence is made directly into potency, into symbol, is music'.[44] Schelling's view of music was essentially Platonic: the forms of music are the forms of the world itself; they spring from the rhythm and harmony of the visible universe. It is not difficult, however, to see in his 'reale Einheit' a possible source for Wendt's preoccupation with musical unity. As for Schlegel, his 'indescribable intuitions of infinity' are so close to Hoffmann that their poetic orientation is all but irrelevant. Wendt, too, with his 'paradise of ideas' and his 'unique, imperceptible world', was caught up in the current of idealism which no German philosopher of his time seems to have been able to avoid.

There was, however, a subtle difference between the points of view of these two critics. Hoffmann held Beethoven's vocal music in relatively low regard; he wrote in the Fifth Symphony review that a musical setting clothes a text in 'the purple shimmer of Romanticism', but that music still strives to break free from any connection with the other arts. Wendt, by contrast, actually preferred Beethoven's vocal music to his instrumental works. He still sought to associate music with ideas and sentiments, and he found in the plot of *Fidelio* a discipline which he had not perceived in Beethoven's other works: a counterweight for the impetuous personality of the composer. Hoffmann and Wendt were really saying the same thing in opposite ways: the former, that music without a text can transcend ordinary human life; the latter, that a text can humanize music and make it more accessible.

It is particularly important to distinguish between Wendt's rather loosely defined emotional interpretation of *Fidelio*, which tends to emphasize music's ability to express ideas, and the most common theory of the eighteenth century, which suggested that music *arouses* emotional states in the listener. Wendt tends to describe the emotional content of music in more objective terms, so that, like Hoffmann, he finds that music *provides access to* the world of emotions being described. For Wendt, it is the text which, above all else, unifies Beethoven's music, and it does this, furthermore, more through its moral than its emotional content.

The last three parts of Wendt's six-part article are devoted to a minute discussion of *Fidelio*. This opera — in many ways Beethoven's most problematic work — had been successfully performed in Vienna for the first time in 1814, in a form substantially revised by the composer.[45] Wendt, however, had heard it in the original version at Leipzig, and knew the revision only from the score.[46] He preferred the original, finding its three-act structure more satisfactory from an aesthetic point of view, and was particularly dissatisfied with the new overture in E major which, he found, did not fit the mood of the drama which was to follow. For the rest, Wendt's treatment of *Fidelio* is nothing less than ecstatic: here is an opera which leaves behind the commonplaces of the musical theater and explores each character's deepest emotions; it clearly belongs in the exalted company of Mozart's greatest works for the stage. The music refers at all times to the events of the plot, awakening from the audience a deep and sympathetic interest. The declamation is truly masterly. In short, song itself seems for once to be more important than the singer: no mean accomplishment for a composer born in the century in which vocal technique had reached its highest point of perfection.

Wendt also elaborates on his earlier comparison of Beethoven with Shakespeare. Some, he says, had criticized the music of *Fidelio* as unnaturally powerful and even ugly; many (inspired perhaps by the 'Kantische Schilderung der Musik' which Wendt had mentioned earlier) still felt that pleasantness and ease of comprehension were the highest aesthetic goals to which music could aspire. Wendt responded to this challenge by suggesting that a great dramatic composer, like a great playwright, must represent life to the fullest extent which art will allow, depicting both pleasure and horror with an Olympian hand. 'We are also given to understand,' he wrote, 'that the music of this opera jangles the nerves of many sensitive natures. We have even heard this from admirers of Shakespeare, who added life's harshest dissonances to the many-voiced choir of his great dramas.' A metaphor like this, if taken seriously, could easily have been the basis for a re-evaluation of musical aesthetics on literary terms. Wendt explicitly refrains from making such an attempt, but his sympathy with Hegel is again apparent in his assertion that 'everywhere that great forces are allowed to develop, great contradictions are also present; Beethoven, however, has created on a truly grand scale and raised his material above the level of ordinary life'.

The concluding pages of Wendt's article are the least interesting from a modern point of view. They are devoted to a narrative of the dramatic situation accompanying each number of Beethoven's opera, with superficial descriptions of the music and painstaking comparisons between the original and the revised version. Unlike Hoffmann, Wendt makes little reference to his aesthetic theories in the course of this analysis, and despite its length (16 columns in all), it could easily be detached from the rest of the text without detracting from the cogency or completeness of the whole. A few points are of interest, however: Wendt defends the original overture (presumably Leonore no. 2) because, though long and rather loosely constructed, it had presented an accurate impression of the mood of the opera. This shows that he took his own theories seriously with regard to instrumental as well as vocal music; a piece full of violent contrasts could, in some circumstances, be preferable to a more unified work, less 'fantastic' and hence more 'classical' in form.

Wendt's fundamental ambivalence toward Beethoven is once again apparent, as he struggles to accept the composer's more adventurous music while at the same time warning against the aesthetic errors it contains. Principal among the latter was the inclusion of the liberating trumpet call from the prison scene, which in this context, he felt, could only be understood as 'a frivolity out of keeping with the deep serious-ness of the entire overture'. Wendt also recommends that Rocco's aria 'Hat man nicht auch Gold beineben' be dropped – it is rather common-place and hence out of character. He may have felt that everyone in the drama, apart from Pizarro, should benefit from the exalted tone set by the principal figures.

Wendt's view of *Fidelio*, then, was not particularly Shakespearean; he admired the opera both for the quality of the music and for the high moral purpose of the drama, but he still mistrusted the more capricious side of the composer's nature. Like Hoffmann, he seems to have viewed the experience of Beethoven's music as a cumulative one. For Hoffmann, the Fifth Symphony carried the listener irresistibly forward into a world both unimaginable and sublime, while for Wendt the very dramatic intensity of *Fidelio*'s darkest moments was resolved by the ending, in which 'every bitter remembrance and every feeling of pain is finally overcome by triumphant joy and delight'. Wendt's foremost concern is for dramatic ef[fect; he would seem to have had] no part in the gradual emancipation of [instrumental music whi]ch [was] to culminate a few years later in Schopen[hauer's] *[Welt als Wille und] Vorstellung*. And yet, strangely enough[, Wendt ends with a quotation] from Schiller which Hoffmann, too, [had used: 'Das Le]ben athme die bildende Kunst, Geist ford[ert] [...] [spricht] nur Polyhymnia aus!'.

Here and else[where ... t]he Romantic view of music, complex a[nd ...], stems from a funda-mental belief in music's ability to lay bare the human soul, with or with-out the assistance of the written word. Far from being the platitude it has since become, this belief in the 'soulfulness' of music was for Wendt's generation a powerful artistic creed, and more than anything else it explains the enormous impact that Beethoven's music had on those of his contemporaries who could hear it with unbiased ears.

Wendt and Hoffmann, then, were both idealists, in the sense that they believed in the existence of a level of meaning deeper and more significant than that conveyed by ordinary speech, and they both found access to it through music. In other respects, Wendt may seem old-fashioned: his preference for vocal music and his apparent belief in concrete affections both recall the traditional emphasis of eighteenth-century theory. The very fact that such opinions were voiced by a professional philosopher, however, is paradoxical from the modern point of view, according to which the history of Romantic music theory was a linear progression toward absolutism.

Actually, the situation was much more complex than this, and it will be shown in succeeding chapters that it is difficult to trace any kind of progress toward a specific philosophical attitude toward music among the critics who wrote about Beethoven during his lifetime. It will be argued that this is partly because such an attitude already existed, and was simply substantially different, as well as more difficult to define, than the absolutist standpoint championed by modern writers. In any case, Hoffmann has long been a favorite subject for studies of all kinds, and he has been enthusiastically adopted to represent the practical embodiment of the musical theories advanced by Tieck and Wackenroder in the 1790s. It is these writers who first suggested that there was a sublime, spiritual dimension to music which could not be put into words, and which made music superior to verbal expression. It has already been suggested that much of Hoffmann's vocabulary can more easily be traced to August Wilhelm Schlegel, but certainly the sublimity which he found in the Fifth Symphony has its roots in late eighteenth-century philosophy, as does the very concept of the creative spirit in art. It is hardly surprising, then, that Hoffmann has been taken as uniquely representative of Beethoven's contemporary critics.

In this view, Wendt appears conservative, despite his idealistic insights. His very theory of drama in particular seems to be anchored in the Aristotelianism of the Enlightenment. According to any strict linear theory of the history of aesthetics, that viewpoint was superseded by the developments which were to culminate a few years later in Schopenhauer's characterization of music. Schopenhauer felt that music was the embodiment of the absolute, thus apparently freeing it from the limitations of 'affection' theory. It is easy to see Hoffmann subscribing to this view, but

Wendt would clearly not endorse it. Was he, then, a true conservative in the context of Romantic music theory?

An answer to this question is crucial to our understanding of later theorists like A. B. Marx, who also differs significantly from the absolutist point of view. It is perhaps best answered by looking at two purely philosophical formulations which also stand on the intricate path between Kant and Schopenhauer, but which deal with the theory of knowledge rather than that of art. The 'subjective' idealism of Fichte and the 'objective' viewpoint of Schelling have never been considered as stages in a linear development: they are too distinct from one another, and they both influenced the succeeding generation. It is here that the explanation of the intriguing contrasts and similarities between our two critics may be found. It is certainly not the case that Hoffmann was a disciple of Fichte, or Wendt of Schelling, but such a pairing brings into focus a conflict between opposing traditions which were nearly as old as the Enlightenment itself, and which were still in active conflict when Wendt and Hoffmann wrote their reviews.

The first, and more familiar, tradition has its roots in the rational, mathematical system of Descartes, which begins by positing the thinking subject as the source of all knowledge. In direct opposition to Decartes' 'cogito, ergo sum' stood Leibniz' dictum that 'the part is less than the whole', which stemmed from the assumption that there exist 'proofs *a priori*, independent of experience'.

It is this latter view which finds its classical statement for music theory in Johann Mattheson's *Volkommene Capellmeister* − not so much in the famous *Affektenlehre* as in what Mattheson calls the general fundamental principle of music ('allgemeine Grund-Satz der Music') − 'Alles muss gehörig singen'.[47] Much has been made of the dependence of Mattheson's theory of fixed and continuous emotional states on Descartes' description of the passions. Bellamy Hosler, however, points out that 'by virtue of giving [the traditional *Figurenlehre*, which held that certain musical figures were suited to particular emotions in an almost mechanical manner] a scientific basis, Mattheson was providing an Enlightenment alternative to the very different passionate utterance theory of musical expression formulated by the neoclassic critics'.[48] Mattheson, then, expresses the objective attitude to musical expression, which Hosler traces not only to Leibniz but to Luther as well.[49] Mattheson 'partook of the traditional German view that there was a "secret affinity" whereby well-ordered sounds would impart their harmony to the sympathetic human soul'.[50]

Something similar to this is expressed in Schelling's belief that the imagination ('Einbildungskraft', or 'In-Eins'Bildung') unifies real and ideal, 'ich bin' and 'es gibt'.

33

As the sun stands freely in the heavens, joining and uniting all in the power of its clear light, so the soul of eternal nature stands in the interlinkage of being itself as the unity and, so to speak, as the divine imagination of that linkage, free and unbounded, as the origin of all feeling existence, which in visible nature pulsates as the heart. And, moving and circulating everything in nature's holy body, it gives rise to each impulse and to the intimacy of all creation.[51]

This trust in a pre-ordained harmony of all things is clearly paralleled by Wendt's insistence on a type of unity which stems as much from dramatic as from musical principles, as well as by his belief in form as the starting point of music history, encompassing expression in the works of Mozart and in Beethoven's music disappearing entirely.

By contrast, the neo-classic critics cited by Hosler insisted that music began as passionate utterance: a purely individual form of self-expression. Hoffmann can also be read in terms of his emphasis on the listening subject, through whose perception alone the spiritual dimension in music is realized. Hoffmann's spirit-kingdom is not an objective form; it is an intuitively perceived reality without shape or boundary, with which the listener must be united for the music to have its effect.

The philosophical counterpart for this view during Beethoven's lifetime might be found in the subjective idealism of Fichte, who abolished the Kantian 'Ding an Sich' in an attempt to reduce all reality to the unification of the 'Ich' and the 'Nicht-Ich'. Fichte's system, though aiming at the same goal of unity sought by Schelling, is fundamentally anti-empirical and subjective; Schelling's system by contrast begins and ends with objectivity. Neither is more or less forward-looking than the other; they simply represent different solutions to the problem of transcending the severe limitations which Kant had placed on human perception. Perhaps, then, it was this same problem which Hoffmann and Wendt were trying to solve musically. Their systems should not be viewed as respectively progressive and conservative, but rather as two equally valid ways of assimilating the new idealism to an explanation of Beethoven's greatness.

Wendt, then, represents the objective–empirical point of view inherited from Mattheson, while Hoffmann maintains the outlook, if not the overweening rationalism, of the neo-classic critics mentioned by Hosler. He simply inverts the system's priorities, concentrating not on passionate utterance by the performer, but on the subjective experience of the listener.

It is thus significant that neither writer is as one-sided as at first appears. Much in line with the various philosophies of the time, they seek unity as the highest goal of art. Thus Hoffmann praises the Fifth Symphony for its unprecedented coherence, while Wendt praises *Fidelio* for incorporating aspects of musical progress without degenerating into formlessness.

Hoffmann simply explains the unity of these works in different terms. For Hoffmann, the abstract spirit-world evoked by the symphony is firmly anchored in the technical aspects of his analysis – a correspondence which will be explored further in Chapter 5. Wendt, on the other hand, saw the specific emotional details of *Fidelio* as unified at least in part by the striving for transcendence which marks the work as a whole. Once again, it is apparent that both writers were saying the same thing in opposite ways: that they were equally inspired by the Romantic tendency to reconcile opposing points of view.

If we are to look for a spirit of the times in their criticism, it should be sought not merely in their desire to transcend ordinary experience – a desire which is clearly inspired by post-Kantian idealism – but in their sincere attempts to reconcile and co-ordinate all opposing aspects of musical experience into a single explanation of Beethoven's work. The importance of these attempts is easily underestimated if the theories of Hanslick and Wagner are seen as the goal toward which musical aesthetics were evolving in the early nineteenth century.

Actually, the writers to be studied in the succeeding chapters will make it evident that the situation was far more complex, and that all the critics who wrote about Beethoven during his lifetime recognized the exaggerated nature of the claims which aestheticians were already making about music, and sought to correct the tendency of those aestheticians to give music a status different from that accorded to the other arts. This rejection of contemporary aesthetic theory is most apparent in A. B. Marx, who will be discussed in Chapter 2. First, however, the present chapter must be completed by examining those writings on Beethoven which appeared in the *AMZ* during the last years of his life.

The later reviews

On June 21, 1813, the armies of Beethoven's one-time idol, Napoleon, were defeated by the British at Victoria, Spain. The mighty political events which had formed the background to most of the composer's life were rapidly drawing to an end, and the man who had proposed to dedicate one of his greatest works to Napoleon ten years before now celebrated the emperor's defeat with one of his worst – and most successful. It is well known that *Wellington's Sieg bei Vittoria* (first performed at Vienna on December 8, 1813, in a concert which also included the premiere of the Seventh Symphony)[52] contributed more than any other single work to the truly popular acclaim which Beethoven enjoyed in the years surrounding the Congress of Vienna.

This acclaim is reflected in the pages of the *AMZ*. The anonymous review of *Wellington's Victory*, printed in April 1816, marks the beginning of a new and rather unfortunate genre in Beethoven criticism. Here, for the first time, any hint of adverse comment disappears, leaving in its place a superficial overview of the work replete with musical examples and easy reverence for the composer's genius. Critical poise is lost, and with it critical purpose; the text reads more like a 'publisher's puff' than a conscientious review. Today it would not be out of place on a record jacket, since its primary aim is to tell the reader what to listen for; only highlights come into play, and difficult questions of aesthetics and artistic goals are completely forgotten.

Two more such reviews, of the Seventh and Eighth Symphonies, followed in quick succession (*AMZ* XVIII, col. 817 and *AMZ* XX, col. 161). Both of these works had been performed for the first time in Vienna on programs which also featured *Wellington's Victory*, and they seem to have profited by the association. Only five years separate the review of the Seventh Symphony from that of the 'Harp' Quartet, Op. 74, cited above as an example of the continuing skepticism, bordering on outright hostility, which Beethoven could provoke even in the years of Hoffmann's preeminence in the field.

It would be a mistake to suppose that this attitude ever vanished entirely during the composer's life; in a footnote to Rochlitz' commentary on the C-sharp minor Quartet, Op. 131, published in 1828, Christian Gottfried Wilhelm Fink, the *AMZ*'s new editor, recalled early anti-Beethoven comments in the *AMZ* and elsewhere and compared them tellingly with opinions held by his own contemporaries on Beethoven's last works. Nor should it be assumed that Beethoven's gradual recognition as the greatest living composer of instrumental music − a recognition which is increasingly apparent in nearly everything written about him in the mid-1810s − turned the heads of the *AMZ* staff when it came to evaluating his newest music. As the following pages will make clear, the man who had once been censured for not writing in the prevailing musical style was occasionally criticized just as sharply for turning his back on his own accomplishments. It must also be remembered that, as will be demonstrated in a later chapter, these reviews were only a small minority of those which appeared even during Beethoven's last years; if the above comments seem to contradict the claim that the composer was universally well received, it is only because the *AMZ* was by far the most conservative source of music criticism in Europe during his lifetime. Elsewhere, the story was a very different one.

These few reviews, too, seem to emerge directly from the world of public acclaim which surrounded Beethoven at the time they were written. For their authors, Beethoven can do no wrong; even the finale of the Eighth Symphony, which seems to have baffled the reviewer more than he openly admits, is praised as an original and spirited work fully worthy of the composer's genius. Hoffmann, Wendt and Kanne had all written for a kind of musical elite; here the intended audience is once again the 'Mittelmässigkeit': the very class of musical dilettantes whom Beethoven's most ardent admirers had previously treated with condescension.

The result is not entirely without insight. In the review of the Eighth Symphony, for example, the author points out that the first movement begins with two very accessible themes and then develops, appropriately, into a character piece in the manner of Haydn: an objective which Beethoven would once have found too limiting. This is the best of the three reviews, however, and even here one looks in vain for a real sense of purpose, or even a convincing account of Beethoven's personal style. The survey of the Seventh Symphony includes, almost as an afterthought, a claim that 'the greatest beauty − the effect of the whole work − cannot possibly be expressed in words. Soon all of Germany, France and England will second our opinion.' Perhaps the greatest challenge a critic can face is that of finding something intelligent to say about a work which is bound to succeed, with or without his encouragement. Everything in these reviews shows the extent to which Hoffmannesque proselytizing was already obsolete; as far as the authors were concerned, Beethoven had already become an institution.

They could not have known that, by 1816, the composer had embarked on a new series of major works which would soon restore him to the position of controversy from which he had so recently escaped. The external circumstances of Beethoven's last years are well known: the deafness, now complete; the legal battles over the custody of his nephew and the latter's attempted suicide; the Viennese public's consuming passion for Rossini; the bafflement produced by the last quartets; and, like a single stunning rebuke to so much misunderstanding and confusion, the triumphant premiere of the Ninth Symphony, where Beethoven appeared in public for the last time, creating an image of pathos that has proved as durable as the symphony itself. If Rossini, who visited the composer during a trip to Vienna in 1822, is to be believed, Beethoven lived and worked during the last years in appalling poverty and isolation: an embarrassment to the aristocratic society which had once accepted him freely.[53]

In the same year, Rochlitz, now retired from the editorship of the *AMZ*, spoke to Beethoven at length. The composer praised reports he had read, presumably in the *AMZ*, of concerts at Leipzig, but, in an oft-quoted diatribe, he attacked the Viennese musical public with surprising vehemence:

You will hear nothing of me here ... What should you hear? *Fidelio*? They cannot give it, nor do they want to listen to it. The symphonies? They have no time for them. My concertos? Everyone grinds out only the stuff he himself has made. The solo pieces? They went out of fashion here long ago, and here fashion is everything. At most [Ignaz Franz] Schuppanzigh digs up a quartet.[54]

What is less well known is that during these last years the European musical press was making a colossal effort – not without success – to come to terms with the new style of Beethoven's last works, and with the challenge of his *oeuvre* as a whole. In the early to mid 1820s, two new journals were founded with a specifically pro-Beethoven bias: the *Berliner Allgemeine Musikalische Zeitung*, edited by Adolf Bernhard Marx, and the Mainz-based *Caecilia*, edited by Gottfried Weber. The most insightful Beethoven reviews of the decade appeared in these new sources, and the contemporary criticism in the *AMZ* must be viewed accordingly.

The new journals, however, were not as harsh with the older one in Leipzig as Schumann would be ten years later when he ridiculed the 'allgemeinste musikalische Zeitung' and the entire state of music criticism as he knew it.[55] Marx was content to teach largely by example, and Weber, as his scathing review of *Wellington's Victory* clearly shows, was not only an apostle of Beethoven but a serious and objective critic as well (*Caec.* III, p. 155). The same can be said of those who wrote about Beethoven for the *AMZ* during the final decade of the composer's life, though, as we shall see, their activities were curiously limited in scope.

Skepticism returns abruptly with a review of the two cello sonatas, Op. 102, printed in November, 1818, but it is now tinged with a profound respect (*AMZ* XX, col. 792). The reviewer expresses his opinion of these works in terms which recall the perplexity of the earliest colleagues when confronted with the music of Beethoven's youth. The tone, however, is apologetic where it had once been harsh; respectful where it had once been condescending. These sonatas, the reviewer believes, stand in relation to the prevailing taste of the time much as certain keyboard works of J.S. Bach had done nearly a century before: austere, uncompromising, and yet thoroughly artistic, they will best be understood by those who are willing to listen to them repeatedly before passing judgment. The entire review recalls nothing so much as the new appraisal of Schönberg which emerged around the time of his centennial in 1974. There is the same emphasis on the composer's links with the past; the same acknowledgment of his intellectual achievement; the same embarrassed admission that his music is nevertheless inaccessible to most of its prospective audience; and the same lingering suspicion that the composer, despite great talent and the highest artistic goals, has been misled by the quest for novelty, and has failed to produce music which will endure.

The Leipzig Allgemeine Musikalische Zeitung

Much warmer in tone, though still not without skepticism, is a review of the last three piano sonatas, Opp. 109, 110 and 111, printed in April, 1824 (*AMZ* XXVI, col. 213). The sonatas of Op. 102, still counted among Beethoven's less appealing works, are now treated as a stage — perhaps a necessary one — in the composer's development: an idea which surprisingly adumbrates the more recent one of a 'Romantic crisis' faced and overcome by Beethoven during the decade of the 1810s.

A new aesthetic attitude emerges in the course of this review, placing it, in its abstraction, close to the spirit of Hoffmann, but rejecting even the earlier critic's style of analysis as superfluous.

The most complete familiarity with human anatomy, light-perspective, coloring, etc., cannot make a portrait into a work of art, and neither does a piece of music become one just because it uses every conceivable contrapuntal and technical device ... Just as the most practiced score-reader cannot enjoy music fully simply by reading the notes ... or reach a suitable final opinion upon it, neither can those to whom a work is unfamiliar be persuaded by written quotations of individual passages through examples. One must hear the entire work in context, performed with understanding. A certain inexplicable something may then persuade us to overlook or exonerate even serious sins against the laws of music. Likewise, the greatest propriety and technical accomplishment, which in reading we recognize with pleasure, may lose all value when heard.

This is very far from the attitude of the earliest *AMZ* critics, who, as we have seen, had their own inflexible criteria of right and wrong in composition, and set little store by the effect a passage made in performance. This author felt that he could do no more than advise the reader on the nature of the music, and describe, sometimes explicitly, the states of mind which it suggests. For example, discussing the first movement of Op. 109, he writes that the Adagio beginning at m.9 has a character of 'melancholy, with lighter moments and several — we will let the English word pass — whims'. The second movement of Op. 110 'paints in tones, one after another: despondency ('Muthlosigkeit'), reassurance ('Ermuthigung'), transport by a higher power ('Fortgerissenwerden durch eine höhere Gewalt'), hesitation before a resolve ('Schwanken vor dem Entschluss'), full encouragement once more, and finally, after a cry of despair, total collapse ('gänzliches Zusammenstürzen')'.

This is not merely a return to the eighteenth-century affections. Except for the 'Schrey der Verzweiflung', it is difficult to connect such fantasies to specific devices or mannerisms in the music itself; they depict psychological images, even offering a hint of mystical fulfillment, and their nature is correspondingly abstract. At times the author recalls Hoffmann directly, as when he describes the second theme in the first movement of Op. 111

39

as 'the loveliest contrast to the powerful, passionate impulsiveness ('dem gewaltigen leidenschaftlichen Treiben') which hardly stops for a moment in this whole movement and which drives everything restlessly forward'.

Here and elsewhere, Hoffmann's idealism appears in a form rather more systematic than its author had intended. Having been broadened to describe these most recent of Beethoven's works, it has lost the sharp focus it had when applied to the Fifth Symphony alone. It has become, in short, a Romantic *Affektenlehre*, handy as an analytical tool in its own right, but still abstract enough to preserve the sense of Faustian striving on which it depends. This kind of watered-down idealism, made considerably more respectable by more talented critics in other periodicals, was to be one of the keynotes of the new Beethoven criticism, where it was invariably designated by the term 'Tonmalerei'. As we shall see, musical programs such as that implied by this review were not uncommon during the 1820s and 1830s. The combination of specificity and other-worldliness which they contain points once again to the sense of priorities I have already sought to document in analysing Wendt's and Hoffmann's reviews; the effortless juxtaposition of idealism with more mundane interpretations.

On the negative side, this critic rejects all but the concluding pages of Op. 111's long second movement as a commonplace set of variations, comparing it to a highly intricate painting done in monotone with a miniature pencil. The nineteenth century had little patience with mere craftsmanship.

With only this review to go on, however, one might suppose that Beethoven's later music was received nearly everywhere with mingled respect and admiration. The *AMZ* was now the most conservative of the three major German-language journals devoted to music, and these sonatas are certainly among the most daring, unprecedented works of their kind. We must read between the lines to discover the real story.

After the lengthy, laudatory reviews of the Fifth, Sixth, Seventh and Eighth Symphonies, it is surprising to find that the Ninth Symphony was not reviewed at all in the *AMZ*, apart from some ambiguous concert reports on the first performances.[56] Neither are there formal reviews of the *Missa Solemnis*, the 'Hammerklavier' Sonata, the 'Diabelli' Variations, or any of the last quartets. Instead, from 1820 on, the *AMZ* critics limited themselves, where Beethoven was concerned, to reviewing folksong arrangements, new editions of earlier music, and incidental works like the trio, 'Tremate, empi, tremate', Op. 116 (*AMZ* XXVIII, col. 494), the *Opferlied*, Op. 121 (*AMZ* XXVII, col. 740), the *Bundeslied*, Op. 122 (*AMZ* XXVII, col. 740), and the choral setting of Goethe's *Meeresstille und glückliche Fahrt*, Op. 112 (*AMZ* XXIV, col. 674). There are also enthusiastic reviews, dating from a few years before 1820, of transitional or anomalous works like the Violin Sonata, Op. 96 (*AMZ* XIX, col. 228) and the song cycle *An die ferne Geliebte*, Op. 98 (*AMZ* XIX, col. 73). There is even an ecstatic review of the Piano Sonata, Op. 101 – an experimental work whose fugal finale anticipates that of the 'Hammerklavier' (*AMZ* XIX, col. 686). That was in 1817, the year after the reviews of *Wellington's Victory* and the Seventh Symphony and the year before that of the Eighth – ten years before Beethoven's death. The astounding fact is that over the next decade, only two reviews of major new works by Beethoven appeared in Europe's largest and most prestigious musical journal. The rest of the late music was virtually ignored.

What explains this extraordinary attitude toward the most famous of living composers? There are only two possible answers: the music was either considered incomprehensible, and hence impossible to review; or else adverse criticism was withheld out of respect for Beethoven. The weight of the evidence supports the second conclusion. The composer died in 1827; the following year a devastating attack on his later works appeared in *Caecilia* (*Caec.* VIII, p. 36). This was followed in 1829 by a less brazen, but no more equivocal, attack in the *AMZ* (*AMZ* XXXI, col. 269). Both articles were submitted by contributors; the latter anonymously,[57] the former under the name of Ernst Woldemar,[58] and neither should be regarded as an editorial statement.[59] They reveal, however, what the formal reviews ignore: Beethoven, in his last years, had become once again both a *cause célèbre* and a *bête noire*.

The *AMZ* article begins with the simple statement that 'since the death of the great master, controversy over his last works has been frequent and often bitter'. After describing the arguments on both sides, and dismissing the favorable ones, the author goes on to attribute Beethoven's alleged decline to a single cause: his deafness. 'Everyone [who has composed],' he wrote, 'will know that there is ear-music and eye-music; that often, that which works brilliantly in score makes no effect in performance, and vice versa. Little by little Beethoven was obliged by circumstances to become a composer for the eye.'

Beethoven's deafness was common knowledge; it had already been alluded to many times in the pages of the *AMZ*,[60] and the relative restraint shown in judging his late music while he was still alive seems to have arisen, simply and understandably, from pity. It was widely assumed that Beethoven, deprived of his hearing, had also lost the critical faculty to correct his own errors of judgment; that a deaf composer was of necessity a poor composer. Neither Woldemar nor the anonymous writer in the *AMZ* questions the value of Beethoven's earlier music; indeed they reaffirm it.

To them, the later works had the poignancy, and even some of the grandeur, of the ruins of Athens which the composer had so recently evoked.

Ironically, the aesthetic argument which is here turned against Beethoven is one that had already been used in his favor, and would be again. It has already been mentioned that apparent errors of method in the last three piano sonatas were excused by the *AMZ*'s reviewer on the ground that they sounded better than they looked on paper. Several years later Hector Berlioz, reviewing the Seventh Symphony, wrote that a certain cross-relation in the finale 'might be expected to result in a terrible dissonance ... but it is not so ... Beethoven did not write music for the eyes'.[61]

Critics of the late music, however, were concerned not with technical errors, but with a general feeling of diffuseness in the structure of the works as a whole; movements drawn out to seemingly inordinate lengths; dissonances sustained at an unprecedented level, as in the *Grosse Fuge* from the B-flat major Quartet, Op. 130. Such concern was especially evident in the concert reports from this period, which, though often rather perfunctory, show surprising agreement. Those from Vienna are generally favorable; the earlier correspondent must have been replaced by a Beethoven enthusiast.[62] The *Missa Solemnis* also seems to have been well received in St Petersburg (*AMZ* XXVI, col. 349) and Frankfurt am Main (*AMZ* XXVII, col. 277). The Ninth Symphony, however, met with skepticism virtually everywhere it was performed. The Frankfurt critic, though praising the work as a whole, criticized the vocal writing (*AMZ* XXVII, col. 279); in Aachen the reaction was the same (*AMZ* XXVII, col. 446), and the Leipzig correspondent wrote that

The last movement ... is played out entirely in the unhappy dwelling places of those who have fallen from Heaven. It is as though the spirits of the deep were celebrating a festival of hatred toward all human joy. This perilous crowd stalks heavily forward, tearing hearts asunder and darkening the divine sparks ('Götterfunken') with noisy, monstrous scorn. *AMZ* XXVIII, col. 853

In Berlin, the A minor Quartet, Op. 132, was described as overlong, rhapsodic and difficult to grasp, despite its many beauties (*AMZ* XXX, col. 363). Even in Vienna, the last quartets were not well understood. The correspondent was skeptical about Op. 132 (*AMZ* XXVII, col. 840), though he praised it enthusiastically after a second performance (*AMZ* XXVII, col. 843). It is difficult to discern an opinion in his report on the E-flat major Quartet, Op. 127 (*AMZ* XXVII, col. 246), but it is clear that most of the public was baffled by the work. As for the *Grosse Fuge*, when it was first performed as the finale of Op. 130, it was met, as is well known, with undisguised hostility (*AMZ* XXVIII, col. 340).

One lengthy article defending the late music did appear in 1828 (*AMZ* XXX, col. 845). Its author, surprisingly, is Friedrich Rochlitz. This is not a formal review, but an essay written on the occasion of ('auf Veranlassung von') the publication of the C-sharp minor Quartet, Op. 131. The *AMZ*'s former editor, now ten years retired, makes a rather wordy case in favor of artistic tolerance. Novel and unprecedented performances, whether they be of new music or of music from an earlier time, cannot, Rochlitz believed, be judged by the same standards applied by critics to mere routine events. When Adam Hiller revived Handel's *Messiah* in Germany, Johann Gottlieb Naumann was opposed to the undertaking; nevertheless, he came to the performance, and was so moved that he recanted his first harsh opinion. Johann Friedrich Reichardt detested Mozart's operas, until at last, in Kassel, he heard them well performed. Beethoven himself had ridiculed Weber's *Freischütz* at the time of its initial success. Though Rochlitz gives no indication that Beethoven ever changed his mind about *Freischütz*, his point is well taken, and the relevance to late Beethoven must have been obvious to his readers. Rochlitz divided the musical public into two groups: those who expect nothing more from music than amusement and those who see it as the key to an inner spiritual life. Superficially this recalls Kanne's distinction between the 'Mittelmässigkeit' and the smaller group of more serious musicians. Now, however, it symbolizes the gap between old-fashioned views of music as mere entertainment and the greater value it was assigned in the intuitional Romanticism of the Schlegels and, ultimately, of Schopenhauer. Rochlitz, like the *AMZ* itself, had moved with the times.

Conclusion

No final verdict was reached on Beethoven's late music during the years which immediately followed his death, either in the *AMZ* or elsewhere. Sensitivity to differences of opinion, however, had always been one of the journal's strong points. Many of the articles discussed in this chapter are transparently tendentious; very few are written with that detached self-assurance which is the gift and the curse of hindsight. The *AMZ* managed, however, to cater for popular taste while at the same time encouraging some of the most advanced critics of the early nineteenth century. It cannot be coincidence that the disappearance of adverse criticism in the mid-1810s was accompanied by a new and rather fatuous style of non-criticism in the positive Beethoven reviews. Good journalism thrives on controversy, and the analytical insights of Hoffmann, Wendt and Kanne would have been impossible without the row of anonymous Beckmessers who continued to dot the *AMZ*'s pages throughout its long life.

43

Nor would they have been possible without the guiding hand of Friedrich Rochlitz. It is appropriate for this survey to conclude with Rochlitz' last Beethoven review, since he remained, even in his last years, a critic of truly exceptional breadth: a cautious admirer of Beethoven; a detractor moved by profound respect. Rochlitz was not a man of genius, and even his journalistic integrity has been questioned on several important grounds; he may have forged a well-known letter from Mozart describing the latter's compositional process, and it is possible that the meeting with Beethoven described above, which he reported enthusiastically in the *AMZ* after the composer's death, never took place at all.[63] As we have seen, he may also have accepted a bribe from the composer 20 years before. Ultimately, it is this peculiar combination of traits which marks both his own work and the *AMZ* under his leadership: old-fashioned, venal, but possessed of a stubborn curiosity and the potential for genuine advancement, both spent a lifetime trying to catch up with the musical giant whose steps always exceeded their grasp.

Rochlitz' retirement was the *AMZ*'s loss. If he had stayed on during the final decade there would doubtless have been more perceptive reviews of Beethoven's major works. There might also have been devastating critiques reminiscent of the earliest years. Rochlitz' most important talent was for attracting good writers; his greatest virtue lay in giving them free rein. After he retired the newest generation of critics was lost to Mainz and Berlin. There were several good reviews, but there were no more Hoffmanns. This, not the failure to reach a consensus of opinion, was the real tragedy of the *AMZ* during the 1820s.

2

Berlin and A. B. Marx

Of all the young critics active during the 1820s, none would have been better suited to take Hoffmann's place on the *AMZ* than Adolf Bernhard Marx. Instead, in 1824, the 24-year-old Marx founded his own journal, the *Berliner Allgemeine Musikalische Zeitung*, and edited it for seven years. He brought to his task a thorough schooling in Hegelian philosophy and was supported by a small but talented circle of Beethoven enthusiasts, among them Ludwig Rellstab, who would shortly found his own journal, *Iris im Gebiete der Tonkunst*. Marx never had the staff or the resources that were available to Rochlitz even in the earliest years of the *AMZ*, and to a large extent the story of contemporaneous Beethoven criticism in Berlin is his own story. In the first year of his journal, he began to supply that series of informed, sympathetic reviews of Beethoven's recent works that had been so conspicuously absent from the Leipzig paper, supplementing them with profound editorials that set forth his own views both of the nature of criticism and of the history of art itself. These views, though highly personal, are indisputably influenced by Hegel, and they show that Marx, like his philosophical mentor, shared the same preoccupation as many of the writers we have discussed: the co-existence of real and ideal − of interpretation and analysis − thus making him a true colleague of Hoffmann and the critics to be discussed in the next chapter.

As a writer on music, Marx is better known today than any of the critics discussed in Chapter 1, and deservedly so. He was one of the first to codify the thematic approach to musical analysis which has been the mainstay of classroom teaching, textbook writing, and program annotation, for better or worse, over the last century and a half. He was an articulate and informed exponent of the philosophical movement which gave birth to the murky and influential German term, *Gesamtkunstwerk*. He was also an engaging and skillful writer, and one of the earliest serious biographers of Beethoven. As a journal editor, however, Marx was a failure. He was unable to keep his enterprise solvent, unable to attract capable and objective correspondents, and thus ultimately unable to fulfill his own ambitious aims in the periodical press.[1] The reasons for this failure will be examined in the following pages.

It is no exaggeration to say that Marx the theorist has all but obliterated Marx the critic. Even his much-discussed Hegelianism, manifestations of which are evident throughout the critical writings, is more taken for granted today than sympathetically understood. Hegel is not now a fashionable philosopher, and it is difficult to imagine the thrall in which he held the Prussian intelligentsia of his time. W. T. Jones writes in his *History of Western Philosophy* that, during Hegel's last years in Berlin, 'something almost approaching a cult developed around him, which Hegel did nothing to dispel, since he had come to the conclusion that his theory was a statement of the final and complete truth about the universe'.[2]

Even in his earliest writings, though, Marx applied Hegelian philosophy to music in a highly personal way, and their inherent interest makes these writings an important guide both to his own later work and to early nineteenth-century musical thought. For this reason I have decided to consider everything that Marx wrote on Beethoven in this chapter, but to ignore *Iris*, which was not founded until after the composer's death, and thus played no immediate role in the controversy begun by Marx – a controversy over the status of a living composer whose career was still subject to the historical trends which Marx sought constantly to define and understand. Clarification of these trends, as applied by Marx and his associates to the music of Beethoven, will be one of the primary objectives of this chapter.

Marx's aesthetic theories

In his biography of Beethoven (first published in 1859), his *Lehre von der musikalischen Komposition* (1837–47), and many other treatises and articles, Marx left behind a more systematic theory of musical aesthetics than any of the writers discussed in the last chapter. Nor was this philosophical bent limited to his mature life as an academician. Although he began his career as a critic, he seems to have felt compelled from the first to give an added dimension to his writing through explanations of the nature and function of expressive devices and musical form. His monograph on tone-painting, published independently while he was editing the *BAMZ*,[3] thus adds to the common view of Marx as a systematic thinker the significant knowledge that the nature of his thought changed little over his 40-year career. In some of his later writings, Marx did adopt a drier, more technical style of formal analysis, thus initiating a type of pedagogy which has survived into the late twentieth century. Both in his earliest and his latest works, however, one finds a kind of active criticism which depends on extra-musical ideas and associations as well as on preconceived models of form − in which the two, indeed, stand together. The primary interest of the biography, and the reason for its inclusion here, lies in the *tour de force* which Marx accomplished in applying this style of criticism to nearly every piece of music that Beethoven wrote. Marx seems to have been determined to leave no questions unanswered. The biography makes compelling reading even today because it presents Beethoven's stylistic development as an historical process, culminating in a small number of pivotal works.

One such work is the 'Eroica' Symphony. The 'Eroica' was never reviewed in the *BAMZ*, where Marx preferred to concentrate on recent publications. In the biography, however, Marx treats it as a monumental achievement, and focuses on it the full array of critical ideas already set forth with regard to Beethoven. Chief among these are the following: (1) each major work presents a psychological image, not just in its initial movements, but in the progress of the whole; (2) one of the devices used to create this image is a significant amount of evocative tone-painting (Marx uses the term 'Tonmalerei', and, as will be seen in the next chapter, he was not the first to apply it in exactly this manner); (3) progress is an indispensable condition of genius; and (4) Beethoven, by following the course of progress, has begun a new epoch in the history of music. From these four points, taken together, emerges that particular view of Beethoven which is characteristically Marxian. For the sake of clarity, these points will be discussed as they are set forth in the biography and in the monograph *Ueber Malerei in der Tonkunst* before returning to the *BAMZ*. In this way, the philosophical underpinning of Marx's reviews can be made clear without any cumbersome dependence on the dialectical process of which their author was so fond.

Marx devoted 33 pages of the biography to the 'Eroica'. On the first of these, he made quite clear his view of the work, and of music in general.

What did Beethoven want? What could he give? Simply a composition of great and noble design? So our aestheticians would advise him − those aestheticians, old and new, who see music only as a play of forms, who expect only the most generalized evocation of unspecified feelings, since it is incapable of 'expressing the concrete'. Beethoven had a different point of view. As an artist, he could do nothing with lifeless abstractions; to create life, life from out of his own life, was his calling, as it is for all artists. The artist knows what his art is capable of; he before all others; he alone.[4]

In *Ueber Malerei*, Marx included a rhapsodic analysis of the 'Pastoral' Symphony, addressed to 'three young ladies', which seemed deliberately designed to confound aestheticians and traditional analysts alike.

I would draw your attention to a figure from the first theme which appears on p. 17 [presumably mm. 150ff.], underneath which the triplet figures of the viola and violoncellos playing in octaves rush down into the gentle range of the clarinets and bassoons, the basses repeat the root of the chord in quiet pulses; and at the fifth, but deep down below, the horns resound until it breaks forth, brighter, like golden sunlight on rocky cliffs, and everything rejoices, everything, everything rejoices, and the hills seem to tremble in the life-giving breath of Being and then everything becomes still in the beautiful ebb and flow of rest and peace.

'But where do you interpret all of this?'

I possess Solomon's secret of the speech of birds.[5]

This passage is fairly typical of a discourse which goes on, with occasional awed interruptions from the 'three young ladies', for four pages, and in which it is evident that Marx has gone far beyond the sketchy program supplied by Beethoven for this symphony. It is not exactly analysis, but neither is it an abstract fantasy in the manner of Hoffmann. Marx does not evoke a supra-sensory world to explain the music; he actually relates concrete images from the here and now to specific passages in the score, for no more compelling reason than the obvious one: they are what this particular piece of music suggests to him.

This is not Marx's usual style of interpretation, but it is not far from it. It was not only into avowedly programmatic works like the 'Pastoral' Symphony that he was willing to read programs as specific as this one. In the biography, he warned against the perils of a too-subjective approach.[6] There is no reason to doubt, however, that in his own private ear he heard and understood music in just this way. To a trained analyst today, the result, when set down on paper, may seem childish, appropriate only in an apostrophe to three young people of unspecified age. To Marx, exactly the opposite was true: the ability to 'hear' the visual and psychological images suggested by music was the mark of a sophisticated listener in step with his time. This idea is expressed clearly in Marx's earlier writings,[7] and is repeated throughout the biography. It is the basis of Marx's analysis of the 'Eroica'.

This does not mean that Marx countered Hoffmann's lofty idealism with a return to more mundane realities. He makes it clear from the first that what Beethoven depicted in the 'Eroica' was not a commonplace battle, but 'die Schlacht als Idealbild' − an idealized combat rather than an earthly one.[8] The funeral march from the symphony was for Marx a piece whose significance far transcended the death of any one man.[9] Hoffmann would have preferred to abandon all specifics (it is certainly significant that he used fewer and vaguer visual images in describing Beethoven's music than he did for either Haydn or Mozart), while Marx clung to them with conviction; this is the most important difference between them.

Marx's visual images, of course, have nothing to do with either the *Affektenlehre* or the rudimentary theories of *Tonmalerei* developed during

the eighteenth century. It is these theories which were constantly con-
founded by aestheticians and practiced by composers, with charming results
that can be heard most notably in Haydn's *Creation*. By 'tone-painting'
Marx means something much more pervasive, and apparently more esoteric
as well, since he compares it to the speech of birds, which, like Hoffmann's
and Wendt's spirit-worlds, all can hear but few can understand.

While Hoffmann's treatment of the Fifth Symphony was punctuated
by reference to the supra-sensory world, Marx's analysis of the 'Eroica'
abounds in concrete associations. The two orchestral chords with which
the symphony begins are a call to attention ('Hört! Hört!); what Marx calls
a turn to the minor mode in the fourth measure of the theme is compared
to Napoleon restraining his reinforcements from entering too early in the
battle; the restatement of the theme is like 'martial music on the morning
of the day of battle'.[10] Marx even discovers that the first four measures of
the main scherzo theme are identical to a line from an old German soldiers'
song.[11]

More important to Marx than these pictorial details, however, was the
unity of the entire symphony – the 'Heldenweihe' which Beethoven carried
throughout. Marx had already observed a similar unity in the Piano Sonata,
Op. 2, no.1, in F minor: one of the first of Beethoven's major works to
be discussed in the biography. There it had been a unity of overall tragic
mood, understood in psychological terms. Whether Beethoven would, or
could, have expressed in words what the sonata expresses is to Marx
irrelevant. What matters is not simply that it begins and ends in the minor,
but that it presents a series of images that fit logically together. In the first
movement, for example, the subsidiary theme is closely related to the
opening, retaining its rhythm and reversing its direction. Any interpretation
which is made of these themes may, Marx points out, be disputed, but the
similarity between them is a matter of fact. They belong together, just as
the four movements of the cycle belong together, distinguishing Beethoven's
sonata from earlier works in which movements were thrown together
without regard for unity.[12] Elsewhere, Marx had written that while
Haydn's works were all different expressions of the same content,
Beethoven's were unique.[13]

Like Amadeus Wendt, Marx had a rather peculiar view of music history.
His determination to show Beethoven as the first great master of instrumental music led him, for example, to the curious claim that Haydn's
oratorios were more important than his symphonies or quartets.[14] Haydn,
he felt, did not take solo keyboard music quite seriously. Beethoven was
the first composer to make the piano strive to be something beyond itself,
and this seems to have been Marx's ideal in instrumental music.[15] In all

respects, then, he was determined to show that Beethoven made a significant step beyond his predecessors in the development of music as an art form. It is in interpreting this idea that Marx first shines forth as an indisputable disciple of Hegel.

Marx's interpretation of music history has been summarized as follows:[16] at first music was nothing but a free play of tones with no meaning beyond themselves (the 'Kantische Schilderung' once again); many composers, beginning with Monteverdi and Caccini and continuing through Bach, Handel, Haydn and Mozart, were able to give it a specific extramusical meaning, largely through the device of *Tonmalerei*; but Beethoven was the first composer to raise the meaning to a sufficient level of clarity that it gave unity and coherence to an entire composition. Here was a full-fledged Hegelian triad, comparable in musical terms to the more familiar one of art–religion–philosophy advanced in the *Aesthetics*.[17] Just as art is considered by Hegel to be the most immediate form of human awareness, philosophy the most complex and consequently the most advanced, so Marx saw music progressing from a simple play of form to an entirely different kind of expressive force: one combining purely musical technique with non-musical elements that expand their potential and give them an added dimension. Marx even goes so far as to compare the early development of music to a kind of mystical religion which delights in aimless movement and growth.[18] In both cases the crucial factor for progress was to be the objectification of human feelings which accompany the basic mystical experience;[19] an objectification which in music was most perfectly carried out by Beethoven. Beethoven, in other words, had taken the expression of concrete feeling in music as far as it could possibly go; later composers could only repeat the attempt with greater or lesser success.[20] Under Beethoven's guidance, music had become as much like the other arts – or rather, as much like the ideal toward which all the other arts strive – as it would ever be, and Beethoven could thus be credited with bringing the specific resources of music to bear in that characteristically Romantic struggle for a mighty synthesis of all the arts.[21]

Marx's view of Beethoven could thus not be farther from that of Hoffmann, with whom he shares the trappings of German idealism. For Hoffmann, listener and music had been equally subjective when compared to the supra-sensory world which the music evoked. For Marx, the ideas depicted in Beethoven's music were as objective and concrete as possible, and in that objectivity lay their strength. It is the combination of this objectivity with Marx's idealism – the belief that music strives to evoke a higher level of reality than that suggested by the commonplace images of his interpretations – which shows why Marx came into conflict with the aestheticians who created the 'absolutist' view of music.

Marx's early writings, in particular, make it clear that he rejected the aesthetic theories of his philosophical models, including Hegel. One of the primary goals of aestheticians, from Alexander Gottlieb Baumgarten through Schopenhauer, had been to distinguish between the natures of the various arts, by ascribing to each a unique purpose and quality. Hegel was among those who assigned to music a relatively low position in the hierarchy of the arts, while Tieck, Wackenroder and Schopenhauer had claimed, in vindicating music from the charges of meaninglessness leveled by earlier critics, that the very vagueness of music was its foremost virtue. This celebrated idea perhaps has its origin in Baumgarten's distinction between man's higher and lower cognitive powers, and his claim that art was not governed by the same rules as the intellect and therefore required a separate science – that of aesthetics – to explain its effect. Marx's bitter denunciation of aestheticians in the biography might be taken to refer to Eduard Hanslick, whose *Vom Musikalisch-Schönen* had appeared a few years before. Actually, Marx had included an even more virulent attack on 'Kunstphilosophen' in *Ueber Malerei* 30 years earlier. In this treatise, it is clear that what appalled Marx about aesthetic theory was the distinction it created between science and art, which resulted in denying music the ability to express ideas, however much it might strive to realize the absolute source of ideas themselves.

Consequently, in defining the expressive powers of music Marx turned not to Hegel's *Aesthetics*, but to the epistemological system first advanced in the *Phenomenology of Spirit*. In this system, each subject strove to realize its object, thus elevating both to a new and broader subjectivity. In the triad advanced by Marx the subject was the old French view of instrumental music, which denounced the lack of unity and coherent meaning in the early eighteenth-century Italian *sinfonia* style. The object was the German view epitomized by Mattheson, according to which music represented universal affections, thus 'painting' (to use Marx's term) attributes of the natural world. The third member of the triad was a higher awareness in which the objectivity of the ideas was balanced by the subjective complexity of musical logic. The result was a new type of unity arising from the juxtaposition of apparent opposites, which Marx found to be represented in Beethoven's music.

The significance of Marx's position is profound. He apparently believed, to use the terminology peculiar to German idealism, that in the new Romantic aesthetic, music had no object, no grounding in the everyday world, precisely because the science of aesthetics assumed a fundamental distinction between art and reality. Marx made no such distinction. For him, music was governed by the same principles as science or history. It is precisely this attitude that is lacking in the so-called 'absolutist' view of music.

Even Hegel, in line with the other German idealists, dedicated much of the discussion of music in his *Aesthetics* to defining the differences between music and the other arts. Far from sharing Marx's optimism about musical progress, Hegel saw the instrumental music of his time as decadent. He clearly preferred music to act as an accompaniment to poetry and the human voice. For Hegel, the charms of more independent music, about which he admits to having only the sketchiest knowledge, depended on spiritual sensations which could not be precisely defined, and which thus spoke directly to the inmost soul.

While he never explicitly rejected this outlook of his philosophical mentor, Marx was certainly familiar with it, and chose simply to ignore it. He certainly believed, like Wendt and Hoffmann, in the 'soulfulness' of music, but he attributed it to music's ability to take emotions and images which were universally comprehensible and transform them through a formal development both dynamic and unified in its conception.

As will be seen in Chapter 5, Hoffmann took exactly the opposite approach, anchoring the metaphysical dynamic dimensions of the Fifth Symphony, which he characterized in emotional terms, in what he considered the rather commonplace (hence worldly) nature of its thematic material. Most aestheticians, Marx apparently felt, had not taken this precaution, and were thus fundamentally wrong in their understanding of music.

Again and again, Marx cites the evidence of the composers themselves in support of his belief that music can portray objective ideas. In the biography he poses the questions: 'Is not music, by virtue of its inability to indicate things and objects, unsuited for the presentation of objective content? Does not this content lie in the merest superscription and − in your subjective imagination?' Marx's answer is an appeal to authority:

Our subjective imagination? − Let us consider what the pronoun represents: nothing less than all the great composers ... from Bach and Handel ... to our own time. They have all known how to find this potential in their art, and have built their life's calling upon it. Or else − if you dare to say it − they have all been fools, who have not understood their own line of work.[22]

If all the greatest composers believed in music's ability to express concrete ideas, then that potential was indisputable. For Marx, no stronger refutation was possible.

It might be supposed that those views would influence definitively Marx's attitude toward criticism: both his own and that of his subordinates. This was not entirely the case, as his introductory article to volume I of the journal makes clear.[23] Marx was not so much interested in the ideas of his critics as he was in their intellectual integrity; they must be sufficiently systematic to present to the reader the criteria on which their judgments were made. Most previous criticism, Marx felt, had not met this challenge, and was correspondingly meaningless.[24] In studying the reviews in the *BAMZ*, one must thus make a distinction between Marx's own writings and those by other authors. Despite its editor, and despite the indisputable bias of most of the published reviews, the *BAMZ* was not always pro-Beethoven to the point of simple discipleship. Marx was careful not to mention Beethoven's name in the introductory article (except in a brief footnote), but he did rail against those who expect absolute consistency from a journal. He clearly believed that informing and educating the readers was a more important goal.[25]

Beethoven reviews in the *BAMZ*

In the following pages I will survey the criticism in the *BAMZ* much as I did that from the Leipzig *AMZ* in the previous chapter. Instead of proceeding chronologically, however, I will begin with those articles that appeared under Marx's name, and will conclude with those that appeared anonymously or were signed by others. In this way I hope to make clear the difference between Marx's own distinctive view of Beethoven, as outlined above, and those of his contributors, as well as to evaluate the extent to which all *BAMZ* articles lived up to Marx's own published expectations.

It is not always easy to tell which articles are by Marx. Most reviews in the *BAMZ* are signed, unlike those in the Leipzig *AMZ*, which usually appeared anonymously. The signatures, however, are frequently only initials, the most common among them being 'v.d.O..r.' Marx and Rellstab signed at least some of their articles with their full surnames, but there are several articles attributed simply to 'M.'. One of these, a review of the score of the C major String Quintet, Op. 29, is listed in the index to volume V as being by Marx. An unsigned article in the first volume is also ascribed to Marx in the index, though its gently disparaging tone and dialogue form are quite different from Marx's usual manner. I will begin, therefore, with those articles that are definitely by Marx, and proceed to those of dubious authenticity.

Marx's first Beethoven review for the *BAMZ*, of the Piano Sonata in A-flat major, Op. 110 (*BAMZ* I, p. 87), is remarkably similar in form to an *AMZ* review. It consists of a few introductory, explanatory paragraphs followed by highlights from each of the four movements, with appropriate commentary. The author's insight, however, is deeper than one would expect from an average *AMZ* critic. He begins by speaking directly of Beethoven's deafness – the great misfortune under which the composer had labored for several years – and goes on to interpret the sonata as a gentle look backwards into happier times. The first movement, he says, shows what a great composer can make out of the simplest material: for example, the opening melody and the 32nd-note appoggiaturas which follow it. The second movement, which had driven the *AMZ* critic to such heights of exegetical fervor, is seen by Marx as a simple folk melody in which Beethoven expresses his great emotional distance from the world of gentle pleasures he has just conjured up. Strange as it may seem to modern ears, 'Verzweiflung' – despair – was apparently the universal response which this movement suggested to its first hearers. Finally, the arioso and its variant can serve as a model to anyone who wishes to write variations without destroying the sense of the original melody, and the fugue which follows proves that counterpoint need not be an academic exercise; it can be made to live in its own right and sound as viably as the other movements of the sonata.

In this short review Marx has something significant to say about each movement; only his comments on the first movement, though, are really penetrating, because he allows himself the freedom of fanciful emotional interpretation. It is hard to imagine that the same associations were meant to apply to the despairing second movement or the arioso; the 'backward glance at happier times' is a characterization of the first movement alone. As yet, then, Marx had not fully applied his own principle of looking for a coherent meaning in each work, either because of limitations of space or because he had not formulated such an image for this sonata. Later, in the biography, he remedied this deficiency to some extent by comparing the harp-like arpeggios in the first movement ('im ossianischem Sinne der Abschied vom trauten Saitenspiel') to those with which the sonata ends – but this reads more like a momentary rationalization than a real attempt to interpret the work as a whole in such terms.[26]

A review of the *Meeresstille und glückliche Fahrt*, published later in the same year, is more thorough, but less favorable (*BAMZ* I, p. 391). Marx finds that the music, though well written and pleasing, does little to amplify the meaning of the poems; indeed, it hinders it. In support of this idea Marx sets forth a theory of poetry, rather than one of music. The greatest poets, he says, sometimes write works in which the fundamental idea is not explicitly present or is only revealed at the very end. One such poem is Goethe's

Ueber allen Gipfeln
Ist Ruh',
In allen Wipfeln
Spürest du
Kaum einen Hauch;
Die Vögelein schweigen im Walde,
Warte nur! Balde
Ruhest du auch.

in which the idea of oneness with nature which Marx sees as permeating the entire poem is not actually stated until the final line. Another such poem is *Meeresstille*, on which the first half of Beethoven's 'cantata' is based:

Tiefe Stille herrscht im Wasser;
Ohne Regung ruht das Meer
Und bekümmert sieht der Schiffer
Glatte Fläche rings umher.
Keine Luft von keiner Seite!
Todesstille fürchterlich!
In der ungeheuern Weite
Reget keine Welle sich.

In this poem, Marx believed, it is not the description of the ocean which is of primary importance, but rather the deathly fear of the lonely man caught up in its midst. Beethoven's setting of the penultimate line reflects this; on the word 'Weite' the sopranos jump up a perfect eleventh, from e' to a'', while the basses fall an octave to low G. Marx identifies this as a cry of anguish from the lonely sailor, thus interpreting the poem as a monologue. He is unable to believe that the peaceful music of the opening lines could come from a man in such distress, and he is particularly critical of Beethoven for yielding to the exigencies of musical setting by going through this mood change twice in the course of the piece.

Marx repeated these opinions, with the criticism of the music somewhat toned down, in the biography.[27] It is apparent, then, that he was willing to find fault with Beethoven on occasion, even though he rarely did so. This review certainly lives up to his own standards, in a way that the previous one did not: it both gives a judgment and explains the criteria by which the judgment has been reached. These are, of course, poetic criteria; what they show us is that Marx, in evaluating a musical setting of a poem, thought in terms of right or wrong. An interpretation − the correct interpretation − of the poem should be apparent in the musical setting. Otherwise, it cannot be counted fully successful, no matter how appealing the music is in itself.

For a fuller view of Marx's reaction to Beethoven's vocal music we must turn to his review of the Ninth Symphony, published in the third volume of the *BAMZ* (p.375). This symphony received wide coverage in the *BAMZ*'s concert reports, as well as in those of the Leipzig journal. In either journal, however, no critic but Marx appreciated the work completely, and no other writer liked the finale. It is this movement that becomes the cornerstone of Marx's interpretation.

Marx points out that, despite *Fidelio* and many other vocal works, Beethoven had been recognized primarily as a great instrumental composer. His latest works, in particular, had opened up new possibilities in instrumental music that had not been previously suspected.

Endless, as in a landscape or in unmeasurable nature, are the possible shapes and combinations in instrumental music. Now the life of nature extends to human expression and song, and one tries to hear in it human meaning and song-speech; now that which is portrayed loses itself in its element, simple tone, and the simplest forgotten form shapes itself once again in many different combinations into a great, meaningful whole, as leaf upon leaf represents a tree.

Song, on the other hand, represents human nature, and to conclude a symphony with song is to show the triumph of humanity over the world of nature. There is thus no need for overall unity; the second half of the symphony simply transcends the first half, which takes on the character of an introduction. Marx seems to have felt that Beethoven achieved exactly the right tone for his setting of the *Ode to Joy*: a point upon which other critics of the time disagreed.[28] More importantly, he believed that the simplest type of song is inherently human, while the most complex instrumental music still symbolizes nature. Furthermore, it was the human side of music which interested Marx. If Hoffmann had reviewed this symphony, he surely would have found the instrumental complexities far more interesting than the vocal finale. Wendt, like Marx, might have taken the opposite point of view. Neither of the two earlier critics, however, would have thought much of the finale of the Ninth Symphony. No doubt Hoffmann would have found it too simplistic, Wendt too crass for his liking. Marx enjoyed the simplicity for its own sake, as the antithesis of instrumental complexity.

He seems almost to have been suggesting a new triad — instrumental music, vocal music, Ninth Symphony — to explain the nature of this monumental work. Each member of this triad would then strive, according to Hegelian aesthetics, to become the next one, in the literal sense of the word. Just as art strives to become religion, and religion philosophy, so instrumental music strives to embrace the word, and, this accomplished, the Ninth Symphony was the inevitable next step. In the biography, Marx made it even clearer that he saw the Ninth as the unsurpassable culmination of Beethoven's symphonic work.

That he did not understand his work in this manner the sketches for the Tenth Symphony make clear. If nevertheless dark forebodings of the approaching end troubled him – who can know? It is certain that a unique and fundamental sound ('ein eigenthümlicher Grundklang') reaches us from this work.[29]

It is not so clear that Marx actually preferred vocal music to instrumental. Like Wagner two decades later, he seems to have believed that the Ninth Symphony implied a new type of music; unlike Wagner, he believed that Beethoven had already achieved all that was possible in this respect. For Wagner, as is now commonly recognized, the text of his music dramas only helped to illuminate the absolute (and here at last we arrive at an historically authentic usage of the term) properties of the music itself. For Marx, however, it was precisely the pictorial and emotional clarity of both music and text which distinguished the Ninth Symphony even from Beethoven's earlier works. Musical meaning, he believed, became more and not less specific with the passage of time, and this paradoxically explained the deep psychological impact of modern music.

Two further reviews shed some light on Marx's interpretation of Beethoven's late music. 'From Beethoven's most recent tone-poems ("Tongedichten"),' he says in reviewing the Elegy, Op. 118,

there speaks at times such a tender, heartfelt, radiant emotion, that one is tempted to find therein a premonition of approaching death; they are dreams and sensations that travel beyond the music, beyond the earth itself, their sound brought forth with the lightest breath – sighs of longing or of parting – and quickly dispersed. No composer has given us anything so far from his earlier fantasies, for none has been so thoroughly set free from the world, from love and hate, the admiration and indifference of society so completely cut off and closed up within himself as he, God's beloved hermit.

In this area of his life and work (which are the same thing) belongs the present song, which nevertheless no sensitive friend of music should ignore. One must lose oneself in the most dreamlike regions of sound in order to understand the soulful language of the singer.   *BAMZ* IV, p.373

This is the entire review. There is no analysis of the work, no theory: simply a heartfelt appeal for understanding of the new Beethoven, 'der gott-beseligte Einsiedler'.

The same could be said of a review of the two quartets, Opp. 132 and 135, published in the fifth volume of the *BAMZ* (p.467). Marx begins by saying that Beethoven's latest quartets go so far beyond what one expects of this genre that it is appropriate, in place of a formal review, to give a few words of introduction to the music. For Marx, these quartets represented a significant step in the progress of musical art; he confidently predicted that in the future they would present no difficulties to the performer, just as Haydn's quarters had ceased to be difficult for Marx's contemporaries. Marx compares the quartets to a painting by Rubens, in which one must first become acquainted with a mass of detail before proceeding to understand the sense of the whole. In short, he urges patience on his readers, much as the *AMZ* critic had done when confronted with the cello sonatas, Op. 102. Marx, however, showed more understanding and sympathy than that earlier critic.

Of the articles whose authorship is in doubt, the most intriguing is the first (*BAMZ*I, p. 95). As mentioned above, this review of the Piano Sonata, Op. 111, is cast largely in the form of a conversation among the author, a student named Edward, and an unnamed music director, and its tone is largely unfavorable. The author, recalling the earliest *AMZ* critics, writes that he had long recognized Beethoven's talent, and had advised the composer to write more naturally: advice which apparently went unheeded, since he confesses himself at a loss before Beethoven's most recent works. The conversation itself, however, reads like the sort of thing Marx might have contrived in order to further his own ideas. The young Edward launches into a spirited defense of Beethoven; he finds the second movement of the sonata to be a representation of the composer's own funeral procession, a premonition of which is described in considerable detail. When the music director objects that art should comfort, and not disturb, Edward indignantly exclaims that 'comfort is for the weak. Holy art instructs us, showing us and letting us feel what we must bear.' Form, he says, is nothing other than the manifestation of an idea, and he takes as a sign of the godliness of art the fact that each person can understand it in an individual fashion. By far the greatest part of the conversation is given over to arguments of this sort, making the article as a whole look like a theory of art rather than a review − a theory which is delivered back-handedly by the author's main opponent. The theme is reminiscent of Amadeus Wendt, but it also fits in neatly with Marx's own Hegelianism: great art does not simply please; it must illustrate all aspects of human life in an original and inspired way, thus presenting a microcosm of life itself, while at the same time pointing forward to a higher type of existence. Form is only a framework employed for convenience by the composer, who fills it with his own ideas. Marx might well have disguised himself as an opponent of Beethoven in order to deliver such a message.

A review in the sixth volume of the *BAMZ* (p. 169), of the Quartet, Op. 135, is signed 'M.' and is almost certainly by Marx. Though short, it mingles a theme already set forth in the review of Op. 110 − the glance backward into happier times − with a thorough exposition of the author's critical principles. These principles, which he claims to derive from Beethoven himself, are already familiar: each piece of Beethoven's is based on a fundamental idea ('Grundidee'), which when understood can clarify the meaning of the most obscure passages. A quotation from the scherzo is offered as proof of this claim. This figure, repeated 46 times by the three lower instruments, seems at first, the author says, to be sheer nonsense. Unfortunately, he does not explain how his own 'Grundidee' − that of a wistful look backward − does anything to clarify the passage in question.

A review of some of the later incidental music, including *The Ruins of Athens* and *King Stephen*, is short and superficial; these works, says 'M.', do not belong among those in which Beethoven expanded the frontiers of art (*BAMZ* VI, p. 329). The final review by 'M.' of the score of the C major String Quintet, Op. 29 (*BAMZ* V, p. 445), is more valuable, not for its content but because it serves to remind one of two important facts: this quintet, largely neglected today, was in Beethoven's time one of his most popular works, and, furthermore, like most chamber music at this time, it was originally published in parts. The sincere wish expressed here and elsewhere in the *BAMZ* for more score publications shows at once the journal's scholarly bent; such a plea was not likely to appear in the Leipzig *AMZ* in the 1820s.

One other point is worthy of mention here. The first movement of this quintet, like many of Beethoven's middle and late works, includes a secondary theme in a key related to the tonic by a third: in this case the submediant, A major. Much has been made of this Beethovenian predilection for third-related keys, which is commonly viewed as a bold anticipation of Romantic harmony. Marx, however, found it unworthy of mention in his brief survey of the quintet's highlights. More importantly, when discussing the works of this period in the biography, at no point does he mention third-related keys as in any way unusual, despite some fairly extensive analyses. In the proper perspective this is perhaps not surprising: third relations are frequent in Haydn, both between movements and within them, and even that perennial symbol of late eighteenth-century musical fashion, Karl Ditters von Dittersdorf, went so far as to introduce a subsidiary theme in the flat submediant into one of his quartets.[30] In and of themselves, apparently, third-related keys held no surprises for Beethoven's contemporaries.

In summary, then, Marx can be seen to have been somewhat more constrained as a reviewer than his own optimistic prospectus would lead one to expect. Many of the reviews are rather cursory, allowing only for a brief survey of the piece or a statement of principles: rarely both. Even the most elaborate review, that of the Ninth Symphony, falls short of the comprehensiveness that Marx apparently desired: he promised to include further details in a later review, which, however, was not forthcoming.

Marx had trouble, then, in combining a thoroughgoing explanation of his critical principles with an equally systematic overview of the piece under discussion. As a critic, he would have to be ranked below Kanne, Wendt and Hoffmann, each of whom presented a personal view of Beethoven with more force and consistency in his reviews. Marx, though he edited his own journal, did not allow himself the sort of space which the Leipzig *AMZ* routinely gave to Hoffmann. His largest contributions to the *BAMZ* were his theoretical articles, in which the subject of Beethoven was avoided. He was not a critic in the same sense as Hoffmann; his best work was in his treatises and books: especially in the biography. It is only when these are taken into account that his interpretation of Beethoven, as presented above, becomes as compelling as those of his predecessors in Leipzig. It is important to remember, however, that while Marx could be more sophisticated than his criticism suggests, he still felt this type of writing to be worthwhile. One reason for this may have been his position within the musical culture of Berlin, a generally conservative city in the midst of which the *BAMZ* must have seemed radical and provocative despite its insufficiencies.

Of Marx's co-workers, the one who wrote most frequently on Beethoven signed his articles 'v.d.O..r'. Like Marx, he was evidently a capable writer and an imaginative critic. He too, however, wrote no articles on the scale of Hoffmann's or Kanne's, to say nothing of Wendt's. Four full-scale Beethoven reviews by him appeared: two in the first volume, one in the third volume and one in the fourth. Of these, two are of major works – the cello sonatas, Op. 102, and the Quartet, Op. 127 – and two of works which are now considered less important – the Scottish songs, Opp. 107 and 108, and the bagatelles, Op. 126. At the time the reviews were written, there may have been a different perception of the relative importance of these works, since the review of the Scottish songs is longer than that of the cello sonatas and as long as that of the quartet. Even so, however, it covers only six columns, and is devoted mostly to unenlightening comments on the felicities of individual songs (*BAMZ* I, p. 159). The other reviews are more insightfully developed, and must have seemed more helpful to readers at the time.

The review of the cello sonatas (*BAMZ* I, p. 409) is also much more favorable than its Leipzig counterpart. The writer describes these works as being in Beethoven's newest manner, apparently unaware that they were already nearly a decade old. He passes over the second sonata, in C major, fairly quickly, describing it in terms of highest praise. The other sonata, in D major, is treated at greater length. The first movement meets with great approval, and the conclusion is judged highly original. The second

60

movement is found too monotonous in tonality, though not without many beautiful spots. Finally, the writer admits, almost apologetically, that he does not much care for the fugue with which the sonata concludes. He hastens to point out that Beethoven could write more appealing fugues, citing the one in Op. 110 as an example. He then details the four qualities which he believes any good fugue should have: thoroughgoing originality, technical facility, beautiful and natural melodies in all voices, and a convincing position in the context of a larger composition.

The review of the bagatelles, Op. 126, is more interesting because it follows a consistent principle throughout: that of the 'Grundidee' already championed by Marx. Needless to say, with such small works as these it is scarcely necessary to argue in favor of a unified conception binding each one together. What is interesting is that the reviewer, like Marx, associates specific images with each of the first four bagatelles – no. 1, for example, portrays the sensation we feel when we discover a pair of birds in their nest in springtime – but then, unlike Marx, admits that not all listeners need react to music in this manner in order to understand it. Some, he says, prefer 'to let the beauties of a piece of music strike them without mediation'.

The review of Op. 127 – the last review of 'v.d.O..r' to appear (*BAMZ* IV, p. 25) – contains more theory and less description than its predecessors. The writer describes having a great deal of difficulty understanding the quartet, and only becoming familiar with it through repeated hearings. The thrust of the review is that one must always give Beethoven credit for artistic integrity; it makes no more sense to criticize individual passages than it does to point to the head of the possessed child in Raphael's *Transfiguration* and say 'this head is not beautiful'.

The same inability, or unwillingness, to combine principles clearly set forth with thoroughgoing critical judgments is shown by all the other critics who wrote about Beethoven for the *BAMZ*. The single extended review by Rellstab, of the *Bundeslied* 'In allen guten Stunden' (*BAMZ* III, p. 34), is largely descriptive; unlike most of Marx's articles, it contains no aesthetic theory at all. More interesting than this are two reviews printed in the first volume: one anonymously, of the Piano Sonata, Op. 109 (p. 37), the other, of the eleven bagatelles, Op. 119, signed 'N.E.' The theme of the former review is that Beethoven could not go on writing forever in the style of his youth, but that his admirers could still find much to value in his later works, despite the widespread perplexity which they had caused. The writer faults the first movement because it has no 'leitende Idee', by which he apparently means not a theme but an emotional state. The whole, despite beautiful moments, is somewhat disturbing ('etwas Unbefriedigendes'). The second movement he likes better, regretting only that it is so short. It has 'a very excited passion' and, since it is in sonata form, he sees it as the real first movement of a two-movement sonata, with the previous movement only a sort of whimsical addition. The interpretation of the last movement is predictable; each variation receives a few descriptive adjectives – the second is 'rhapsodisch und frei gehalten', the third 'kräftig und keck' – but there is also some analytical discernment: the subject is correctly placed in the alto voice in the fugal variation (no. 5) and the whole episode is described as a 'cadenza' in which the *composer* shows off his virtuosity before returning to the mood of the beginning.

The review of the bagatelles takes the same approach as that of Op. 126 by 'v.d.O..r' discussed above; individual bagatelles are assigned rather fanciful (to modern readers, at least) extra-musical interpretations (*BAMZ* I, p. 128). No. 1, Allegretto in G minor, receives an especially detailed exegesis. It is, the reviewer says,

the lament of a young man who has lost his beloved. Time has already exercised its right; despair has subsided and resignation dominates. One perceives the expression of a gentle sorrow. Gladly, then, the young man summons back his remembrances of past happiness. He revels in them, but they increase his sorrow; wild depression leads to exhaustion, the gentler sorrow returns, and, lost in it, he sinks completely into slumber.

It is a measure of our own distance from the interpretative world of this review that a piece which now seems so simple and unpretentious could suggest such an emotionally overladen interpretation.

By far the most significant of the anonymous articles is a three-part mini-treatise on 'the symphony and Beethoven's achievement in this area', which appeared in the first volume of the *BAMZ* (pp. 165, 173, 181). This begins with a survey of the history of the symphony, which is traced back to the earliest operatic overtures and forward through Haydn and Mozart. Mozart, the author felt, had originated a particular type of symphony, characterized by a 'pure lyrical tendency', which strongly influenced Beethoven. Beethoven then developed the symphony in three important ways. After his earliest symphonic works, which followed the Mozartean model, he went on, in the Fifth Symphony, to portray specific states of mind in musical terms. In the 'Pastoral' Symphony, he developed the form in a different way, by including extra-musical references. Finally, in his most successful symphonies, among which are counted the Third and the Seventh, the two approaches are combined. Of the funeral march in the 'Eroica' he says, recalling Marx, that it is 'too big to lead to the tomb of a single man. Who does not, after hearing the warsong of the first movement, perceive in this Adagio a picture of a bloody battlefield?' Likewise, and with equal assurance, the first movement of the Seventh Symphony is held to represent 'the glowing south, a rustic people with the souls of warriors, the quick, bold pattern of the warrior's life'. All questions of authorship aside, this article, both in its view of history and its evaluation of Beethoven, is very close to Marx's own spirit.

Conclusion

If a reason is to be sought for the failure of the *BAMZ*, it might well lie in the reluctance of its critics to face up to the standards imposed by Marx. The average *BAMZ* review is not much different from an average review in the Leipzig *AMZ*. Both journals cultivated the same type of article; typically, an introductory paragraph or two, describing the nature of the work under review, is followed by an analytical discussion, designed to familiarize the reader with the work's most outstanding features. The Leipzig journal, however, had greater resources from which to draw, including a staff of writers spread throughout the cultural centers of Germany, and it had a 26-year tradition behind it by the time Marx's first issue was published. Helmut Kirchmeyer has pointed out that Marx was forced to draw, for his correspondence sections, on writers who were little more than publicity agents for the theaters whose concerts they were ostensibly reviewing.[31] These sections are correspondingly of much less interest than those in the *AMZ*. The time and energy which Marx was forced to devote to assembling this staff must have severely handicapped him in his role as a critic.

The value of the *BAMZ* today is primarily as an historical document. It shows that there existed, in Germany during the 1820s, a different view of Beethoven's late works from that which was apparently held in Leipzig, and among the *AMZ*'s readership. Ultimately, its failure may also show the relative precariousness of this position in conservative Berlin; serious critics may have understood and appreciated late Beethoven, but the general public was unconvinced. Occasionally, the reviews, like that of Op. 109, even make reference to this public reticence; the critics were aware that they were fighting for an unpopular cause, and even if, like Marx, they chose to ignore the fact in their writing, they did so by deliberate choice. When Robert Schumann inaugurated his own journal in the 1830s, he began by attacking all the journals that were then in existence, including the venerable *AMZ*, in no uncertain terms.[32] Marx, however, limited his criticism of the *AMZ* to a few comments in the concluding article to his first volume – hardly an auspicious place for so bold a foray. Marx did not have enough of the crusader's spirit to make his journal into a *cause célèbre*.

Marx does show us, however, beginning in the *BAMZ*, that other important critics besides Hoffmann felt that metaphysical interpretation could be combined with more seemingly mundane approaches to the same music. His style of criticism, which attempts to invest each of Beethoven's works with what we would today call programmatic significance, attests as well to this belief, since Marx's programs are never separable from his idealization of the composer. He also had a courageous view of Beethoven's work as a unified *oeuvre*, and it was this that he was to embody, many years later, in the biography. That book, written nearly 30 years after the demise of the *BAMZ*, remains his most enduring monument of Beethoven criticism, and it is to this that I will return in Chapter 5, where Marx will be directly compared with his contemporaries.

3

Other German sources:
the controversy over the late music

A great deal has already been written about German music criticism in the
early nineteenth century, but there remain large gaps in our knowledge of
the subject, which have until now made a balanced assessment of
Beethoven's critical reception in Germany impossible. This is especially true
in the English-speaking world, where even the secondary sources are
frequently difficult to obtain. There are at least two scholarly works from
the early twentieth century, those by Eugen Brümmer on Beethoven's
reception in the Rhenish press[1] and Georg Kaiser on Carl Maria von
Weber's musical writings,[2] which shed significant light on certain aspects
of the subject, yet are almost totally unknown in America. Even more
important are two journals founded during the last years of Beethoven's
career which add considerably to our knowledge of his reception by the
press.

Though the Mainz-based *Caecilia* is even less familiar today than the
BAMZ, it contains several of the longest and most carefully considered
reviews of Beethoven's late works ever to appear in print. These have,
through a combination of ignorance and oversight, remained totally
obscure.[3] Predictably, the only exceptions are the few negative articles on
Beethoven which appeared in *Caecilia*: one by Gottfried Weber which deals
at length with *Wellington's Victory* (*Caec.* III, p. 125), and the other by
Ernst Woldemar, whose denunciation of the late music was described in
Chapter 1.[4] Both of these will be examined in detail below. A more
intriguing picture of the fate of Beethoven's late music in Germany,
however, emerges from the unfamiliar, favorable reviews, as well as from
the theoretical side of Weber's writings.

Similarly, the *Wiener Allgemeine Musikalische Zeitung* (formally
*Allgemeine Musikalische Zeitung mit Besonderer Rücksicht auf den
Österreichischen Kaiserstaat*), published from 1817 until 1824, provides a
view of later Beethoven, particularly the Ninth Symphony, which in the
context of our present knowledge of the subject may seem surprisingly
sympathetic. Robert Haas has pointed out that it is virtually impossible
to find negative comments on Beethoven in the Viennese press after the
time of *Wellington's Victory*, and the *WAMZ* was edited in its later years

by Friederich August Kanne, an ardent disciple not only of Beethoven but of the late music in particular.[5] Kanne's review of the Ninth Symphony is comparable in stature to those which appeared in *Caecilia*, and it is equally favorable toward the work and the composer. It too will be examined in detail below.

The goal of the previous chapters has been, in part, to show that the German critics' treatment of Beethoven was both more varied and more favorable than has hitherto been recognized. In the present chapter, this picture will be rounded out by focussing on the controversy surrounding the late music, as represented primarily in the two journals just cited, and on the attitudes toward musical aesthetics which that controversy represents. The chapter will be divided into four major sections, dealing respectively with Woldemar and the arguments against late Beethoven, the views of the journals' editors, the reception of the Ninth Symphony, and that given to the other late music. In this manner, it will be shown that even the most widespread notion concerning that music – that it was misunderstood and little appreciated until the end of the nineteenth century or the beginning of our own – is not, for the most part, supported by the evidence of the criticism.

The Woldemar case

As we have seen, a vigorous attack on Beethoven's late music was begun shortly after the composer's death; its primary exponents were an anonymous writer, presumably Amadeus Wendt, in the *AMZ*, and the Berlin music critic Ernst Woldemar in *Caecilia*. Of the two, Woldemar was far more bitter, since he accused Beethoven, through the insanities of his late style, of damaging Germany's international reputation for musical pre-eminence. Two criticisms in particular stand out from this chauvinistic diatribe: Beethoven, Woldemar felt, had lost his musical good sense because of his deafness, and had disregarded Horace's dictum according to which each work of art should be a simple and unified whole.

Woldemar's 'Aufforderung' soon led to a defense of Beethoven by the Leipzig organist C.F. Becker, later an affiliate of Schumann's on the *Neue Zeitschrift für Musik*, and an angry response by Woldemar (*Caec.* IX, p. 135). This controversy has been summarized in an article by Helmut Kirchmeyer,[6] who clearly views Woldemar as the voice of a majority opinion. Kirchmeyer makes several important mistakes, however: he counts Friedrich Rochlitz as a detractor of the late music, and attributes the lack of negative reviews in the *AMZ* solely to his respect for the composer.[7] Rochlitz, of course, had retired as the *AMZ*'s editor in 1817, leaving the journal to be managed during the following decade directly by the firm of Breitkopf und Härtel.[8] It has already been seen that neither Rochlitz nor C. W. Fink, who eventually succeeded him as editor, was an enemy of late Beethoven. Is Kirchmeyer to be trusted, then, in his claim that a general disapprobation of these works lay beneath the tranquil surface of Beethoven criticism during the 1820s, and that the composer's death alone was required to bring this volatile situation into the open?

The answer to this question must be a partial one, since it is possible that at no other time was conservative opinion so poorly represented in the musical press. It is clear from the *AMZ*'s concert reports that audience reaction to performances of late Beethoven was divided as it had never been before, and that some works, like the *Grosse Fuge*, Op. 133, were universally condemned. This must have continued to be the case for many years, since Kirchmeyer's example of the resistance encountered by Richard Wagner when he tried to perform the Ninth Symphony in Dresden in 1846 is beyond dispute. That symphony, like most of Beethoven's late works, was longer, more iconoclastic, and above all more difficult to perform and understand than virtually anything within the public's experience, and it remained so for a very long time. Since the most conservative Beethoven critics had always been far behind public opinion in recognizing the composer's merits, it thus seems eminently likely, as was suggested in Chapter 1, that a great deal of adverse criticism was withheld out of respect for the ageing composer. Even the *BAMZ*, in its concert report on the first performance of the Ninth Symphony, published an essentially negative reaction (*BAMZ* III, p. 213), and it is possible that other such opinions were waiting in the wings.

What is remarkable is that, despite Wendt's and Woldemar's calls to arms, these continued to be withheld even during the last years of the 1820s, when Beethoven's death should have made such respect superfluous. No spate of condemnatory articles appeared in the *AMZ*, and, as has been seen, the *BAMZ* continued its pro-Beethoven stance with the greatest possible indulgence toward the late works.

The case of *Caecilia* is perhaps even more telling. Woldemar called upon the editor to draw attention to the inferiority of Beethoven's recent works, and the latter, in a lengthy footnote, explained that he had already done so, citing his comments on *Wellington's Victory*, an ostensibly unfavorable review of the String Quartet in E-flat, Op. 127 (*Caec.* V, p. 145), and an article by Rellstab which cites some disparaging remarks allegedly made by Carl Maria von Weber (*Caec.* VII, p. 18). All of these claims are misleading. Weber's attitude toward Beethoven, as reported by Rellstab, is enigmatic. He expresses himself a warm admirer of the composer but deplores the recent tendencies shown by his music. Nevertheless, he is said to have reported enthusiastically on his meeting with Beethoven in 1824, after having submitted his *Euryanthe* to the master's judgment. Weber's case will be examined in detail below; as will be seen, it is unlikely that he ever wrote the series of bitter critiques that Schindler attributed to him. If he deplored later Beethoven, he usually kept his silence. As for Rellstab, it is unlikely that, as Kirchmeyer suggests,[9] his account of Weber's alleged opinions indicates agreement with them. Although he is known as a musical conservative, Rellstab was one of Marx's closest associates, and one looks in vain in his collected writings for a hint of adverse criticism toward Beethoven.[10] After a performance of some of the late quartets in Berlin, which seems to have been more successful than those in Vienna, he wrote an appreciation of these works for the *BAMZ* (*BAMZ* II, p. 165). It is also well known that several song texts by Rellstab, including that of Schubert's famous *Ständchen*, had first been submitted to Beethoven, who declined them. As warm an admirer of earlier Beethoven as he may have been, Rellstab would hardly have made this tribute in the last years of the composer's life if he had not felt that his poems were likely to receive a worthy setting.

What, though, of Gottfried Weber? Do his comments on *Wellington's Victory*, which is hardly a late work, indicate a general antipathy toward late Beethoven? Since he wrote no formal reviews of this music, apart from a short and favorable one of Op. 127 (*Caec.* V, p. 239), one must judge primarily by the ones he chose to print. After Beethoven's death, these were without exception favorable. In volume 8 (1828) of *Caecilia* there appeared two reviews of the Ninth Symphony, the first 26 pages long, both accepting it as an unquestioned masterwork (*Caec.* VIII, pp. 231, 256). In the next volume there were no fewer than four substantially positive reviews: two of the *Missa Solemnis* (*Caec.* IX, pp. 22, 27); one, a more or less explicit reply to Woldemar, of the quartets, Opp. 131, 132, and 135 (p. 45); and the last an extensive analysis of the Ninth Symphony, the *Missa Solemnis*, and Op. 131, 27 pages in length (p. 217). It is true that all of these works had been published by Schott, which also published *Caecilia*. The *AMZ*, too, however, was owned by a firm which printed Beethoven's music, and at no point while he was still alive had any of that music received comparable critical attention, favorable or otherwise. Some adverse comments on the *Missa Solemnis* and Op. 131 in the last-cited review also show that *Caecilia* was not blinded by any obligation to its parent company. Weber and his journal must thus be counted among the greatest posthumous admirers of late Beethoven.

Whatever may have been the opinion of the public about these works, then, the press continued to take their challenge seriously, even after Woldemar. He and Wendt remain Beethoven's sole detractors during this period. Their charges, furthermore, have a familiar ring which undermines their own primary objection to the late music: that it was the work of a man who had lost his musical judgment. It did not take much imagination to suggest that a composer who had gone deaf might write for his inner ear and produce music which seems sheer madness in performance. The only criterion by which that madness is judged, however, is an old one: lack of unity. Woldemar's other criticisms are nothing but rather malicious invective, which only make it clear that he heard the late music as a series of diffuse ideas with no rational organization. The main difference between this and negative reactions to Beethoven's earlier music was the degree of its intensity. Before, as has been shown, lack of unity was not usually seen as a final reproof – a reason to reject the music out of hand – and as time progressed and Beethoven became more familiar, it began to be forgotten. In later years, however, it once again surfaced to explain the unfamiliarity of the composer's newest style. To Wendt, who had never been an ardent admirer, it seemed that Beethoven had simply pushed his former obscurities to the point where they could no longer be endured.

There is thus little to be learned from studying these negative reviews. They present no new aesthetic arguments, showing themselves to be based on instinctive hostility, rather than on a reasoned rejection of a style whose objectives the critics were able to understand. Much more can be learned from the attitudes of the pro-Beethoven editors of *Caecilia* and the *WAMZ*, even though, in the former case, at least, these differ radically from those of the writers they employed.

Weber and Kanne on tone-painting

Gottfried Weber has earned a prominent place in Slonimsky's *Lexicon* for an article he wrote on the subject of tone-painting, attacking *Wellington's Victory* as unworthy of Beethoven. This is not a review, nor is it primarily devoted to Beethoven's music, but it deserves attention because it concentrates on one of the crucial issues in progressive German criticism of the early nineteenth century. We have already seen that, for Marx, tone-painting was not an occasional curiosity, limited to works like the 'Pastoral' Symphony, which explicitly portray scenes and events. It was, on the contrary, one of the fundamental expressive devices of music, and Marx's vivid imagination was able to find examples of it even in works whose designated character was totally non-programmatic. In this respect, he was the complete antithesis of Hoffmann, who admired Beethoven's instrumental music for its quality of abstraction, and would have found explicit tone-painting naive.[11] Of the two, Hoffmann now represents the more familiar position. Thanks in part to Schopenhauer's glorification of instrumental music in *Die Welt als Wille und Vorstellung* (1817), Beethoven has in our own time been considered to be the hero of abstract thought in art and, for this reason, of German idealist views about music.[12] Paul Henry Lang, in the little-known review quoted in the introduction to this book, embodied this position in his claim that Beethoven, the arch-symphonist, represents the antithesis of programmatic musical thought.[13] According to Lang, it was only the French who were unable to think of music without the help of literary association: for example, the extra-musical programs which Berlioz, Lang's *bête noire* and one of the greatest champions of Beethoven in France, applied to his work. Marx, in this view, was an anomaly: a German, an admirer of Beethoven, but a man incapable of abstract thought about music. Quite apart from his opinions on *Wellington's Victory*, then, it is interesting to know where Gottfried Weber, another devotee of Beethoven, stood on this disputed issue.

Like Marx, Weber points to the contradiction between theory and fact: tone-painting is constantly condemned in theoretical writings, but it is nevertheless practiced regularly by composers. Weber, however, unlike Marx, does not simply assume that those composers know what they are about. He takes the paradox as a significant aesthetic problem, and he develops a theory to resolve it. Music, he says, is exactly analogous to speech; both communicate on a level of understanding which, technically at least, makes symbolic gestures obsolete. Primitive and uneducated men may rely on gestures to communicate, but in civilized conversation these are kept to a minimum: a slight motion of the hand, for example. Likewise, in the elevated style of composition, which Weber seems to equate with liturgical music, outright tone-painting is inappropriate. A descending figure should not be used to illustrate the phrase 'descendit de coelis', nor an augmented second to illustrate the magnitude of one's own sin. When the style becomes more intense, however, as in the *Dies irae* of the Requiem, some degree of tone-painting is not only appropriate but necessary, just as an excited speaker would tend to gesticulate more than a calm one. In non-liturgical religious works, like Haydn's *Creation*, word-painting is also called for when specific images appear in the text. In comedy, too, it is an essential form of expression. In opera, it can be used to create scenic effects, in which case it need not correspond to the words being sung.

It should be clear from these examples that Weber had in mind a rather different kind of tone-painting from that advocated by Marx. He was thinking primarily of vocal and dramatic music, and believed tone-painting justified only when it suited the expediencies of text or stage, without doing violence to the more exalted moods of the music itself. Weber seems to have felt that instrumental composers used tone-painting only rarely, and that such instances must be judged individually according to the effect they create. His sole example is *Wellington's Victory*, which he describes at length in order to show that Beethoven, in this work, had not painted a battle in tones, but had simply transferred the sounds of battle – patriotic songs and artificial gunfire – directly into his score. In a footnote, Weber indicates his relief upon discovering that this piece was first written for a mechanical orchestra, and may thus be taken as a joke. The reader is left wondering what he might think of more accomplished tone-painting in a serious instrumental work.

There is no doubt, however, about Weber's view of the purpose of absolute music; according to a parenthetical insertion its highest goal is to express the emotions. In this respect, his attitude corresponds to that of eighteenth-century theory,[14] which Beethoven's contemporaries are often held to have rejected. Unlike Marx, he certainly did not see tone-painting as an essential Romantic device: a means of conveying ideas and hence an important step in the progress of musical thought. He saw it instead as a vestige of the very earliest stage of consciousness, when both music and speech were more demonstrative than they have since become. Likewise, he still believed in the power of instrumental music to speak a comprehensible language, rooted in the everyday world of the emotions, and was thus far from Hoffmann's abstraction. It would perhaps be closest to the truth to say that Weber was a pragmatic critic rather than a theoretical one; his analogy between music and speech is based on observation and personal preference, and interpretively it represents a compromise position, rejecting both the extremes of those aestheticians who had condemned tone-painting out of hand and the opposite one of embracing it freely. His attitude toward this issue shows us that he was not a Romantic, but a traditionally oriented critic who happened to like Beethoven, and was interested in understanding why. This may explain why most of the reviews of Beethoven in *Caecilia* were written by others. In any case, the conclusions those critics reached show just how difficult it was for a person writing in the rising tide of Romanticism to appreciate late Beethoven on Weber's terms. His position is important because it shows that their interpretations, especially those of the Ninth Symphony (which we shall examine shortly), were not as prosaic as they may at first appear. They too breathe a Romantic spirit which was by no means common currency in the third decade of the nineteenth century, and which marks their views as representative of the attitude of most German idealists toward Beethoven.

Kanne's view of tone-painting, set forth in a lengthy article appearing in four installments in the *WAMZ* in 1818, is as different from that of Weber as is the Romantic aesthetic of Hoffmann and Marx from the old theory of the affections (*WAMZ* II, pp. 373, 385, 393, 401). His interpretation of music is an idealist one which allows of no restrictions; instead, music

draws the human heart in its flight through the aether, through all the joys and sorrows of the world – and through the light of dawn into the blue aether of heaven – and shows it stormclouds from afar, which threaten to advance, and lets it experience a foreboding of the depths of the underworld, without overwhelming it in horror, but carries it again aloft, gently on beautiful waves into the restful groves.

This is almost a paraphrase of Hoffmann, but it also gives more than a hint of Schelling: one of the first, as Einstein has pointed out, to speak of a spiritual dimension in music,[15] while still clinging to the visible universe and thus encouraging visual imagery. While a painter, however, can evoke only one image at a time, a musician, according to Kanne, is a 'Geistermahler' who, like a poet, creates different images in succession. He cannot portray the legs of a hero, but he can show his steps; not his actual arms, but the power which they embody; not his mouth, but the words which issue from it. Instrumental music, in other words, does not create concrete images, nor does it evoke stereotyped emotions. Rather, it shows with unparalleled vividness the entire emotional world of its subject, which can be understood only with the inner eye, in the presence of a characteristically Romantic longing. The boundaries between the arts are deliberately blurred by Kanne, since in his opinion they all aim at the same goals in different ways. This could be understood, however, only by those who were prepared to recognize it. 'There is something else,' he wrote, 'something higher and deeper, in the process of finding a subject to observe the object of art, namely a breadth of education and a depth of spirit. If these are present, then there will be no difficulty in understanding musical painting.' The overtures to *Don Giovanni, Egmont, Iphigenia in Tauris* and *Medea* are suggested as works which evoke images in this manner.

Marx, then, was not an isolated example; musical idealism did not necessarily imply any positive break between music and the other arts. It has already been seen that Amadeus Wendt, too, was able to combine an idealistic viewpoint with a specifically literary, and hence non-abstract, bias; yet he was neither a conservative nor a dilettante, at least as regards the philosophical basis for this synthesis. A professional philosopher, he clearly understood what he was doing. It has already been remarked that Hoffmann and Wendt said the same thing in opposite ways. Wendt's preference for the written word, when combined with the other-worldly view of music at which he broadly hints, is analogous to Hoffmann's shunning vocal music while clinging to, and indeed expanding the vocabulary of, harmonic and formal analysis. Marx might be said to resemble Wendt in his preference for worldly associations within an otherwise transcendental, Hegelian view of Beethoven's position in music history.

Kanne, on the other hand, resembles Hoffmann in his tendency to idealize the images which music creates. Like Hoffmann, too, he insisted on making these images dependent on thematic events. In fact, as will be seen in connection with his analysis of the Ninth Symphony, he tended to contradict his own theory in order to dramatize the surface details of the music. All four writers, then, held views of music more complex than those usually associated with nineteenth-century musical idealists. Instead of calling attention exclusively to music's deeper unity and the vagueness of the images it creates, they insisted that it must be grasped intellectually as well. Was their attitude so widespread as to provide a genuine alternative to the theories of Romantic aestheticians about music? The writers to be discussed later in this chapter give evidence that it was. Many of them followed Wendt's lead, if not his musical taste, and drew explicit parallels between music and poetry, to the extent that in their writings the essential difference between instrumental and vocal music often appears to be forgotten. At the same time, these writers were concerned with developing a new kind of analysis, which today may seem old-fashioned, but which at that time was both radical and universally accepted: a sure sign of the unconscious acceptance of its precepts.

What those precepts were will shortly become apparent, since it is in the Ninth Symphony that poetry and a tradition of abstract music were brought together for the first time, literally demanding that the listener adopt an aesthetic position. Fortunately, the first critics of this symphony, Kanne among them, rose to this challenge, producing some of the most intriguing and unexpected documents in the history of music criticism.

The Ninth Symphony

Of all Beethoven's late works, the Ninth Symphony, though for many years rarely heard, was the most notorious during his lifetime and immediately afterward. Everywhere it was performed, it was awaited with eager anticipation; everywhere opinions were divided. In a recent dissertation David Benjamin Levy has surveyed the early performances of this symphony, and the reactions it provoked, in five major cities: Vienna, London, Paris, Leipzig, and Berlin.[16] In all the German cities, he has found, the reaction was the same; initial skepticism was followed by very gradual acceptance, which arrived about mid-century under the batons of a few gifted conductors: Otto Nicolai in Vienna, Felix Mendelssohn in Leipzig. In Vienna, perhaps due to Beethoven's enormous prestige, it was better received than elsewhere. Always, however, the sticking point was the finale. Nothing – not the unprecedented size of the work nor the extraordinary difficulty of its execution – produced such opposition as this movement, which was censured, vilified, or described as tasteless and trivial, everywhere the symphony was performed. The possible reasons for this rejection are manifold. Schiller was then a much admired poet, and many may have felt that Beethoven's setting did not do justice to the lofty sentiments of the *Ode to Joy*.[17] The choral part is notoriously difficult, and it may often have been badly performed. As Marx suggests in his review, many people had difficulty grasping the relationship between the finale and the rest of the symphony.

The crucial issue, then, was this: how was a symphony of such dimensions, and such unusual form, to be reconciled with the limited aesthetic sensibilities of its first hearers? Any critic approaching the work must have had this question forced upon his attention, together with several possible solutions. He could, of course, condemn it, like the *AMZ*'s and *BAMZ*'s Leipzig correspondents after the first performance in that city. He could treat it as program music, taking Beethoven's hint and seeing the finale as a resolution of the themes introduced in the earlier movements. Like Marx, he could give his own interpretation of the finale and its relationship to the rest of the symphony. Or he could simply analyze the work in detail, leaving his readers to draw their own conclusions. The one thing he could not do was to superimpose an abstract but verbal interpretation in the manner of Hoffmann, since, as Marx's review suggests and Hoffmann would certainly have acknowledged, the use of voices in the finale places the entire symphony in a different world from that of its predecessors. It is specific where the Fifth Symphony was abstract, and there is never any doubt about the meaning of the finale, which forces the message of Schiller's poem upon even the least musical of listeners. For this reason, the early reviews are all the more interesting for what they tell, or refuse to tell, about the state of the ideal of absolute music in Beethoven's Germany.

Kanne's approach to the Ninth Symphony is almost antithetical to that of Marx (*WAMZ* VIII, pp. 149, 157). He assigns a different theme to each of the first three movements, with the finale neither transcending nor resolving, but actually uniting these themes. Thus, the first movement is a gigantic fantasy, full of blue fire, rolling waves and Hoffmann-like apparitions. Kanne mentions the contrast produced by the singing use of the wind instruments, but in all he obviously regards the effect of the movement as oppressive, since he cites the scherzo as providing relief. Indeed, he seems to wish for the first movement to be followed directly by the song-like Adagio. The scherzo, however, is sufficiently comic to satisfy him, and he interprets it, unlike the first movement, programmatically. The staccato runs of the wind instruments seem to him to portray Colombine dancing with Harlequin, and the various modulations show them hopping boldly about. The timpani strokes on F beginning at m. 248 portray Harlequin's sword, while the large jumps in the bass in the following measures show us 'den langarmigen Pirot'. Kanne also speaks of the manifold imitations in this movement as though they were personalities designed to entertain the listener.

The Adagio, meanwhile, is for Kanne a simple song which offers spiritual relief after the turbulence of the preceding movements. Kanne speaks evocatively of the way the melodic line 'soars from the comfort-seeking sixth'[18] before the final cadence (mm. 15 – 18), and of the lyrical lines given to the bass instruments in the first section of the movement and their contrast with the higher registers. It is evident that for him this movement was primarily a play of tone colors, subtly juxtaposed to create an effect of the greatest melodic expansiveness.

So far, then, Kanne has struck a notable compromise, anticipating the style of Marx, between selective commentary on the technical aspects of the music and purely fanciful interpretation. Neither is self-sufficient; in the Adagio, for example, the idea of the melodic prominence given to the sixth is considered only by virtue of its emotional effect, while the shape of the line, climbing 'wieder auf eine höhere Klangstufe', is clearly only a metaphor for the final struggle which precedes true relaxation. Rarely, however, do these images become specific enough to serve as more than a vague guide to the meaning of the music. Only in interpreting the scherzo do Kanne's fancy and his own theory of tone-painting appear to gain the upper hand, apparently because of the fanciful nature of the genre itself. Kanne must have believed, then, that he was interpreting, not his own experience of the music, but the intention of the composer, which was that the first movement should overwhelm, the second amuse, and the third give solace to the listener.

How was the finale to combine these three ideas? The answer seems to be that it is, quite simply, a gigantic conglomeration of all the different elements of music: an enormous synthesis at which the earlier movements had only hinted. 'All movements of this work', he wrote, 'carry the stamp of the gigantic, the tremendous, in their entire economy. Consequently . . . [Beethoven's] powerful tempos drag the listener along, as if in a torrent, from one emotion to another, and scarcely give him a chance to be himself.'[19]

This was not, however, the way that Kanne had described those movements before, except possibly the first. In discussing the second and third movements, his emphasis was rather on the stability of the emotions they represent, thus apparently contradicting his own theory of musical expression. Likewise, in describing the finale, he emphasizes the classical sense of unity which Beethoven imposes through fugal techniques and attention to form. Kanne's paradoxical belief seems to have been that this effect was increased by the sheer diversity of the movement. How this was achieved we can only guess, since Kanne provides no analysis comparable to that of Marx to support his far-reaching claims. He does offer one hint, however: 'Beethoven felt that, due to the application of such manifold energies, such heaping of apparently so much heterogeneous material, still a greater measure of all powers needed to be added. Therefore he introduced the Turkish march in the middle of his chorus.'[20]

Kanne is at pains to deny that Beethoven was indulging in a real Turkish spirit here, but he must have felt that the nature of the contrast, so abrupt and complete, corresponded to the differences among the earlier movements, and thus increased the bond between these and the finale: a bond which, as he had already pointed out, had been set up at once by the recapitulation of their themes at the beginning of the movement. For Kanne, then, the finale was by no means a Marxian resolution of the preceding movements, nor did it transcend them, as Marx himself had hinted in his review. Rather, it recalled their diversity while at the same time imposing a gigantic unity of its own: a unity compounded of a greater variety of materials than had ever been used in a symphony before, and transcending the limits of a single movement to encompass the entire work in its plan. Only because the previous movements had been so diversified was such a heterogeneous finale possible: one which at the same time employed, as Kanne clearly recognized, every standard device of symphonic development and organic growth.

The most striking thing about Kanne's review is how little he says of the work's most important innovation: the introduction of voices into the finale. For Kanne, the chorus apparently added no new dimension to the symphony which its form did not already imply; it was simply one more element of diversity in an already diversified structure. He makes little of the bass recitative which plays such a prominent role in the introduction to the finale, never thinking to connect its implied vocal nature to the actual use of voices later on. In this manner, any programmatic interpretation based on the significance of the *Ode to Joy* is implicitly rejected. This is all the more surprising since, as we have seen, Kanne was by no means averse to creating programs where none was specified by the composer. It can only be concluded that he felt such an explicit manner of thinking to be appropriate only to a musical joke, a scherzo, and not to an entire symphony employing classicizing tendencies throughout, and which depended upon abstract form for its overall unity. There is thus a significant parallel between this review and the earlier one of the 'Eroica' in the *AMZ*, which may have been written by Kanne before he became familiar with the aesthetics of Romantic idealism, and which also largely avoids the themes of heroism and tragedy pronounced by the composer. Even in his later writings, Kanne was apparently unwilling to read meaning into music on any but the most immediate level: that of the emotionally or pictorially significant phrase.

No greater contrast could be imagined than that between this review and the first of the three reviews of the Ninth Symphony printed four years later in *Caecilia*. The author of the latter was Franz Joseph Fröhlich, a professor at Würzburg University who was also a noted violinist and conductor and an accomplished composer of symphonic works. Fröhlich had founded an institute for the performance of choral and orchestral music, and was thus in an unusually good position to appreciate the introduction of a chorus into the symphony itself, as well as to follow the intricacies of Beethoven's score.[21] He saw the symphony as nothing less than Beethoven's musical autobiography. He refers to the widespread skepticism which the work had provoked, and admits that he initially shared this feeling. Only after careful study of the score did he become convinced that it was an aesthetic whole: that indeed it was the greatest symphony ever written. The process by which he arrived at this decision involved not only musical study of the work but theorizing about the history of the symphony. Anticipating Marx, Fröhlich states that Beethoven was the first composer to use the symphonic form to convey ideas, and like Marx, he cites the 'Eroica' and 'Pastoral' Symphonies as prime examples. He also claims that, according to Beethoven himself, a psychological idea lies behind each of his works, not just the symphonic ones, and it is to be regretted that more of these have not become known. The Ninth, however, was something entirely new: an actual fusion of music and poetry. In this symphony, thanks to the text of the last movement, the idea is clear. The theme is the transcendent power of joy to overcome both everyday sorrows and the larger issues which oppress mankind. In Beethoven's case, the larger issue was deafness, and, says Fröhlich, the composer had only realized the redeeming power of joy after great spiritual struggle. The symphony portrays this struggle and its resolution, beginning in D minor and ending in D major with the choral tribute to joy's divine spark.

This may not seem a very imaginative interpretation. It combines the obvious view of the symphony as a tribute to joy with the now familiar one of triumph through progression from minor to major in a multi-movement work. The latter idea, however, had apparently never been suggested before, nor would it be again until Berlioz wrote about the Fifth Symphony in such terms, fully ten years later. This is particularly striking in view of the perhaps disproportionate significance which has since been given to the view of Beethoven which that idea implies. It is permissible for a modern writer to speak programmatically about psychological struggle in works like the Fifth and Ninth Symphonies, while for virtually any other music of this period, such interpretation is generally shunned as naive.[22]

In Beethoven's time, the situation was reversed. Emotional views of music were the rule of the day, whether those of the old-fashioned affections, of Hoffmann's spirit-world, or of the more specific rhapsodizing of Marx. No writer before Fröhlich, however, Marx included, had ever thought to attribute any emotional motivation at all to Beethoven's long-range progressions from minor to major. We have seen how Hoffmann disregarded as much as possible the seemingly obvious triumph of the Fifth Symphony's last movement. Kanne, in his review of the Third Piano Concerto, made nothing of the C major coda in the last movement, while the 'Pathétique' Sonata was championed in the *AMZ* because its finale returned to the mood of the opening. The 'Moonlight' Sonata found approval for the same reason. Other works by Beethoven in minor keys tended to be undervalued; we have seen that the reviewer of the 'Appassionata' Sonata preferred the D-flat major variations to the outer movements. With the exception of these works and the Violin Sonata, Op. 23, no other minor-key work by Beethoven was reviewed at all until the late period. Whatever psychological significance these works may have had for Beethoven, that significance was far from obvious to his contemporaries.

Fröhlich, then, was suggesting something genuinely new. What followed was the largest and most specific emotional interpretation of a Beethoven symphony (or any other work of Beethoven) yet published, followed by a lengthy discussion of the aesthetic issues involved in this type of analysis. Those issues were current ones: Fröhlich was responding to an article printed in the *AMZ* the year before, but the controversy had actually begun when Grétry published his *Mémoires* in 1789, and it was one which was to have great significance for the aesthetic anomaly of the 'Choral' Symphony. Grétry had maintained that good instrumental works conveyed such specific ideas that they demanded to be set to words, citing Haydn's 'belles symphonies' as a genre likely to benefit from such treatment.[23] Haydn's works, he wrote, were a vast dictionary, from which one could draw ideas that could not be repeated except through words.[24] Karl Spazier, in translating Grétry into German in 1800, had ridiculed this notion, which seems at first glance to stem from the mistaken zeal of an operatic composer for a familiar style of text–music association.[25]

Actually, the issue was more complex than this. Nowhere is the difference between the Romantic generation and that which preceded it more apparent than in their respective views of the relationship between music and the written word. Even so systematic a philosopher as Immanuel Kant, in his *Critique of Judgement*, accepted without question the idea that music was analogous to spoken language.[26] In Mattheson's *Volkommene Capellmeister*, we read that a listener should 'completely grasp and clearly understand the motive, sense, meaning and force, with all the phrases and sentences pertaining thereto, as if it were real speech'.[27] Comparisons between music and language continued to be made throughout Beethoven's lifetime, but their implications gradually changed, and the transition is perhaps nowhere better represented than in the pages of the *AMZ* and *Caecilia*.

The first step in what was to prove a new direction was taken by Rochlitz in the first year of his editorship of the *AMZ* (*AMZ* I, col. 433). According to Rochlitz, those who, like Grétry, wished to set texts to pre-existent music were fundamentally mistaken, since they attributed to those words a flexibility which they did not possess. Like most of his contemporaries, progressive and conservative alike, Rochlitz felt that music's subject was the emotions, and that those who denied music the ability to express were simply unable to understand it. At the same time, however, he recognized the unique character of musical expression: that it possessed nuances and subtleties which correspond to the nature of thought itself. Just as a person would not be able, after an hour of particularly profound emotion, to describe in detail all of the psychological changes he had undergone, so it was impossible to give a specific emotional narrative of a piece of music, or to assign it more than an overall expressive character. Language, by contrast, contained so many parts of speech which were merely essential, and had nothing to do with the emotions, that it was impossible to write a text that would sufficiently correspond to the musical subtleties already explained. A composer could draw his inspiration from poetry, but never the other way around.

Responding to this challenge, A. Apel, writing in the *AMZ* seven years later, suggested another interpretation of Grétry (*AMZ* VIII, cols. 449, 465). He might have meant, Apel said, that the ideas conveyed by music could also be expressed in poetry, or, for that matter, in any of the other arts. A symphony, that is to say, if not actually set to words, could at least have a poetic counterpart. If this were the case, the paradox created by Grétry would be resolved, because music and poetry are actually sister arts. Music consists of a harmony of tones, but double counterpoint presents another element: a harmony of the ideas expressed. In order to silence doubters, among them Rochlitz himself, who had also been skeptical about this type of poetic 'translation', Apel actually composed a poem as a companion piece for Mozart's E-flat major Symphony, K. 453. The largo maestoso introduction became a paean to Eros and Anteros, the first elements of Creation, while the Allegro moderato explored the themes of childlike delight, mature sorrow, and the power of love to overcome difficulties. This part of the poem contains the prophetic (and probably Schiller-inspired) words:

> Rasch verspottend jeden Zügel
> trägt ihn bald der Freude Flügel
> durch der Brüder muntre Reihen
> Feste täglich sich erneuen.

Apel was proposing, then, that music conveys, not poetical ideas, but ideas in the abstract, whose poetic form was only another possible manifestation of their potential. This is a much more advanced notion than any Grétry probably intended, suggesting as it does the transcendent and at least partially inaccessible world of much contemporary German thought: a world which Hoffmann was to evoke again four years later. For the German Romantics, it was a central concern that access to this world, which Kant had so austerely denied, should be achieved through art, and, for some at least, through music alone. Apel, however, does not sever the link between music and poetry; he affirms it, thus showing himself a forerunner of Amadeus Wendt more than of Hoffmann.

Apel also apparently laid the issue of music and poetry to rest, in the *AMZ*, for more than 20 years. It did not surface again until the publication, in 1825, of the second volume of Rochlitz' *Für Freunde der Tonkunst*. Rochlitz' book contains a 'Commentatiuncula in usum Delphini', the story of a court-clerk in an obscure German backwater who receives at last the issue of the *AMZ* which contains Apel's poem, and is moved by it to relate his own experience with Beethoven's variations from the Piano Sonata in A-flat major, Op. 26. He claims to have found in these variations nothing less than the history of his own life.[28] Rochlitz probably meant to imply that anyone could have read into the same music anything he pleased, and the review of this volume published in the *AMZ* the same year makes it clear that this was how he was understood at the time (*AMZ* XXVII, col. 433). The reviewer also shows that he saw the difference between Apel's approach, with which Rochlitz had taken issue specifically, and that of Grétry; he refers with scorn to various attempts since Apel's time to relate instrumental music to specific concepts (i.e. ideas) and express them in words, rather than merely setting words to music, which was doubtless all that Grétry had intended.

This was the context, then, in which the article originated to which Fröhlich felt compelled to respond. Entitled 'Soll man bey der instrumental-Musik Etwas denken?', it appeared in the *AMZ* in two installments in August, 1827 (*AMZ* XXIX, cols. 529, 545). It is cast in the form of a conversation between two men, Wolfgang and Friedrich, who take diametrically opposite positions toward the question posed by the title of the article. Friedrich's opinion is clear from the very beginning; he had heard an Andante by Mozart, and it reminded him of a story, because all good instrumental music could best be understood in terms of an underlying text. In listening to Mozart's quartet, he had heard clearly four singing voices, and could hardly resist the temptation to perform the work vocally. This was, of course, a reversion to the position of Grétry, and Wolfgang counters it with a series of arguments from which his own ideas only gradually emerge. The basis of these is that:

Music puts us in mind of exactly all that which is to us closed off, stiff, doubtful, confused, cumbersome, and wants to be clarified and reconciled; that which other languages, art-forms, and influences from life attempt in vain. The more a man guards his life from rigidity through freedom of feeling, the more he sees all existence filled with the poetry of life, the better he will understand music.

These feelings, however, should not be thought of as a text; they should not be demanded of the artist, nor searched for in ourselves, because man feels without reflection intervening.

The latter part of this quote perhaps reflects Schopenhauer, who nine years earlier had called music 'as direct an objectification and copy of the whole will as the world itself'.[29] Wolfgang's theories are, of course, divested of the Schopenhauerian reverence for a higher consciousness, but, in this anonymous article (it is signed 'F. L. B.'), one component of that philosopher's aesthetic is clearly expressed: the idea that music, unlike the other arts, speaks to the listener directly, without mediation, and explores a world of inchoate feeling which would otherwise be totally inaccessible. Hoffmann had felt likewise, and Rochlitz had anticipated this to some extent with his talk of nuances and subtleties in music of which poetry was incapable; but he still believed these to be nuances of conscious thought, and hence relatively unmysterious. Now the barrier between man and his unconscious was removed, and music stepped in to occupy the gap.

It was this interpretation of music, which more than any of the writings encountered so far recalls the modern view of Romantic musical aesthetics, that Fröhlich felt he had to reject. He used the Ninth Symphony as the prime example of a perfect union between music and poetry, in which Beethoven had transcended the abstraction of his earlier music and made it possible at last for the symphony to become a truly popular art. It had not done so, he believed, because long, abstract symphonies were difficult for the uneducated public to understand. The public was not to blame for this, but appreciation for symphonic music should be heightened through proper schooling. In the meantime, it would be beneficial if accomplished poets would illustrate the subject of each new symphony; their poems would be printed in the program, and the basic feelings which they suggest (Fröhlich uses the Marxian term 'Grundidee') would then be developed by the music according to its own powers. Haydn had already shown how this could be accomplished in the orchestral version of his 'Seven Last Words', which in effect had used entire symphonic movements to illuminate the meaning of fundamentally simple texts. With clues such as these, the proper manner of playing the music would be conveyed to the interpreters, and this could only facilitate the understanding of the work.

At the same time the symphony would not become a mere mongrel; rather it would be heightened, as we thankfully see it in the highly developed works of Beethoven's genius. The strongly oratorical art, which we find in Haydn's and Mozart's marvelous symphonies, would become at the same time bearer and messenger of a high poetical outlook, in which the essence of oratory in words would be combined with that of music.

Obviously, if a symphonic composer were actually to incorporate vocal music into his work, as Beethoven had done, the possibilities for such development would be virtually unlimited; joined together, poetry and music could illuminate each other, showing what an enormous effect either alone was capable of. Listeners would be encouraged not to think of absolute music as empty form, but to see instead its oratorical ('rednerisch') potential and appreciate it as a whole.

Fröhlich, then, takes Apel's view of the exact correspondence between musical and poetic themes and reduces it to a more generalized system in which a few fundamental concepts from the poem serve as the guidepost for the development of purely musical ideas. At the same time, however, Fröhlich refuses to sever the relationship between music and speech which the previous generation had so carefully established. The Ninth Symphony is seen by him as a basically simple structure, showing the way from struggle to resolution through joy, and it must have taken considerable insight, as well as faith in the composer's control over musical unity, to perceive such straightforwardness in a work which at the time was so uniquely gigantic. For Fröhlich, however, unlike Hoffmann or the Romantic aestheticians, this unity worked itself out on the level of the everyday world; although Beethoven's symphonies strove to express a new level of meaning, it was also comprehensible in more traditional terms. Fröhlich was still an idealist, or he could never have written about music's mysterious powers in the terms he did, but, as should by now be apparent, this seemingly simple philosophical position allowed for an almost infinitely wide variety of interpretations of the role of music in conveying abstract thought.

Fröhlich's worldliness is immediately apparent in his treatment of the opening of the first movement. The initial interval, he says, lacking the third degree, portrays ambiguity, and thus evokes a sorrowful feeling of longing. Where Hoffmann would have seized upon that longing, however, and made it the cornerstone of his interpretation, Fröhlich sees it as immediately resolved by the appearance of the tonic and the entrance of the unison theme at m. 17. This, says Fröhlich, is the expression of a powerful spirit, and since that same spirit is able to resist all of life's obstacles, it is natural that it should form the focal point of the movement's unity. The opening idea (mm. 1–6), meanwhile – Fröhlich seems not to have noticed, or not to have cared about, the motivic connection between this and the following unison passage – is used throughout to portray tenderness, sorrow, and impulsiveness: the first two through the already-mentioned ambiguity, the last through the effect of increasing power which always accompanies it. The 'deeply stirring' accents of mm. 21–5 complete the picture of an uncommonly powerful soul, while the tender phrases of the winds in mm. 28–30 show the milder side of this noble personality. The opening returns – this time it is also described as 'gentle', but no reference is made to the shift from the fifth on A to one on D – only to give way, in B-flat, to a surge of even more powerful energy. This is increased through effective imitation (mm. 55–61) and a series of modulations, by which term Fröhlich apparently understands any introduction of accidentals into the basic key structure. In these opening measures may be found the key to the form of the movement, and the rest is described only generally as the struggle of the soul therein portrayed, often powerful, sometimes surrendering to tender feelings, but always recognizably the same.

Fröhlich thus provides an emotional counterpart for the type of modern harmonic analysis which has had so much success in reducing Beethoven's most complex structures to a few fundamental key and intervallic relationships.[30] A modern analyst – even one who, like Leo Treitler, claims to follow nineteenth-century principles – might see the move to the flat side at m. 24 as the crucial turning point in the overall form of the first movement, while for Fröhlich, the fundamental emotional elements are introduced within a similarly short span. These are: tender longing for promised joy (mm. 1–16), striving, unconquerable heroic strength (mm. 17–20), tragic pathos (presumably mm. 21–4), and the sweet, still longing perception of joy itself (mm. 28–30). Although he doesn't say so specifically, it may be surmised that Fröhlich would see the B-flat major second theme as a manifestation of the last-named emotion, mm. 102ff. as a return to the conflict of tragic pathos and tenderness (juxtaposing as it does the martial rhythm first heard in m. 27 with similar melting figures in the winds), and mm. 160ff. not as the beginning of a new section but as a cyclical return to the mood of the opening. He may have felt that it is only musical logic which turns what would be a pedestrian progression of a few basic feelings into a tightly organized and dramatically interesting whole. It is likely, though, that Fröhlich would have tried to describe this process further if he himself had been a gifted poet. Like many of his contemporaries, he clearly felt that the written word played an important role in unravelling the mysteries of music. These mysteries Fröhlich himself does not attempt to resolve, except by urging that the performers should have the deepest possible understanding of the psychological themes developed in the Ninth Symphony, in order that the work may produce its full effect.

Fröhlich's interpretation of the scherzo is less specific in individual details, but also more dynamic, more oriented toward the overall form. In the first movement, questions of form had been ignored, presumably because formal dynamics were among those aspects of the music which Fröhlich felt unable to describe precisely in words. In the scherzo, however, he was able without difficulty to connect his basic poetic idea: that of a search for joy, with the bipartite structure and its juxtaposition of major and minor tonalities. The first section shows a heightened struggle of the same personality we had encountered earlier, moving mercurially through a succession of moods and emotions, until finally, in the 2/2 section, it gives way to a vision of joyful fulfillment. This vision, however, asserts itself in vain; the struggle inexorably resumes, to conclude the movement with unresolved energy.

What Fröhlich neglects to mention is that this is nothing more than the standard triple-meter dance movement with trio, moved to an unaccustomed position within the symphony, and with an unusual duple-meter refrain, but nevertheless recognizable and familiar. Beethoven, he seems to be saying, had invested this familiar structure with a new level of meaning and poetic clarity: one which even he could never hope to repeat in the same way. This, not the technical innovations just mentioned, is the real novelty of the movement, and its fundamental simplicity brings that movement within the realm of concrete thought. As we have seen, Marx also saw the symphony as progressing toward a type of music that was more immediately comprehensible, by virtue of its simplicity and its use of the written word, than anything in Beethoven's earlier symphonies. For Marx, the finale simply transcended the previous movements, making the symphony into a two-stage *Gesamtkunstwerk* in which the shady obscurities of instrumental music were forever redeemed by the very composer who had formerly handled them with such mastery. Fröhlich may reflect this view in some ways, but he was also distinctly different from Marx, and his manner of emotional interpretation was in many ways original with him.

This is especially evident in his view of the slow movement. Here, he once again chooses to ignore the overall form: that of a set of double variations, and instead to concentrate on the meaning, already firmly established in the earlier movements, of the principal tonalities, B-flat major and D major. The former is known from the first movement to be the key in which Beethoven chose to express most thoroughly the tender side of his character, showing a longing after joy not yet fulfilled. D major, by contrast, was in that movement the key of joy itself, just as it was, in the scherzo, the key in which joy in its purity had been glimpsed for the first time in the symphony. Now, in the succession of B-flat major Adagio and D major Andante, longing (here expressed as a feeling of rest after the struggle of the preceding movement) is directly juxtaposed with joy itself. Joy, however, cannot subdue the longing, which then returns in more dynamic form (m. 43). The appearance of the second theme in G major at m. 65 suggests a new emotional direction, which is fulfilled by the turn to E-flat at m. 83. A new seriousness has been introduced: a deep source of feeling to soothe the longing heart. This is heightened, only to return to the original emotion at m. 99. With the introduction at this point of 12/8 meter, the music becomes more agitated, and the conclusion of the movement is largely an expression of the various emotional states to which longing is still susceptible in its as yet unsuccessful search for fulfillment.

Fröhlich thus sees the variation form as significant only insofar as it expresses a gradual heightening of a few fundamental emotions. Motion (first the stillness of the opening, then the increasing power of mm. 43ff. and 99ff.) and key are everything in this movement, since they highlight the gradual unfolding of a character, but form itself is never mentioned. Fröhlich's attitude seems to be that each new form creates itself out of

85

factors too complex to be indicated in more than a rudimentary way. The third movement, then, stands halfway between the dazzling clarity of the scherzo, with its unambiguous dramatization of the quest for joy forestalled, and the unfathomable complexities of the first Allegro.

The finale receives from Fröhlich the most complex interpretation of all. The beginning, not surprisingly, is seen as a renewed search for joy, in which the various directions hitherto attempted are interrupted by a bass recitative representing unsatisfied longing. It is interesting that neither Kanne nor Fröhlich — the latter with his explicitly poetic interpretation of the entire symphony — makes much of the implied vocal character of this recitative, whose connection with the later choral section seems so obvious. Instead, Fröhlich seems to see the entire introduction as raised, through the combination of such brief and meaningful fragments, to a new level of narrative specificity, achieving something at which Beethoven had only hinted in the previous movements. Only in this sense is it possible for him to say that the recitative beginning at m. 80 'speaks forth' ('ausspricht') the picture of joy, while those before had signified only longing.

The introduction of the 'joy' theme, its development, and the entry of the chorus are described in predictable detail. The next point at which Fröhlich is forced to elaborate on the interpretation which he has already given in all its essential aspects comes with the beginning of the Turkish march in B-flat major. We have seen that for Fröhlich B-flat was the key of longing, while for Kanne this entire section could be understood only in the context of the enormous diversity of the symphony as a whole. Fröhlich, however, sees it as contributing to the unity of the movement through furtherance of a poetic idea; namely, that all creatures on earth should share in the source of joy. This, then, is a journey to the depths of the earth, in which the lowliest creatures, represented by the bassoon and bass drum, gradually join with all the others as the orchestral instruments and sections enter one by one. This picture is then completed by the tenor solo and men's chorus, representing mankind. The orchestral fugue which follows exhibits generalized rejoicing, resolved at last by the simplicity of the joy theme returning in D major. Only after this journey downward is it possible, like Dante, to ascend to heaven in the section which follows.

Fröhlich's comments on the conclusion of the movement are less specific, probably because obvious textual associations here give way to fugal development of the basic ideas. He never questions, however, that Beethoven in this 'instrumental' conclusion has absorbed in the deepest sense the meaning of the poem, illustrating again and again the universal rejoicing he had so carefully prepared.

This review has been dealt with at such length because it is the first to be considered so far, except for Hoffmann's of the Fifth Symphony (which will be further discussed in a later chapter), which combines such a detailed analysis of any work of Beethoven with a thoroughgoing extra-musical interpretation. For Fröhlich, as for Hoffmann, the two ideas – interpretation and analysis – were largely inseparable.

Indeed, Fröhlich's analysis, unlike Hoffmann's, is not really an analysis at all, since the only building blocks it recognizes are emotional ones. Form and harmonic structure emerge only when, as in the scherzo and slow movement respectively, they happen to correspond exactly to the emotional fabric of the work. Fröhlich did not attempt any such approach to the first movement, probably because, as has already been suggested, he felt incapable of providing a commentary for a work of such complexity. Likewise, in the finale, he tends to talk about the fugal sections only in the most general terms, reserving specific description for the first half of the movement, in which the poetic ideas are clearer. This does not mean that Fröhlich preferred music which was always comprehensible to him in terms of the written word. He makes no such distinctions, seeming to stand in awe of the entire symphony. In this sense, he was perhaps closer to Hoffmann than is immediately apparent, since for all the obviously programmatic nature of his approach to the symphony, he was restrained enough to reject programmatic commentary where he felt it to be inappropriate, preferring, like Hoffmann, to evoke an entire range of feelings almost at once.

Considered as a whole, then, his review falls somewhere between Hoffmann and the more specific formal–programmatic approach of Marx, in which each aspect of the music is linked as closely as possible to an extra-musical event or idea. Once again, Fröhlich must be considered a true original, defining a style of analysis which had no real precedent and which, despite these differences, may have influenced the later Marx profoundly.

Less sophisticated interpretations are presented in the other two reviews of the Ninth Symphony in *Caecilia*. The one immediately following Fröhlich naturally seems, in comparison, somewhat cursory. Written by a Dr Grossheim, of Cassel, it contains no real analysis of the score, and it may be read as a refutation of the then current idea that Beethoven had not properly understood Schiller's *Ode*. The alterations which he performed on the original text are defended, even if they are not properly explained. Grossheim believed that 'when poetry and music appear together, the first is master, the other servant', but he nevertheless felt that Beethoven was writing a pure tribute to joy, and thus did not need to set the entirety of Schiller's poem. As for the relationship of the finale to the remainder of the symphony, Grossheim explains this as a marriage of opposites. Beethoven had suffered more than most men, and was thus unable to portray joy without first showing joylessness. There is no question here of any spiritual progress, as with Fröhlich; Beethoven simply juxtaposed these two opposite states, leaving the listener to draw his own conclusion.

The third review dealing with the Ninth Symphony in *Caecilia* is the longest of all, covering 27 pages with additional musical examples. It also treats the *Missa Solemnis* and the Quartet, Op. 131. Written by Beethoven's friend Ignaz von Seyfried, author of the notorious *Beethoven-Studien*, it offers the additional perspective on this music of someone who knew the composer personally. Unfortunately, Seyfried says nothing about Beethoven's motivation in composing this gigantic work, although he clearly rejects Fröhlich's programmatic view of the symphony as a whole. Seyfried's approach to analysis is also more purely technical than that of Fröhlich; he describes rather than explains, by quoting all the major themes but saying little of their interrelationship. He chooses to ignore the problem of the finale. It had been suggested, he relates, that Beethoven should write two conclusions, one choral, one instrumental and of more manageable length, and publish them both, as he had done with the String Quartet, Op. 130. As it was, one could deal only with the work as he left it, and Seyfried praises the finale not for its unusual form but, like Kanne, for its mastery of fugal and symphonic technique. He divides the movement into 20 different sections, according to the changes in tempo, and comments individually on the particularly lengthy ones. Thus he too avoids the question of the bass recitatives in the introduction, preferring to ignore the aesthetic issue − that of an implied weakening of the boundary between instrumental and vocal music − which they seem to force upon the listener. Indeed, for Beethoven's generation in Germany, this issue seems simply not to have arisen. Seyfried also makes nothing of the violent contrast which begins the Turkish march section, and which had led Kanne and Fröhlich to such radically different interpretations.

The middle movements receive from Seyfried more emotional commentary than the others, which might be taken to mean that he preferred these movements to the enormous symphonic structures which surround them. Like Kanne, but unlike Fröhlich, whose view of the scherzo was more complex, Seyfried sees it as essentially a humorous piece, presenting a sharp contrast to the mood of the opening movement. He clearly appreciates the effect of the trio, which he sees as a glimpse into a different, friendlier world, but he refuses to read any meaning into this contrast, preferring to see the entire movement as an abstract (his own word) instrumental piece which calls for no additional, extra-musical idea to explain it.

Lest Seyfried be thought an enemy of verbal interpretation, however, it should be noted that he reads into the slow movement, as Rochlitz' fanciful clerk might have done, a picture of human life: the trouble, hopes and sufferings which precede the release of 'der arme Staubgeborne' back into the breast of the earth, and God's just reward. 'Whether our master thought and wanted precisely that,' Seyfried writes,

can admittedly not be ascertained for certain. That, however, as in the moment of consecration he received his ideas from above, turning there with all his soul – for precisely his innermost impulses made this necessary – such, or some similar feelings rose up in him, can, by more precise knowledge of his deep nature, his heart filled with purest religious inclinations, be almost unconditionally maintained, even proved with nearly logical evidence.

The nature of this thought, with its tortuous Teutonic succession of clauses and careful qualification, shows Seyfried either unsure of himself or conscious that disagreement might arise. It is more difficult to determine where he stands on the issue of musical programs, for that is what is really being debated here. His cursory analysis of the slow movement, which follows this quotation, makes no reference to any of the stages in the hypothetical life's journey which has just been outlined in the previous paragraphs. Like Apel, Seyfried seems to believe that the ideas embodied in a piece of music can also be explained in other terms, but, perhaps conscious of Rochlitz' parody, he shies away from any specific coordination of musical and extra-musical ideas, preferring to describe the entire movement as having a gloomy, closed, almost melancholically rapturous character.

Seyfried, then, largely avoids the challenge of the Ninth Symphony, preferring to speak in generalities and interpret only where he is not likely to arouse controversy. That he believed in programmatic interpretation seems likely, but he was either too insecure, or had insufficient imagination, to apply it to the symphony as a whole. He thus stands somewhere between Kanne, who largely rejects such interpretation, to the point of ignoring the text of the finale, and Fröhlich, whose clear vision of the entire symphony is ultimately limited only by his reluctance to be too specific about Beethoven's symphonic forms.

None of these writers, of course, saw Marx's inner necessity for transcendence in the choral finale, which was observed in the previous chapter. Fröhlich comes closest, since he sees the entire symphony as springing from a spiritual progress through suffering to joy. While his manner of associating ideas with specific passages in the music seems, however, to go hand in hand with the Marx of *Ueber Tonmalerei*, written at about the same time, and to adumbrate the style of the much later biography, it is clear that Fröhlich had none of Marx's Hegelian obsession with progress, and would not sanction a view of the symphony in which the first movement and the finale sprang from essentially different worlds.

The first interpreters of the Ninth Symphony, then, seem to have very little in common. Nevertheless, they all endorse the quality of abstraction which Lang believes to be essential to German idealist musical thought, and they all accept Kanne's view of tone-painting, according to which instrumental music suggests visual and poetic images. Paradoxically, therefore, they all combine abstract and programmatic interpretations within the fabric of their individual reviews, without apparently giving much thought to the interpretive problem which this creates. They all liked the symphony, they all took the use of a chorus in the finale more or less for granted, they all endorsed the unprecedented contrasts which Beethoven introduced, and, perhaps most important, none of them, Marx excepted, made any interpretive distinction between the finale and the rest of the symphony. It is as though they all felt that the contrast in genre between instrumental and choral music – between abstraction on the one hand and the unambiguous meaning of the text on the other – simply did not exist. This attitude is symbolized by their uniform failure to see any special significance in the symbolic meeting place of instrumental and vocal music: the bass recitatives in the finale.

Of course, part of their confusion was probably due to the relative currency of C. P. E. Bach's theories of instrumental music. Many of Bach's fantasies for clavichord contain passages of instrumental recitative, so that this idea in itself was hardly a novelty to Beethoven's first critics. William Weber has found, through careful studies of concert programs from the early nineteenth century, that instrumental music made up a much smaller proportion of the repertory during this time than has widely been supposed, and that vocal and instrumental works were often performed together.[31] The choral finale of the Ninth Symphony could hardly have been as much of a novelty as its unique form suggests. Perhaps the first critics of this symphony were simply not used to making the strong distinction between music with and without a text that has since become commonplace.

In any case, there was substantial common ground among their disparate interpretations, which, given the writers' lack of sympathy for each others' views, must stem from premises shared by all progressive German critics, of whatever persuasion, in the early- to mid-nineteenth century: a period which extends from the hypothetical first writings of Kanne to the final ones of Marx. What those premises were is by no means obvious. These reviews, however, were written at a time when technical analysis, developed extensively in the eighteenth century by Heinrich Christoph Koch and others at the level of the individual phrase or period, was being extended to include the more all-encompassing concepts that later became nineteenth-century 'textbook' form. At the same time, the validity of the Matthesonian *Affektenlehre*, some version of which held a kind of universal sway during the eighteenth century, was being challenged by the much-quoted 'absolutists', Tieck, Wackenroder and Schopenhauer among them, who saw music, especially instrumental music, as the key to experiences deeper and more inaccessible than those of everyday life. The impulse generated by their views, however, was once again paradoxical. Far from being exclusively abstract and analytical, this impulse was strongly interpretive, as virtually every one of the writers cited in this section makes clear in a highly individual fashion. Freed from the limits of the old affections, music could explore uncharted territory which challenged the resources and the vocabulary of its foremost exponents. As we have seen, even the fundamentally conservative Rochlitz acknowledged a special psychological depth in musical emotion which the other arts could not achieve, and which defied precise description.

The new emphasis on poetry and music as sister arts, with its idealistic overtones, not only reconciled this viewpoint with the older notion of correspondences between the arts, but made it plain as well that, even if in the new aesthetics music could be interpreted through means more subtle than any previously employed, these could paradoxically still be expressed in words. Most literate German musicians at the time read the *AMZ*, and thus could not help being familiar with the basic outlines of this theory. Certainly the writers cited above were conversant with it. What they seem to have in common is an unspoken belief that abstract and specific interpretations are not incompatible: that, indeed, it is possible to relate this unprecedented range of musical meaning and expression to the technical features of the music revealed by analysis. How this was to be accomplished is by no means obvious, and ultimately only Hoffmann and Marx were able, as will be seen in Chapter 5, to reconcile technical analysis with extra-musical interpretation in a manner which was fully convincing. Nevertheless, the resemblances noted above can only be explained on the assumption that this is what, with their unique, poetically inspired interpretations, Kanne, Fröhlich and Seyfried were trying to do. It was at least partly their belief in the feasibility of such a synthesis that led them to undervalue the expressive significance of vocal music, with its seemingly more flexible emotional range, when compared to the first three movements of the Ninth Symphony. Beethoven's instrumental music might, as Wendt had suggested, seem vague and amorphous when compared to the crystalline

91

clarity of emotion in *Fidelio*, but for those with greater vision, this music could be understood psychologically as precisely as any poem, and in that strength lay the more sophisticated formal integrity which Wendt would deny it. For these writers, then, the finale of the Ninth Symphony was merely an affirmation of this extra dimension, in a movement which, they rarely fail to acknowledge, is instrumentally conceived.

The other late music

We have seen that Beethoven was not neglected by the press during the last years of his life, despite his treatment in the *AMZ*. Compared to the Ninth Symphony and the *Missa Solemnis* (which will be discussed shortly), however, the other late music received relatively short shrift. The 'Hammer-klavier' Sonata, which Beethoven himself considered the high point of his work in this genre, was never reviewed in any of the journals we have discussed, nor were the 'Diabelli' Variations or the Quartet, Op. 130. Opp. 131 and 132 were dealt with only in articles defending the late music in general, and never reviewed in their own right. All the other major late chamber and piano works, except for Opp. 109, 110 and 127, each of which received at least two reviews, were reviewed, somewhere, exactly once.

The works which were ignored have one obvious point in common. They all contain, in their original versions, at least, long, difficult fugal finales. It is known that the *Grosse Fuge* from the quartet was completely misunderstood, and it can only be conjectured that the other fugues fared similarly. These works, then, were ones which contemporary critics, even the most sympathetic ones, preferred to avoid. It has already been seen that the anonymous critic in the *BAMZ*, despite his generally sympathetic outlook toward Op. 102, did not like the fugue in the second sonata, although he found that in Op. 110 much more acceptable. Seyfried, too, as will be seen, fell afoul of the fugues in the *Missa Solemnis*. Since he and the other critics just discussed raise no objection to the use of fugal techniques over shorter spans in the Ninth Symphony, it seems likely that what offended the first hearers of the other late fugues was not their nature but their extraordinary length. Nobody before or since Beethoven has ever written a fugue lasting 20 minutes, and his first hearers can certainly be forgiven if they found these works to be mere intellectual exercises, and highly dissonant ones at that, unfit for serious attention. This is the most that will ever be known of the initial reaction to some of the most unusual works in the history of music.

Reviews of the other late chamber music appear both in the *WAMZ* and in *Caecilia*. With the founding of the former journal in 1817, Beethoven gained a significant forum in the periodical press, and although its format changed four years later, when Kanne became editor, concentrating on concerts and theoretical articles rather than on reviews of publications, Kanne's article on the Ninth Symphony cited above hints at the acclaim that the other late works might have received had the *WAMZ* survived past 1824. As it was, the Viennese journal reviewed mainly middle-period and transitional works. The Seventh and Eighth Symphonies are both praised extravagantly, in the first (pp. 25, 37) and second (p. 17) volumes respectively, but with no more insight than was shown in the *AMZ* at about the same time. Three reviews of later music, however, are of somewhat greater interest. The 'Archduke' Trio, Op. 97, is reviewed in the first volume, and the critic is less ploddingly methodical in his analysis, but also more prone to make generalizations about the individual movements (*WAMZ* I, pp. 125, 139). Of the first, for example, he writes that the modulation to the submediant is characteristic of the composer: a point which even Marx seems to have missed in discussing similar works. Likewise, the scherzo and trio are described as contrapuntal masterpieces, with the modulations in the trio producing a particularly striking effect. Once again, Beethoven's use of counterpoint *per se* does not seem to have aroused opposition. This is not a profound review, but at least it avoids the pitfall common to many critics at the time: unimaginative, quasi-analytical description of the music which goes into great detail and says little or nothing of value.

Even in the *WAMZ*, one reads, in an otherwise favorable review of the Piano Sonata, Op. 90, that 'high originality, which sometimes borders on the peculiar, characterizes all the works of this composer' (*WAMZ* III, p. 483). This was written somewhat after the height of Beethoven's popularity, but before the enigma of the late music partially revived his reputation as an eccentric composer of highly original but irregular works. Evidently, that impression never completely died away, even in Vienna.

A review of the Violin Sonata, Op. 96, in volume III (p. 633) is more fanciful, suggesting the picturesque ideal of Kanne and Marx. The slow movement, for example, 'might be called an eclogue; so tenderly as the Arcadian shepherd complains to the trees, the bushes, the spring and the flowers of his love-sorrows, just so does he breathe his feelings in tones, and Chloe cannot remain insensitive'.

Apart from Kanne's review of the Ninth Symphony, however, these are the best of a not very distinguished group, and they are hardly worthy of the same attention as the longer reviews in *Caecilia*. Unfortunately, the Mainz journal, too, was capable of dealing superficially with the late chamber music. The review of Op. 127 in volume V (p. 145), cited by Gottfried Weber in response to Woldemar as an example of his ostensible opposition to late Beethoven, turns out to be a defense of the quartet. It is based on the same premise taken by Rochlitz a few years later: that it needs to be heard repeatedly in order to be understood. Weber's own review of this work, printed in the same volume (p. 239), is perhaps deliberately ambiguous. Beethoven's latest music, he says, goes far beyond the boundaries set by his earlier works, and while this may not be an example of genuine progress – while, indeed, one may prefer the earlier works – the later ones are nevertheless interesting to study: an opinion to which Woldemar would have taken strong exception. Weber leaves the reader to draw his own conclusions by studying the score, explicitly rejecting both the analytical and the interpretive approach to reviewing; he, at least, does not suggest that they are compatible. Weber, then, found the late music of Beethoven intriguing, its means entirely unprecedented, and was willing to leave it to others to come to terms with the music more precisely.

The reactions to the chamber music, then, are not only shorter, but less positive than those to the Ninth Symphony. Even here, however, the range of opinion does not include any negative reviews whatsoever, and the spectrum is completed by an adulatory one (*Caec.* IX, p. 45). Written by a von Weiler, this is not a formal review; it could hardly have been intended otherwise than as a reply to Woldemar, whose letter had appeared earlier the same year. It contains a by now familiar argument: that the late quartets need to be heard many times, and performed many times by the same players, in order to be satisfactorily understood. It also offers an interesting hint at the author's personal interpretation of Beethoven's late music. He points out that certain earlier works of Beethoven had been criticized for embodying clear ideas rather than stereotyped emotions: the 'Pastoral' Symphony and the *La Malinconia* movement from Op. 18, no. 6 are given as examples. The author implies that in the late music Beethoven had continued the theme represented by these works, and given specific titles to many individual movements. The 'Heilige Dankgesang' in Op. 132 is cited as the most successful of these, while the meaning of the finale of Op. 135 is less clear to Weiler. It may be supposed, however, that he believed even the movements without superscriptions to convey ideas: he refers to Beethoven as a 'Dichter', and suggests that any performance of these quartets must grasp the central idea in order to be successful. He also defends the late music by virtue of its originality: the fact that it avoids imitation of others' or even Beethoven's earlier works. At the center of his interpretation, though, lies the notion that each movement must convey an idea *clearly* in order to be grasped.

Weiler, then, resembles the writers on the Ninth Symphony discussed above, in a way that Weber did not. He was a true Romantic, and he once again reveals that among progressive writers it was not considered inappropriate for a piece to convey a specific idea, or even an entire extra-musical program. Some, like Hoffmann and Schopenhauer, may have praised the ambiguity of instrumental music, but the majority of the critics among their contemporaries — writers who were clearly no less Romantic or idealistic — preferred a manner of interpretation which we would now call programmatic, and which emphasized the links between music and the other arts. Literary metaphors abound in the reviews which have been discussed, and indeed this style of interpretation appears to have originated in Germany in the period now under discussion.

Far from being, as Lang implies, a kind of French malapropism, surviving with little alteration from the days of Grétry, it was absolutely central to German musical thought throughout the 1820s and beyond. This is not as surprising as it first appears if it is seen in the context of the intellectual premises repeatedly demonstrated in this chapter: the effortless juxtaposition of the ideal and the worldly, the fanciful and the analytical, the musical tone and the written word. These are, I believe, the parameters of German musical thought at this time, and it is surely significant that they are no less evident in the shorter, less philosophical reviews just discussed than in the longer ones. Only a truly unconscious assumption could be so universally accepted.

The final part of Seyfried's long review, dealing with Op. 131, is the least satisfactory. Although no enemy to the work, he did not like it as well as the other two, and reduced his treatment of it to the point of insignificance. In all, then, the reviews of Beethoven's late chamber music in *Caecilia* have very little new or original to say, and their value is limited to their support of the interpretive tendency discussed above. Nowhere do they even approach the significance of the reviews of the Ninth Symphony. Fortunately, with the *Missa Solemnis*, the same critics found another work which they considered worthy of their attention.

Fröhlich's review of the *Missa Solemnis*, which this time was the second of the two printed in *Caecilia*, tells us more about the author's philosophical position than any of the other tributes to late Beethoven which appeared there, and consequently it provides valuable evidence in support of the conclusions just discussed. What in the Ninth Symphony review was only implied here becomes explicit; Fröhlich seizes upon the occasion of the sacred text to develop a theory of Romantic art with far-reaching consequences. Like Chateaubriand and Schlegel, he saw in the mysteries of Christianity the essence of Romanticism. He also quotes Jean Paul, who in turn echoes Schelling's Platonism: 'If the Greeks called the fine arts a kind of music, so is romanticism a music of the spheres.'

95

When he writes, however, of a world-soul inhabiting the entire universe; of a relationship between the material and the ideal, at which earlier mythologies had hinted, but which reaches its highest perfection in Christianity, offering redemption to saint and sinner alike, he shows himself to be an idiosyncratic Hegelian. In the review of the Ninth Symphony, this attitude may have led him to disregard the differences in genre between instrumental and vocal music. In this review, Fröhlich explains the nature of that disregard. Older composers, he says, had used instrumental ritornellos in vocal works to prepare the entry of the voices, and from then on the instruments were used only to accompany while the voices dominated. Beethoven had abolished that distinction, and for that reason Fröhlich is able to speak of the *Missa Solemnis* in terms which show his own aesthetic ideal even more clearly than had his interpretation of the Ninth Symphony:

[Beethoven] allows both choirs − that of the voices as well as that of the instruments − when it is feasible, to step forth independently, ending through his genius the belief, consecrated through a hundred years of practice, that instrumentation must be subordinated to song. Every work of the great Creator is the prize of his hands; everything created joins in with the holy rejoicing; why should not this be intoned by the individual instruments, as well as by the chorus, independently of words? ... Here [at the beginning of the 'Gratias' in the Gloria] the instruments do not merely form the transition to the following expressions of pious thanks ... these feelings are so accurately developed by the instruments before the entry of the voices, that the hearer finds in the spoken word only a strengthening of the excitement and outlook which have been formed in his soul.

What Fröhlich seems to be saying here, whether he recognized it or not, is that vocal music had become superfluous, because the instruments can express the same sentiment just as clearly and just as specifically as any text. His metaphor comparing the orchestral instruments to the inferior orders of creation, which also appears in the discussion of the Ninth Symphony, should not be taken to mean that only the voices can simulate human thought, for in fact Fröhlich implies the exact opposite. In his Romanticism, every creature, no matter how lowly, is equally imbued with the spirit of the Creator, and for Fröhlich the instruments themselves seem to have a life of their own which justifies this evocation of divinity. The voices, by contrast, are present only by virtue of their liturgical function, which Fröhlich has already suggested is secondary in this Mass, too large to be performed in any church service and hence comprehensible only as a grand sacred oratorio.

Once again, then, we see that an absolute musical idealism, supported by the broadest possible philosophical pedigree, and fervently endorsing the capabilities of instrumental music, need not imply any difference between the nature of the interpretation required by music and that employed for the other arts, especially poetry. For Fröhlich and others of his generation, vocal music was really analogous to poetry, since both differ from instrumental music only by their use of the word. Music, however, suffers nothing by comparison to poetry, but it is closer to the source of the ideas themselves. This was the real paradox; for the Germans, the apparent confusion between abstract and specific interpretations which has already been observed was simply another way of expressing their faith that the unique qualities of music could be brought down to earth, while at the same time losing none of their uniqueness.

Even more perhaps than his approach to the Ninth Symphony, Fröhlich's treatment of the *Missa Solemnis* shows his awareness of the notion that in developing the abstract forms of composition, Beethoven was also clarifying the expressive potential of music.

At the 'Domine deus', the first thought, with its lively impetus, returns, and here too may be found a peculiarity in the handling of the Gloria. This is that just as a principal feeling dominates all the individual pieces, to which all the emotions developed in the neighboring sections limit themselves as subsidiary parts, so there is also a principal theme, which continually returns, and which is thus the focal point of the whole.

It is interesting to see how easily Fröhlich makes the connection between 'principal feeling' in the subsidiary sections − a concept which, as has been seen, links the voices and instruments together − and 'principal theme' in the movement as a whole. He seems to feel, furthermore, that in the 'Domine fili', which, he points out, is related to the opening idea of the movement, Beethoven has transformed the emotional character of the theme, making it into a subsidiary section of the 'Domine deus', which in turn is unified by the return of the opening mood, and theme, at m. 210. Fröhlich, in other words, sees in mm. 174−279 of the Gloria a monothematic ABA form whose very articulation in part depends on the listener's sensitivity to the emotional character of the theme in its different appearances. That sensitivity, in turn, depends upon awareness of the close thematic connection between mm. 192ff. and the opening of the movement. Since the key to this connection may be found in the presentation of the theme at this point by the wind instruments, which, unlike the following vocal section, contains the exact melodic outline of the opening, contracted into the interval of a diminished fifth, it may be assumed that Fröhlich is once again imbuing abstract form with specific emotional connotations, rather than taking his cue from the text.

Fröhlich's analysis of the fugue with which the Gloria concludes shows how precisely he can underlay even this most 'instrumental' of forms with an emotional theme, albeit a simple one of generalized rejoicing. The opening of the fugue is described only technically, but with the introduction of the subsidiary 'Amen' theme at m. 459, Fröhlich speaks of the combination as producing a feeling of wonder – whether at the divine mysteries or at the technical devices employed by Beethoven is not clear – culminating in the unison which begins at m. 488. The solo voices at m. 500 are answered by the chorus 'with deeply felt emotion', while it is left to the wind instruments to express through their imitations the feeling of joy. The rejoicing then builds toward the final Presto, which not only pours forth the height of praise, but, Fröhlich implies, rounds out the form of the movement with the return of the opening theme and text. The fortissimo beginning at m. 546 expresses the greatest enchantment. The held tones show emotion surging forth, and the short rhythmic figures and striking modulations add to the total effect.

Fröhlich thus shows here explicitly what he had only hinted at in his review of the Ninth Symphony; he believed that the most complex fugue could express the meaning of a text just as precisely as a less complicated and emotionally more straightforward setting. Despite the simplicity of the emotions expressed, what he wrote was not just a generalized evocation of them, but a formal description of the fugue itself, encompassing not only the obvious large-scale divisions but technical devices – pedal points, close imitations, dynamic contrasts, modulations – as well. Any of these could, for Fröhlich, have interpretive overtones, which depend at least as much on their position within the overall structure – a gradual crescendo of rejoicing – as on their association with specific words. So little significance is given to the latter that Fröhlich could have been describing an instrumental work: in terms, however, both poetic and analytical in their intent.

Having illustrated Beethoven's technique in the Gloria in such detail, Fröhlich is deliberately less specific about the rest of the Mass. It is always clear, however, that he felt this to be both a difficult and an unusually rewarding work: one that enters more deeply than most Church music into the sacred mysteries. Clearly, then, even apart from its religious purpose, Fröhlich found the Mass to be the ideal text for Romantic composition, and for Beethoven in particular. The words, despite their often dogmatic nature, offered for the most part only the most generalized hint at their ideal expression, and it was this that Beethoven was able to achieve through music as no-one had ever done before. That that music was essentially abstract often goes without saying, though Fröhlich states that at one point it may even seem to contradict the text. It is clear that he felt an uncommon sort of text – music relationship to be operative in the *Missa Solemnis*, and that its essential quality was paradoxical: it avoided the obvious suggestions of the text, but at the same time made its deeper secrets breathtakingly clear. In this respect it is interesting that Fröhlich does not mention the martial note introduced by Beethoven into the 'Dona nobis pacem', preferring to see the entire 'Agnus dei' as a struggle between cries for mercy and deep spiritual contentment, with the latter eventually gaining ascendancy. Clearly, then, he saw the Mass as a drama enacted on an essentially musical level, rather than on the obvious one of traditional text-painting. Weber had taken such tone-painting seriously, but Kanne, and Fröhlich too, all but ignored it in favor of the new ideal of a purely musical drama filled with concrete meaning.

The significance of this distinction is perhaps obscured by the latter writers' retention of the term 'Tonmalerei', but as has been seen, for the Romantics this term had a new set of connotations which conservative theorists like Weber never imagined. It allowed music to be treated as an autonomous art, but at the same time demanded that it be grasped not only by Romantic yearning but by the intellect as well. This somewhat extravagant claim may be meaningless to any generation not reared in the shadow of Kant's epistemology, but it is precisely such a role in bridging otherwise incompatible experiences that Kant assigned to the faculty of imagination, and he believed that all art realized a synthesis, anticipating that suggested by these critics. The latter, in qualifying but not contradicting the claims made by Romantic aestheticians concerning the spiritual nature of music, can truly be placed in the mainstream of post-Kantian thought, along with Schelling, Fichte and an entire generation of 'synthetic' idealists. They simply claimed for Beethoven's music what these writers had claimed for human thought in general: that it could unify seemingly contradictory points of view.

Neither Grossheim nor Seyfried possessed the degree of analytical sophistication shown by Fröhlich in his treatment of the Gloria, and Seyfried, furthermore, apparently did not share Fröhlich's unqualified admiration of the *Missa Solemnis*. Thus their descriptions are fairly routine, never attempting to explain the uniqueness of Beethoven's accomplishment. Both of these writers, however, mention the military nature of the 'Dona nobis pacem', which Fröhlich had chosen to ignore. For Grossheim the use of an 'ängstlich Paukenton' required no special comment, nor did the introduction of recitative, which, in this entirely vocal movement, seems to have occasioned no more or less surprise than the use of instrumental recitatives in the Ninth Symphony. Seyfried, however, was appalled by this passage.

What these strange trumpet-fanfares, the mixing in of recitative, the fugued instrumental section, which only destroys the flow of ideas ... what the hollow,
unrhythmical, bizarre timpani strokes are intended to mean, only dear Heaven
knows. No-one felt compelled to question the master about this: he never clarified
himself precisely on this point, and thus took the secret with him into the grave.

Seyfried also admits that he liked the Gloria and Credo less than the rest
of the Mass, and seems to have had particular difficulty understanding the
long fugues in these movements.

The *Missa Solemnis*, then, presented greater obstacles to at least one
critic's understanding than did the Ninth Symphony. Perhaps Seyfried,
despite his praise of Beethoven's setting of the *Ode to Joy*, was not as well
prepared as Fröhlich to acknowledge that abstract, 'instrumental' forms
could convey the essence of a text. It seems more likely, however, as has
already been suggested, that he simply found these fugues too abstract –
overly long and not sufficiently interesting musically. In any case, the
aesthetic issues involved in Beethoven's treatment of the religious texts seem
not to have crossed his mind, except to arouse his more conservative
instincts against the composer's attempt to introduce the sounds of war
directly into his plea for peace. In this respect, his objections are similar
to those of Weber toward *Wellington's Victory*. It could be, however, that
he found this example of old-fashioned text-painting to be unworthy of
Beethoven's high purpose in this setting of the Mass. As Seyfried says of
the music, we will never know for sure.

Epilogue: the strange case of C.M. von Weber

It has been seen that the nature of German music criticism during this period
has given rise to substantial misunderstanding. Before leaving Germany
for France, it is necessary to pause momentarily to examine yet another
misconception with far-reaching implications. Many modern writers have
taken it for granted that Carl Maria von Weber was Beethoven's harshest
critic in the press, bar none. To the best of my knowledge, however, apart
from a partial examination of the evidence by John Warrack in his
biography of Weber, there has never been an attempt in English to evaluate
fully the veracity of this legend. Its very sources are correspondingly unclear.
Of all the reviews printed in Weber's collected writings, there is not a single
one which treats Beethoven with anything but respect and admiration.[32]
There are, in other words, no documented reviews by Weber criticizing
Beethoven. How, then, did the tradition arise?

It appears to have three sources. The first is Weber's unfinished novel
Tonkünstlers Leben (1809), in which the instruments of an imaginary

100

orchestra are overheard discussing some recent compositions, among them the 'Eroica' Symphony. The instruments are appalled by the work, and a viola begs that they be given instead an Italian opera, which will at least allow them a chance to sleep now and again. It is not clear whether Beethoven or Italian opera is being satirized here. Discussion then turns to a new symphony recently arrived from Vienna.

First, we have a slow tempo, full of brief, disjointed ideas, none of them having any connection with each other, three or four notes every quarter of an hour! – that's exciting! – then a hollow drum-roll and mysterious viola passages, all decked out with the right amount of silences and general pauses; eventually, when the listener has given up hope of surviving the tension as far as the Allegro, there comes a furious tempo in which the chief aim is to prevent any principal idea from appearing, and the listener has to try and find one on his own; there's no lack of modulations; that doesn't matter, all that matters, as in Paer's *Leonore*, is to make a chromatic run and stop on any note you like, and there's your modulation. Above all one must shun rules, for they only fetter genius.[33]

It has apparently been taken for granted by virtually everyone that this passage refers to Beethoven's Fourth Symphony, for no better reason than the fact that it follows the discussion of the 'Eroica' cited above. As Warrack has pointed out, however, the description does not fit.

There are no silences longer than a quaver until just before the Allegro, no general pauses at all, nor are there any 'hollow drum rolls' ('dumpfer Paukenwirbel') or 'mysterious viola passages' ('mysteriöse Bratschensätze') ... It seems likely that, since Weber deliberately avoided mention of any particular work here but did not hesitate to name the Eroica previously, he was attacking a generalized target.[34]

Tradition aside, then, *Tonkünstlers Leben* provides little evidence of any enmity toward Beethoven. More serious is a letter written by the 23-year-old Weber to the publisher Nägeli on May 21, 1810. 'You seem to see me from my quartet and Caprice as an imitator of Beethoven,' Weber wrote,

and flattered as many might be by this, I don't find it in the least pleasant. Firstly, I hate everything bearing the mark of imitation; secondly, my views differ too much from Beethoven's for me to feel I could ever agree with him. The passionate, almost incredible inventive powers inspiring him are accompanied by such a chaotic arrangement of ideas that only his earlier compositions appeal to me; the later ones seem to me hopeless chaos, out of which break a few heavenly flashes of genius proving how great he could be if he could tame his rich fantasy. Though of course I cannot enjoy the gift of Beethoven's great genius, I do at least believe I can defend my own music from a logical and technical point of view, and produce in every piece a definite effect.[35]

Clearly, this letter does not show contempt for Beethoven; it evinces a healthy respect for a very different creative personality, which Weber admits he is unable to understand. Much in line with the thought of his time, Weber sees Beethoven's music as disunified and fantastic. The admittedly harsh impression given by the phrase 'hopeless chaos' is tempered by the references to Beethoven's 'heavenly' genius; the young Weber evidently saw the older composer as combining the best and the worst extremes of the musical cosmos, producing 'incomparable novelty'.

These sources, both from the earliest years of Weber's career, are certainly authentic, but they are far from conclusive. Even if Weber did mistrust Beethoven in 1810, there is no reason why he should, much later, have launched into a series of 'bitter reviews' that marked him forever as the composer's mortal enemy, as Anton Schindler has claimed. Such allegations stem from Schindler alone, and, without exception, they are all obscure and undocumented. Schindler's claim, first made in the original edition of the biography, published in 1840, is that Weber, after hearing Beethoven's Seventh Symphony, declared the composer 'ripe for the madhouse', and that he sent from Prague, where he was then living, the above-mentioned reviews. When Weber submitted his *Euryanthe* to Beethoven several years later, he is supposed to have received him cordially even though he knew Weber's opinions of his music. There is no quotation from any of these reviews, nor any indication of where they may be found.[36]

Nevertheless, the significance of Schindler's charge is clear. By the time of the Seventh Symphony, Weber was a mature musician, and such criticisms as he made at this time cannot be taken merely as youthful indiscretions. But how reliable is Schindler? A thorough examination of his charges against Weber appears in Georg Kaiser's 1910 dissertation *Beiträge zu einer Charakteristik Carl Maria von Webers als Musikschriftsteller.* Kaiser finds that, after the biography appeared, Schindler's allegations were promptly refuted in the *Blätter für Literarische Unterhaltung* and the *Neue Zeitschrift für Musik.*[37] 'Schindler's book,' wrote the *Neue Zeitschrift*, 'also contains a deficiency, which includes the most malicious untruth, and which one can see at once must stem from personal hatred.'[38] The *Blätter* also referred to a deficiency ('Ausfall') 'which is certainly rooted in misunderstanding'.[39] It is not clear if these denials are directed primarily at the charge against Weber's criticisms or at the claim that *Euryanthe* was submitted to Beethoven at all. In a later edition of the *Blätter*, however, Schindler backed off somewhat from the former charge, admitting that the information he had received might not withstand closer scrutiny, and that the reviews he had in mind might have been written by Baron von Lannoy.[40]

Nevertheless, in *Beethoven in Paris*, published two years later, he indicated that drafts for these criticisms had been found among Weber's papers. This claim also appears to be based on rumor rather than first-hand knowledge; the information is attributed to none other than F. A. Kanne,[41] who is personally supposed to have informed Beethoven of the reviews' existence shortly after Weber's death. Schindler does not appear, before making this claim, to have taken the trouble to consult the edition of Weber's *Hinterlassene Schriften* which appeared in 1828. Had he done so, he would have found no trace of the incriminating documents.[42] Kaiser, who perused Weber's personal papers in preparation for a new edition of his writings, did not find them either.[43] In the third edition of his biography, published in 1860, Schindler then attempted to substantiate his claim even further. Quoting from the *Tonkünstlers Leben*, he added that 'after the above specimen of blindness and malice one may not doubt the existence of a much harsher criticism, in which Weber, after hearing the A major symphony, declared our master ripe for the madhouse. This also appeared in print and sooner or later it too will probably be found.'[44] It never has been, and neither could Kaiser, after a painstaking study of the periodicals of Weber's time, which unearthed more than two dozen formerly unknown critiques, find a trace of any of Schindler's 'bitter reviews'.[45]

One further point needs to be considered here. If it is true, as Schindler claims, that Weber submitted the score of *Euryanthe* to Beethoven for revision after the unsuccessful premiere, he seems not to have considered the insuperable difficulty which this fact presents to his case. If the mature Weber were in the habit of maligning Beethoven in the press, what conceivable reason could he have had for committing a work of great personal significance to the older composer's guidance? In the face of this material and psychological evidence, Schindler's obstinacy appears to stem indeed from personal hatred. It is certainly not supported by the evidence as it existed in Schindler's own time.

Weber's case is important because it symbolizes the kind of misunderstanding that commonly arises where nineteenth-century Beethoven criticism is concerned. Few illusions can have had such a magical fascination as that of Beethoven's ungracious reception in the musical press. From Schindler's time until our own, the temptation has been to show that a genius of Beethoven's stature was either neglected or maligned, and that temptation becomes stronger when a figure of Weber's renown is involved. Even Weber's biographer John Warrack, after partially vindicating his subject from the charge of anti-Beethovenism, feels compelled to claim that 'most of [Weber's] colleagues had found the greatest difficulty in following Beethoven beyond the First Symphony, and the musical journals of his day are depressingly unanimous in their failure to understand what he was about'.[46] Such a blatant misrepresentation can stem only from a careful reading of Slonimsky or a highly selective reading of the primary sources. Like Schindler, many modern writers would clearly like to believe in a theory which is not supported by the bulk of the evidence. It has been shown in this chapter that that theory does not apply even to the reception of Beethoven's late works in Germany. The chamber and solo music may have been relatively neglected, but there is no reason to suppose that, apart from the long fugues, it was less well liked or understood. Even Woldemar seems to have directed his tirade primarily against the Ninth Symphony and the *Missa Solemnis*.

Contemporaneous Beethoven criticism, then, may well have been more often misunderstood than was the music itself. The same confusion is evident in our modern perception of the attitude in Germany toward absolute music and 'literary' interpretation. It has been seen that actual texts were considered of secondary importance in understanding music, but that even instrumental music was often considered analogous to poetry or painting in its effect, the only difference being that it was more potent than either. I will repeat, therefore, by way of conclusion, what has been the major theme of this chapter: that literary interpretation of music – the creation of explicit parallels between the 'sister arts' of music and poetry – originated during Beethoven's lifetime, and was a distinctly German contribution to nineteenth-century aesthetics, no less than was the glorification of 'absolute' music found in Schopenhauer and Hoffmann and underscored by Lang. That glorification did not, except in a few individual cases, imply any distinction between the character of instrumental and vocal music. On the contrary, it made the latter a mere continuation of the former, while at the same time confusing many of their essential qualities. It was partly for this reason that the writers discussed above found no paradox in the idea of an instrumental recitative. It was for this reason, too, that many with less imagination found great difficulty in understanding the Ninth Symphony. Since France has been claimed as the birthplace of program music, the fate of that symphony and other works of Beethoven there makes an extremely interesting comparison, and it is to that subject that I will now turn.

4

French Beethoven criticism

'The history of "Beethoven in France",' wrote Leo Schrade in 1942, 'is one of the strangest chapters in the records of the human mind.'[1] Schrade believed that veneration of Beethoven in later nineteenth- and early twentieth-century France had reached the status of a religion, and that the composer's work was in some way essential to the French national consciousness during that time. His case is based principally on the testimony of Berlioz, Rolland and other French Beethoven 'disciples', and is thus open to challenge on purely empirical grounds. In the review of Schrade's *Beethoven in France* cited earlier, Paul Henry Lang took advantage of exactly this weakness to deliver a withering critique of the book, which unfortunately marks the beginning and end of its *Rezeptionsgeschichte*.[2] Despite his dubious view of German musical aesthetics, Lang is generally convincing, but he begins by attacking Schrade in purely theoretical terms, and in this part of the review he is less persuasive than elsewhere. He claims that Beethoven's abstract symphonic music was inimical to the nature of French thought, and that that music could not even have been properly understood, let alone worshipped, in France. Here Lang falls victim to the same mistake of which he accuses Schrade; he depends too heavily on the example set by Berlioz – specifically that of his so-called 'program symphonies' – and does not pay enough attention to the reaction of earlier French critics of Beethoven, or for that matter to the evidence of Berlioz' own writings on the subject. As will be seen, these lead unanimously to a very different conclusion.

Lang's view of French musical taste, however, is still sanctioned by the same kind of popular legend which has enshrined an essentially false view of Beethoven's critical reception in Germany. It is true that the French had a tradition of operatic and vocal performance which was unparalleled in Germany, and may have made it difficult for them to come to terms with Beethoven's new symphonic style. It is worth considering, however, whether a more useful thesis than that advanced by Lang can be found to explain the differences between the reactions to Beethoven in the two countries, and indeed, whether those differences are as significant as has commonly been believed. In the following pages I will try to show that they are not, documenting this conclusion by looking in detail at the initial reception of Beethoven by major French critics, progressive and conservative alike. Much of the material of this chapter has already been dealt with by others. Ingeborg Grempler, in *Das Musikschrifttum von Hector Berlioz*,[3] discusses each of Berlioz' reviews of the Beethoven symphonies. More recently, Peter Anthony Bloom, in 'François-Joseph Fétis and the Revue Musicale',[4] has devoted a lengthy chapter to Beethoven's reception by Fétis and, incidentally, other leading critics. It will thus be unnecessary to describe each of these reviews in turn, as I have done in the previous chapters; instead, I will proceed by comparing French reaction to a few crucial works, in order to determine the criteria on which the evaluation and the analysis, if any, have been made.

Early performances

Beethoven's music was not generally known in France until after his death, and the writings discussed in this chapter thus stem for the most part from a later period than those previously examined – mostly from the mid- to late 1830s. There were, however, earlier Beethoven performances – and reviews – in the concert halls and newspapers of Paris. This period, too, is well documented, having been treated in several sources, including Schindler's *Beethoven in Paris*, Schrade's book, and Bloom's dissertation.[5] Bloom points out that critical reaction was quite similar to that of the *AMZ* correspondents who heard the same music performed in Germany. For example, the prominent woodwind writing in the First Symphony was consistently singled out, either for praise or blame.[6] Only the first few symphonies were heard, however; Schindler, though never a reliable observer, reports that when the 'Eroica' was first attempted by a Parisian orchestra, it was met only with laughter.[7]

By 1828, the average concert-goer in Paris probably knew Beethoven's later symphonies, and virtually all of his non-symphonic music, only by repute. Thus it was possible for *Le Globe*, in observing the composer's death, to call him 'the Kant of music', and to make a rather labored comparison between Beethoven's treatment of harmony and Kant's philosophical system (*Le Globe*, April 7, 1827). It is hard to believe that anyone who really knew the music would go to such lengths to praise it while at the same time remaining so clearly hostile. The writer does express a wish, however, to hear again a recently performed Beethoven symphony – probably the only one he had actually heard. The following year, his wish having been granted, he was more enthusiastic. Schrade describes him as 'utterly disgusted at the Germanism of Beethoven', taking this as typical of French opposition to the more impulsive side of the composer's nature. What he actually said was:

It would be difficult to find a musical composition grander, more picturesque, richer in new and learned developments, than this symphony. The third movement in particular is an admirable masterpiece. Its instrumentation is as indefinable as it is strewn with new effects: the rhythm, the melody, the harmony, everything is original, everything is cast into a pattern which could only belong to the metaphysical and mysterious genius of Beethoven. One does discover from time to time the faults of the German school, more *bizarrerie* than charm, more calculation than true inspiration, and a development too subtle, too analytical of the phrases, even the least singing ones, but one is overcome by the vigor and the interconnection of the thoughts, by contrasts as ingenious as they are unexpected, by the truly imposing grandeur of the masses of harmony.   *Le Globe*, May 14, 1828

It is hard to imagine anything further from Schrade's 'utter disgust'; clearly, in at least one case, early opinions on Beethoven in France, like those in Germany, have been misrepresented so as to appear more negative than they actually are. Beethoven certainly provoked adverse reactions in Paris, but it is doubtful whether those who knew his music were ever unreservedly hostile to it. Cambini's famous statement that 'he seems to harbor doves and crocodiles at the same time'[8] is probably characteristic of the conservative French reaction to Beethoven.

What, then, were the 'bizarreries' which prevented these early writers from fully accepting this music, and which they characteristically branded 'Germanisms'? The *Tablettes de Polymnie* spoke of 'the most barbaric dissonances' and a 'fracas of all the orchestral instruments';[9] the *Globe* reporter cites excessive calculation and analysis. Schrade feels that 'what seem to have shocked the French when they first encountered Beethoven's music were the abrupt changes and sudden transitions'.[10] Needless to say, these are exactly what had offended the first German critics in the *AMZ*. We need only recall that Op. 12 was denounced as 'a mass of learning without good method', while other works were criticized for their unusual chord progressions and lack of fluency (i.e. stylistic continuity). Beethoven was constantly advised to write in a more natural, less calculated manner. These were universal reactions, and they did not always imply absolute censure. In the article from *Le Globe* cited above, Beethoven's use of contrast is even cited approvingly.

There was thus nothing unique in the initial French reaction to Beethoven. Even the 'Germanisms' for which he was criticized – particularly the intellectual nature of his style – had found as many detractors in Germany as in France. It should be remembered that Haydn, the other great master of the Austro-German symphonic style, had long since been enthusiastically accepted in Paris, where hundreds of dubious symphonies were published under his name to assure their success. Beethoven's first two symphonies – probably the only ones to be publicly performed in Paris before his death – differ from Haydn's only in their slightly larger proportions, their more heavy-handed scoring, and a characteristically Beethovenian *panache* which the older composer would have found too blatant for his carefully honed style. Haydn also relished analytical development, sudden modulations, unexpected contrasts, and even some surprisingly harsh dissonances, and yet his symphonies were welcomed in Paris while Beethoven's, at first, were not. The unavoidable conclusion is that Beethoven was regarded, as he had been in Germany, as something of a usurper, playing havoc with the conventions of an established form. In neither country did this impression survive closer acquaintance with the composer's work, at least for the majority of the listening public.

The turnabout in French opinion may have come after the Second Symphony was performed at the *Concert spirituel* in 1821. According to Berlioz, the Allegretto of the Seventh Symphony was heard in place of the slow movement, and it was so successful that the entire symphony had to be repeated, after which the first movement and the scherzo, little appreciated before, also met with great applause. After this concert, Beethoven's admirers began to outnumber his detractors.[11] As a result of this enthusiasm, F. A. Habeneck founded the *Société des Concerts du Conservatoire*, which, beginning in 1828, presented to the public a musical repertory in which Beethoven occupied the central position. Schindler and others testify to the extraordinary quality of the *Société*'s concerts, and it is likely that, beginning with the fourth decade of the nineteenth century, Parisians were privileged to hear the best performances of Beethoven's symphonies available anywhere in Europe.

Paris after Habeneck

It was in this context, then, that the three most prominent French critics, Castile-Blaze, François-Joseph Fétis and Berlioz, wrote their reviews of Beethoven's symphonies, and the nature of the *Société* explains their almost exclusive concentration on the composer's orchestral works. Castile-Blaze, like Berlioz, wrote in the *feuilleton* section of the *Journal des débats*, signing his articles 'XXX'. Fétis wrote in his own journal, the *Revue musicale*, and Berlioz published reviews in various periodicals in addition to the *Débats*, reprinting them later in his book *A travers chants*.[12] Each critic, then was writing for a slightly different audience – Castile-Blaze for the artistically inclined intelligentsia of Paris, Fétis for an exclusively musical readership, and Berlioz, ultimately, for the public at large.

Castile-Blaze, as Schrade points out, tried to overcome some widespread prejudices, and he did so with a familiar vocabulary; 'bizarrerie', formerly a term of censure, became in his hands a positive attribute of the music.[13] Less partisan in his outlook, Fétis was probably closer to the French public; he liked and respected Beethoven but had serious reservations about certain aspects of his work, which he did not hesitate to express. Berlioz, however, was a Beethoven disciple, and approached the music with a reverence which far transcends even the most enthusiastic reviews of the other two. Berlioz represented the *Jeune France*, the generation of young Romantics who reacted to art with a supercharged intensity of feeling, and his writing, like most of his music, was a direct outgrowth of this primal experience. These three writers, then, probably provide a representative sampling of French musical opinion during the third and fourth decades of the nineteenth century. Together, they show that Beethoven was able to conquer progressive and conservative alike within a relatively brief time, apparently becoming a genuine phenomenon of French musical taste.

In fact, the appreciation of Beethoven in Germany and in France followed a similar course. The most significant difference was one of chronology. In Germany, conservative criticism was only gradually superseded by the Romantics, whereas in France conservative and progressive criticism were written at approximately the same time. Beethoven's works were also introduced in France in a rather arbitrary order, so that French critics (except for Berlioz, who seems to have acquainted himself with all of the symphonies, at least, at the first possible opportunity) were not always able to place a new work within the context of the composer's *oeuvre*. Despite this limitation, the French seem to have reacted to virtually all of the music in much the same way as their German counterparts. At first, as has been seen, they were alternately receptive and hostile toward something new and unfamiliar, sometimes in the same breath. Upon closer acquaintance, however, they came to accept and value the works of the early and middle periods, despite continuing reservations about certain aspects of the composer's style. Finally, the Ninth Symphony, for many years the sole example of the late music familiar to the French public, produced highly partisan reactions, both pro and con, following its first performance in 1831. Berlioz found it to be the most perfect expression of Beethoven's genius, and the prominent *Conservatoire* musician Chrétien Urhan wrote a lengthy, quasi-mystical appreciation in *Le Temps* (January 25, 1838). Fétis, however, although he liked the first three movements, condemned the choral finale. Berlioz reports that, leaving a performance of the Ninth Symphony with a small group of musicians, he found opinions evenly divided among himself and the others on the merits of the work. One newspaper, he says, found it the culmination of modern music, while another judged it a monstrosity.[14] As in Germany, the longest and most substantial reviews were favorable, but public opinion remained at least partly hostile for many years. Before considering the reasons for this lack of agreement, I will look more closely at French reaction to some of the middle-period works, and at the aesthetic ideas which lie behind them, since it is here that the critics are at their most characteristic.

In certain respects, Berlioz, as the representative of Romantic criticism in France, resembles both Hoffmann and Marx, who stand in a similar relation to their less flamboyant predecessors and contemporaries. Berlioz, however, is less systematic than either of these critics and, despite his enormous enthusiasm, less self-confident in his judgments. Unlike Hoffmann or Marx, Berlioz was a working critic, whose major source of income for many years was his writing. He was forced, in his own words, to attend an unending series of 'recitals by beginners of both sexes, revivals of antiquated operas, first performances of antiquated operas'[15] at a time when he was waging a largely unsuccessful struggle to have his own music performed in France.

The unresponsive Parisian public may have been the target of an amusing short story which Berlioz appended to the Beethoven criticism in *A travers chants*. Entitled 'Beethoven in the Ring of Saturn', it recounts a séance in which the composer's spirit is summoned from outer space and requested to compose a new sonata. Duly dictated, the work proves striking only by its banality. It hints, indeed, at a fourth period in Beethoven's career, honed to the dictates of interstellar taste, but which impresses its earthly hearers as flat and uninspired. The moral of this fable appears to be that 'operas performed and applauded daily ... would be hissed in Saturn, in Jupiter, in Mars, in Venus, in Neptune, in the big and little dippers, in the constellation of the chariot, and to the infinite universe are nothing but infinite platitudes'.[16] This sentence very clearly shows what Berlioz thought of the cult of Meyerbeerian grand opera which was then predominant in Paris. It also shows, however, that he did not believe in any absolute standards of musical aesthetics. Elsewhere, in his article on the 'Eroica' Symphony, he had also expressed doubt about the possibility of defining musical beauty in any way that would be comprehensible to all people; the opposing comments on the Ninth Symphony cited above were mustered in support of this view.

Berlioz, then, was a pragmatic critic. Having been forced to review

110

a good deal of music which he did not like, praising works, like Meyerbeer's
Les Huguenots, of which he obviously disapproved, he was less inclined
than his German counterparts to wax enthusiastic and metaphysical over
music of which he did approve, even when that music was by Beethoven.
This does not mean that his approach to music was fundamentally different
from theirs. The divergence was entirely one of method. The similarities,
and the differences, can best be illustrated by turning to one of his reviews
of a middle-period work. That of the Fifth Symphony will be considered
in detail in the next chapter, where it will be compared directly with Marx
and Hoffmann; that of the Seventh, however, is probably more characteristic, and can thus serve to represent the others, without the necessity of
discussing them individually.[17]

Berlioz begins this review with an ironic jibe at the popularity of the
symphony's second movement, the still famous Allegretto. The custom,
he says, is to consider those works the most beautiful which obtain the most
applause, even though there are beauties of infinite value which are not
of a nature to excite such enthusiasm. Assaults on popular taste were
common in Berlioz; he claims, for example, that apart from this comparatively serene Allegretto, the most popular Beethoven movements in France
were the finale of the Fifth Symphony and the storm of the 'Pastoral': two
of the loudest and least subtle symphonic works in the composer's *oeuvre*.
He also gently ridicules those listeners who had found the main theme of
the Seventh Symphony's first movement to be naive; had Beethoven titled
the movement, as in the 'Pastoral' Symphony, 'Ronde des paysans', this
criticism would never have occurred.

It seems likely, given the circumstances of Berlioz' career and the fate
of his music in France, that these witticisms cover a profound contempt
for popular taste such as he would never have dared to express directly in
a paid article written for the benefit of the public. They show, in any case,
that Berlioz the critic did not represent French musical taste any more than
Hoffmann can be said to represent the *AMZ*'s readership in 1810. One of
his goals in writing was, like Hoffmann, to educate his readers. Lang is
thus correct in challenging Schrade's use of Berlioz and Rolland as star
witnesses in his case for a French Beethoven cult.[18] At the same time,
however, Lang's antipathy to Berlioz the composer has led him to overlook
the implications of the critic's reiterated attitude toward musical programs.
'If this program offends you, repels you, or irritates you,' Berlioz had
written of the 'Pastoral' Symphony, 'discard it and listen to the symphony
as though it were music of no determined object.'[19] Once again, with
regard to the Seventh Symphony's non-programmatic first movement, he
makes it clear that the presence or absence of an extra-musical idea was

to him a matter of indifference, however much it might mean to the public at large. He believed fervently in the power of music to express ideas, but also that it could just as easily be understood without the aid of an idea supplied by either the composer or the critic.

Berlioz goes on to praise the orchestration of the opening, with the entrance of the solo oboe hidden by the attack of the full orchestra, and the rhythmic structure of the first movement: 'never has a rhythmic ostinato been employed with such success'. Then, as was his usual practice, he singles out two passages which strike him as particularly unusual and discusses them in detail. One of these is the harmonic progression in mm. 155–6, in which a 6/5 chord based on A is resolved to an F major triad in first inversion. Berlioz points out that this could have been resolved instead by moving the F-sharp upward to G or by moving the E downward to D, but that Beethoven chose this unusual resolution, emphasizing it by the abrupt shift from fortissimo to pianissimo. The other example which Berlioz cites is that beginning at m. 401: an 11-fold bass repetition of a two-measure motive based on D, C-sharp and B-sharp, this is the passage which was supposed to have provoked Weber's comment that Beethoven was 'ripe for the madhouse'. Berlioz correctly analyzes the harmonic secret of the music – the fact that the winds, brass and timpani play throughout an E pedal which can belong to either tonic or dominant triads, while the upper strings play the components of the tonic triad only when the appropriate note, C-sharp, appears in the bass. The effect, he says, is totally new, and has never been successfully imitated.

Berlioz' most common procedure, then, is not to describe the entire movement, as Marx or Hoffmann would do, but to comment instead on particular moments or passages which seem to him worthy of extraordinary praise. In so doing, he rejects both formal analysis and the necessity of characterizing the movement as a whole, but he is able to evoke considerable detail when it seems important to him to do so. His approach is thus both more and less sophisticated than that of his German counterparts: more so in that it calls for precise and sympathetic understanding of some of Beethoven's most noteworthy innovations; less so in that it does not attempt the same degree of psychological penetration.

This is not to say that, in discussing a non-programmatic work like the Seventh Symphony, Berlioz dispensed with psychological interpretation altogether. He simply failed to apply it systematically. To describe music entirely in technical terms would have been as difficult for him as it is second nature for an analyst today. Thus, although he once again sees rhythmic structure, this time depending on the combination of a dactyl and a spondee, as the most outstanding feature of the second movement, his technical descriptions of that movement are laden with emotional terms and phrases: the pianissimo repetition beginning at m. 19 is full of melancholy and mystery; the countersubject which enters in the violas and cellos at m. 27 is a lamentation; the conflicting rhythms which begin at m. 75 are cries, sobs, and supplications; the end of the entire movement is a profound sigh upon an indecisive harmony, and the rest is silence.

The concluding harmony, Berlioz goes on to point out, is a 6/4 chord; its use here is certainly one of the most unusual features of the movement. More to the point, however, is the fact that in this case technical and emotional descriptions do not simply reinforce one another; they actually coincide. The sigh is the meaning of the unusual harmony, just as the harmony explains the passage's effect. The two go together; each is worth mentioning only because it is explicable in different terms – the sigh as a chord, the chord as a sigh. For Berlioz, then, just as specifically as for the German writers discussed in the previous chapters, analysis and emotional interpretation go together, and are in practice inseparable. What makes Berlioz different from those writers is that he does not concentrate on emotional interpretation; he simply takes it for granted. For him, more perhaps than for the metaphysical Germans, the first priority was always the technical side of musical analysis.

Just how sophisticated Berlioz' approach to that music was next to that of his French contemporaries can best be seen by comparing it with Fétis' view of the Seventh Symphony.[20] Like the French public as a whole, Fétis found the second movement to be the highlight of the symphony; 'this piece is one of the small number which it suffices to name in order to praise it'. He also liked the scherzo, but, as Bloom has pointed out, the first and last movements seemed to him strange, overwrought, and even diseased.[21] After the first performance of the symphony, he was apparently assured by his friends that he would like it better upon repeated hearings, but Fétis was a stubborn man, and he later reiterated his first opinion.[22] He was particularly disturbed by the rhythmic ostinato of the first movement; the same feature that Berlioz had singled out for particular praise. Fétis' more general objections to the symphony centered on two points, both of which have been observed by Bloom. The first is the composer's deafness, which Fétis believed to have already encroached upon his judgment at the time the symphony was written. Like his German contemporaries, Fétis apparently believed that Beethoven suffered in later years from a loss of tonal memory which adversely affected his musical judgment, so that 'to compose was now no more than to dream'.[23]

In describing this music, Fétis reverts to the vocabulary of the first French Beethoven critics – the first movement is 'more bizarre than

113

original' – and like them he was both attracted and repelled. His view of the Seventh Symphony as somehow indicating a loss of Beethoven's creative faculties is, however, both inaccurate (Beethoven was not yet completely deaf at the time of composition, and certainly had not had time to lose his aural memory as Fétis suggests) and typical of his chronic inability to accept anything which violated his pre-established concepts of musical aesthetics. He is constantly attacking harmonies which strike him as unacceptable *a priori*, and he was even accused by Berlioz of trying to revise Beethoven's harmonic 'mistakes' in his edition of the symphonies.[24] He thus resembles, in his attitudes toward Beethoven, some of the early *AMZ* critics, who, while admiring the composer, were utterly inflexible in their condemnation of his stylistic 'errors'. This aspect of Fétis' view of the Seventh Symphony, then, resembles a stage in German criticism which had already been largely superseded 25 years before.

Fétis' second objection to the Seventh Symphony is based on a more advanced, or, as Lang would have it, more characteristically French view of the music. At some unspecified point in his life, Fétis claims, Beethoven had become interested in poetry, particularly the *Iliad*, and this had led to a change in his musical thinking. No longer abstract, it became based upon an essential idea ('idée principale') that was at the root of his approach to his work. Since this secret was not always revealed it was not always possible to appreciate his music fully; 'what might have appeared sublime if the work were known, seems, in one's ignorance, only bizarre or unnatural'.[25] This is not simply a French form of the old doctrine of the affections, since according to eighteenth-century theorists those affections were limited and immediately recognizable. Instead, it appears to be precisely what Lang had in mind when he wrote that 'French genius insisted ... on *meaning*, i.e. literary associations, in its music'.[26] Fétis, Lang would say, was unable to accept abstract instrumental music without some sort of programmatic allusion to back it up, because he instinctively thought of music in literary terms. Music must, in some unspecified way, be *about* something, and if the French were none too clear as to how this idea was to be expressed, it was only because they had not developed a meaningful theory of instrumental music, and indeed were incapable of doing so. This is not, I believe, to overstate Lang's position.

Unfortunately for Lang, and for proponents of a French origin for 'program music' as well, that position cannot be applied systematically to French writers on music, or even to Fétis himself. Fétis never mentions his theory of literary influence elsewhere in his writings on Beethoven, nor does the lack of an accessible 'idée principale' for most of the composer's instrumental music prevent him from declaring himself an admirer of

Beethoven's 'tremendous talent' in the context of yet another article on the Seventh Symphony.[27] Castile-Blaze, whose opinions on that symphony nearly duplicate those of Fétis, despite his generally pro-Beethoven stance, does not even suggest that the work's failings are due to any ambiguity of meaning; apart from some vague and misleading speculations about the relationship between the second movement and the music of the ancient Greeks, he avoids the issue of aesthetics entirely.[28] The case for a literary bias in early French reactions to Beethoven thus rests on shaky foundations: a single reference in Fétis, and the writings of Berlioz, who, as has already been seen, was far from representative of French musical thought. Fröhlich had also claimed that each Beethoven symphony was based upon a literary idea, and, unlike Fétis, he systematically carried though the implications of that hypothesis.

Considerably more light is shed on this elusive subject by the same critics' reaction to the one Beethoven symphony with a specific program, or at least an idea declared by the composer: the 'Pastoral' Symphony. This is not, in the modern sense, program music; in Beethoven's words it is a depiction of feelings rather than tone-painting. It is, however, undeniably less abstract than the symphonies which precede it. It contains numerous extra-musical references: the bird calls in the second movement, the polytonal horn entries at the beginning of the finale, and the entire fourth movement, which depicts a storm replete with thunder rolls in the timpani and other characteristic devices. It is also less adventurous musically, and hence more accessible, than the symphonies which surround it: a fact which the earliest German critics immediately recognized.[29]

It is surprising, then, to find that both Castile-Blaze and Fétis had serious reservations about this work. Castile-Blaze liked the scherzo and the storm, and he praised the second movement, though finding it too long. The first movement, however, he found 'weak in invention, overcharged with insignificant details, with repetitions which are tiring because the motive and the fragments derived from it lack originality'.[30] He speculates that the success which this movement achieved was due only to the name of Beethoven — an indication that already, by 1829, that name commanded considerable respect among the limited public who attended Habeneck's concerts.

Fétis had more thoroughgoing objections, pertaining to the entire genre of descriptive music. Such music, he felt, was at its best when portraying scenes involving action, and was ill suited to depict tranquility. Music could be calm and serene over short periods, and this was effective when used in contrast with more agitated sections, but when extended to the length of an entire movement, it inevitably resulted in monotony. This, Fétis felt, was the great fault of Beethoven's 'Pastoral' Symphony. It was successful imitation, but fundamentally dull music.[31] The 'Pastoral', then, did not fare well with the critics after its first performances in France. Only Berlioz was entirely enthusiastic, choosing his review of this work for a triumphant defense of modern art vis-à-vis the art of the ancient poets, whom he so admired.[32] This was hardly an auspicious start, though, for the work which Lang claims to have been the primary basis of Beethoven's reputation in France. Nor, apparently, was Fétis' rejection of this work based on his instinctive conservatism. He mentions in his review that the 'Pastoral' Symphony is entirely lacking in the eccentric mannerisms which he had found to be so damaging to the effect of Beethoven's music, and which seem to have disturbed him and other French critics because of their unfamiliarity. The style of the 'Pastoral' Symphony struck Fétis as entirely accessible. What provoked his reservations, and those of Castile-Blaze, was solely the work's imitative, quasi-programmatic nature and the limitations which this caused.

Of course, the later popularity of the 'Pastoral' Symphony in France is beyond doubt; why else would Debussy have written so disparagingly of the work in *Monsieur Croche Antidilettante*?[33] Does that popularity, however, indicate a French prejudice in favor of program music, and a consequent inability to understand Beethoven's other symphonies, or is it simply a function of the accessibility of the music? Fétis in particular yields some interesting hints.

First, Fétis, unlike his German counterparts, seems to have confused descriptive music with affective music in the old sense, which allowed only one affection per work or movement. Thus he failed to recognize that the 'Pastoral' Symphony employed the same proportions as any other symphonic work of Beethoven, with less drama, but no less formal articulation. He heard the entire symphony as a series of sketches, each depicting a given scene and never diverging from the basic mood suggested by that scene. He appreciated the scherzo and the storm, since they suggested livelier affections, but he agreed with Castile-Blaze in finding the themes of the first movement to be trivial, and he considered the second movement, which had pleased Castile-Blaze, to be even less successful, due to its slow tempo and the resulting tediousness of the form.

Fétis also made reference to the Aristotelian theories popular in the eighteenth century, which suggested that the first goal of all art was the imitation of nature.[34] Although he apparently accepted this principle as applied to the other arts, Fétis rejected it with regard to music. He never denied that music is capable of imitation; he merely claimed that such imitation is bound to be unsuccessful because of the limits of musical art. He made this claim, moreover, in an almost offhand fashion, without advancing any aesthetic argument to support it. He wrote, in other words, like a man who knows his readers will understand what he is talking about. Those readers were the French musical establishment of the early nineteenth century, and Fétis could usually be counted upon to represent their more conservative instincts.

Probably, then, theories of musical imitation – anything analogous to the German 'Tonmalerei' – were not widely accepted by French musicians at this time, nor was the theory of descriptive music of any kind very advanced. As already seen, the principle of imitation was used by French neo-classic critics to support the theory of music as passionate utterance, rather than literal imitation of nature such as Beethoven implies in the 'Pastoral'. A German critic like Marx or Kanne could treat virtually all of Beethoven's music as descriptive, and hence programmatic, but Fétis always preferred to characterize it in technical terms, criticizing it according to its adherence to some rather rigid *a priori* principles.

Indeed, one looks in vain in any French criticism before Berlioz for any other approach to Beethoven; like the early critics in Germany, the first French critics seem not to have considered the idea of extra-musical allusions or tone-painting as an explanation for the composer's eccentricities. In both countries, this idea seems to have appealed only to the younger critics – those who were the most ardently Romantic, and had fewest ties with the previous generation. In Germany, this meant a large number of progressive critics who were able to reject the limited view of tone-painting still endorsed by Gottfried Weber. In France it meant Berlioz alone, with occasional contributions from such minor figures as Chrétien Urhan (see below) and Joseph d'Ortigue, who succeeded Castile-Blaze as musical editor of the *Journal des débats*. For the older generation, which included both Fétis and Castile-Blaze, descriptive metaphors were of questionable value even in a work with specifically programmatic content like the 'Pastoral' Symphony. In Germany, however, even the conservative Rochlitz had embraced this work without questioning the composer's artistic goals. The critical evidence suggests, then, that early advocates of program music were more numerous in Germany than in France, and that this explains the poor reception which the 'Pastoral' Symphony originally received among French critics.

In fact, one of the most explicitly descriptive passages in the score was particularly uncongenial to Fétis. Bloom points out that in his harmony treatise, he criticized the opening of the finale, where the horn call anticipating the theme directly juxtaposes tonic and dominant sonorities (mm.

5–8).[35] This passage, which so clearly suggests the mingling of shepherds' horns from various directions before the song begins in unison, was unacceptable to Fétis because the tonic pedal was not prepared in advance. It would be hard to find a clearer instance in which a pedantic idea takes place over a descriptive challenge to a critic's imagination.

This is, of course, an isolated instance; the reception of a single work by a few critics can hardly provide conclusive evidence for the artistic outlook of an entire nation. All the evidence of Berlioz' writings, however, suggests that he had to fight a very similar battle to that waged by his German counterparts, against the same entrenched concepts of musical aesthetics. Marx, in the treatise *Ueber Malerei* cited above, railed against those 'Kunstphilosophen' who opposed tone-painting and would thus deny its expressive potential. Berlioz seems to have had similar opponents in mind when he attacked, in his *Mémoires*, those who did not accept music's ability to portray ideas. There is no indication in any of this that the ideal of absolute music belonged exclusively to Germany, or that conservative French musicians were willing to accept, let alone depend upon, programmatic or literary allusions. In France and Germany alike, sensitivity to such allusions seems to have depended upon one's generation, the only differences being that the German Romantics were more numerous than the French ones, and predate them by a score of years.

This division between the generations is emphasized by the French reception of the work in which progressive German critics had found the most perfect embodiment of musical idealism: the Ninth Symphony. David Benjamin Levy, in the dissertation cited in the last chapter, has presented French reactions to the first performances of that symphony, so that it remains only to interpret them along the lines developed above.

Not surprisingly, Fétis found much to admire in the Ninth Symphony, but also much to criticize, especially in the finale. His favorite movement was the scherzo, in which he discerned 'a type of light charming banter', relieved in the trio by a motive 'new and piquant', its development 'a marvel of elegant construction and brilliant imagination'.[36] He also liked the first movement, and found the introduction, though at first seemingly insignificant, to be intimately related to the piece as a whole. The slow movement he liked less well, judging the total effect fatiguing, but reserved his final opinion for a future performance. The setting of the *Ode to Joy*, however, appalled Fétis.

If one pays attention to the meaning of Schiller's verse, one finds nothing in the musical expression that relates to it; Beethoven has even disrupted its order. But the astonishment again increases when after the first development of the chorus

118

in a serious movement, one re-enters the domain of instrumentation only to go through every degree of the most bizarre fantasy as far as the caricature of the theme in rapid movement, in which the speed increases from one moment to the other.[37]

Spohr had been similarly harsh in suggesting that Beethoven did not do justice to Schiller,[38] but in general the progressive German critics in *Caecilia* and the *WAMZ* chose to defend Beethoven on the very grounds that Fétis criticized: Grossheim supported his re-ordering of the verses in the *Ode to Joy*, and Kanne, Fröhlich and Seyfried had all praised the fugal working-out of the vocal material. This may seem merely a German defense of the 'absoluteness' of those techniques, but most German critics were by no means indifferent to the message of Schiller's poem, divergent though their responses to it were.

Fétis, then, found these 'instrumental' techniques too much of a shock to his sensibility, and in this sense he probably represented the Parisian audience, which seems to have had great difficulty in comprehending the finale of the Ninth Symphony, even after repeated hearings.[39] A further article, printed in the *Revue musicale* after the third performance and probably not written by Fétis, praises the instrumental part of the work but again condemns the finale.[40] Here at last may be found an interpretation of the bass recitatives in this movement, which the author sees as 'the formidable voice of a fantastic being to ask for, and to reject in turn, all these diverse subjects, in order to choose finally the one which will become the pivot, the center of the entire composition'.[41] This critic recognized, then, that vocal music and vocal techniques were foreign within an instrumental work, and required special commentary. None of the German critics five years earlier had made this distinction.

Finally, François Stoepel, in the *Gazette musicale* of the following year, wrote as follows of the finale:

Beethoven concentrated on his musical ideas; he had grown in his exclusive occupation with his art. He knew only his God, nature and music. Therefore, when he had grasped the fundamental idea of a movement, he was not preoccupied with the rest. In this sublime hymn by Schiller, Beethoven is equal to the poet in so far as it is an issue of friendship and the divine creator; but as for the rest, there is no trace of musical workmanship with the words, nor any regard to the prosody, no more than to the poetic allegories. It is, in our opinion, from this point of view that one may attempt to analyze this sublime work; it must be judged solely as a musical work, and as such it merits the admiration that it has excited.[42]

The implication of these reviews is that Beethoven was incapable of composing an adequate setting of the *Ode to Joy*; although he understood the difference between instrumental and vocal music, he could not capitalize on it, being too closely bound to traditional symphonic and contrapuntal techniques. When Stoepel speaks of 'musical ideas', it is these techniques that he has in mind. To some extent, as already seen, their excessive use may have been associated in France exclusively with German music. Fétis and the others just cited would probably have agreed with their countryman Grétry that if symphonic music were to be set to a text, the text should be written to conform to the music, rather than vice versa. Stoepel's 'fundamental idea', too, seems to mean something that can best be expressed musically, without reference to words. Beethoven was not preoccupied with 'the rest', by which was meant attention to the details of a pre-existent text, because he did not understand how to set words to music. The distinction in genre between a work with a poetic text and one without, which the Germans had consistently failed to make, was used by the French to Beethoven's detriment as a vocal composer.

Two further points need to be made here: at no time do these critics show any lack of sympathy for the instrumental style of which they see Beethoven as the absolute master, and at no time do they even remotely suggest a programmatic reading of the Ninth Symphony, as a whole or in part. The anonymous author's 'formidable voice', rejecting in turn the themes of the previous movements, comes the closest, but it derives from Beethoven's own text ('nicht diese Töne'), and is not characteristic of the critic's reading even of the vocal sections of the work. The initial reservations about Beethoven in Paris seem to have been largely overcome, much as they had been with Haydn many years before, but the French critics refer constantly to the anomaly of the finale: its unusual form and its apparent independence from the earlier movements. The concert managers seem to have felt this too, because the symphony was often performed in two halves, with the finale alone occupying the second.[43] The Parisians enjoyed at least the first three movements, but any connection between them and the finale − any literary program for the work, such as Fröhlich, under the influence of current German theories on poetry and music, had suggested − was flatly rejected. The French had come to terms with Beethoven by other means.

It seems likely, from the evidence discussed above, that those means were essentially the same ones that had been followed in Germany. The tradition of vocal music, and opera in particular, was much stronger in France, but by the time Beethoven's music arrived there, Haydn and the native French school of symphonic composition, whose importance has only recently been recognized,[44] had accustomed Parisian audiences to abstract instrumental music as well. Even if, like Grétry, they wished to set that music to words, they were not without their counterparts in Germany: needless to say, however, this project was never carried out.

The progressive French critics, however − Berlioz, and in this case

Chrétien Urhan, an admirer of Berlioz and another champion of German music in France – had a great deal to say about the Ninth Symphony's literary overtones. Urhan, echoing Fétis, but recalling Fröhlich as well, whose analysis he seems to have read, claims that Beethoven had in mind a specific poem for each of his symphonies, and that he was inspired both by nature and by great literature, above all Shakespeare. Urhan's debt to Fröhlich is apparent in his interpretation of the Ninth Symphony as a whole, which he too sees as Beethoven's musical autobiography. It is interesting that Urhan, who was only the second French critic to suggest that Beethoven's music was conceived in literary terms, should have built so closely on a German prototype.

In a sense, though, Urhan's view of the symphony is more complex than that of Fröhlich, since he sees no real connection between the individual movements, and interprets the finale not as a tribute to joy, but as a religious statement. He, too, makes a parallel with Dante, but he sees the excursion to the depths of the earth as beginning in the first movement, with the last presumably signifying an arrival in paradise. For Urhan, the trio of the scherzo is not an anticipation of the finale, but an evocation of nature, and the third movement represents the purity of human love. The finale, however, is described as a mystical experience: the merging of the soul with its Creator.

Urhan gives most attention to that passage whose implications the German critics had ignored: the bass recitatives at the beginning of the movement.

Never before had anyone had the idea of making the basses and contrabasses *speak* ... Only Beethoven, in his Symphony in C minor, had attempted this innovation, but that was only an attempt: whereas here the recitative is largely established. It has its role – it is really a voice that speaks.[45]

Urhan is evidently referring to the famous unison passage at the beginning of the trio in the scherzo of the Fifth Symphony. It is difficult to know why he should have seen this as an earlier attempt at speech, but it is clear that, like other Frenchmen, but unlike his German contemporaries, Urhan saw a fundamental difference between instrumental music and vocal music. These recitatives, he says, growl in anger, chasing away in turn the themes of the preceding movements, and preparing the entrance of the *Ode to Joy*. At the same time, Urhan mentions no contradiction between the choral setting of that text and the instrumental techniques which Beethoven employs throughout, and which he must have recognized as such. We can only surmise that he felt this combination to be justified by the movement's mystical intent: that of presenting a union with God, and hence of reconciling opposing forces. In this respect, despite his different view of the music, Urhan's mysticism may be compared directly with the idealism of his German counterparts. It too assumes that transcendental experience is not foreign to the everyday world of man.

Berlioz' approach to the Ninth Symphony shows once again his ambivalent attitude toward musical programs.

Without seeking out the personal ideas which the composer wished to express in this vast musical poem, for which study the field of conjecture is open to each ... let us see if the novelty of the form would not be justified by an intention independent of all philosophical and religious thoughts ... by an intention, finally, purely musical and poetical.[46]

Beethoven, says the composer of *Roméo et Juliette*, had already written eight symphonies; the only way to go beyond this accomplishment was to merge voices and instruments, while at the same time observing the law of crescendo by beginning the work with instruments alone. This explained the unique structure of the Ninth Symphony.

Berlioz, then, like Kanne, seems to regard the use of voices as simply one more element of diversity in Beethoven's symphonic structure. Unlike Kanne, however, he sees the bass recitatives in the finale as the bridge between the instrumental and choral sections, thus showing that he too perceived a fundamental difference between these two parts of the symphony. His approach to the finale is more specifically interpretive than his descriptions of the earlier movements, which he had chosen to characterize only in the most general terms. This may, of course, be a by-product of the multi-sectional structure of the movement. It is clear, however, that Berlioz saw a unity here as well, and that unity was primarily expressive: each section of the finale shows a different aspect of joy. Thus the first orchestral fugue becomes 'the divine movements of an active crowd full of ardor',[47] while the return of the chorus evokes the original simplicity. Berlioz did not, however, find the other movements to be inferior; rather, he considered their complexity too subtle to be adequately expressed in words. The same idea had governed his view of the 'Pastoral' Symphony, which led him to describe the ancient poets as 'inclyti sed victi' – great but conquered – by the supple power of which modern music alone was capable.

Berlioz thus presents a mass of contradictions to the modern reader. He distrusted programs, yet wrote them for his symphonies.[48] Like Schopenhauer, whose musical idol was Rossini, he praised the flexibility of instrumental music, but was strangely attracted to poetry and the human voice, and found in the Ninth Symphony the most perfect example of Beethoven's genius. Such contradictions were to some extent characteristic of Romanticism, and it may be asking too much to expect that they should be susceptible to logical explanation. They can, however, at least be clarified one step further.

It has already been suggested that literary interpretation of music during this period was not a French but a German innovation, and, on the basis of the evidence discussed in this chapter, it may be added that what seems to characterize French musical aesthetics generally during the early nineteenth century is not an antipathy to abstract composition, but a sensitivity to the unique properties of vocal vis-à-vis instrumental music, and an ability to value each in its own right. To Berlioz, the boundaries may have been less clear than they were to Fétis, but they nevertheless determined the unique form of the Ninth Symphony, in a manner which his German counterparts would have found it difficult to understand. There were exceptions, of course; Hoffmann seems to have genuinely preferred instrumental to vocal music, while Wendt exactly reversed his priorities. Both of these writers clearly understood the differences in potential between the two genres, although Wendt clothes *Fidelio* in the same idealistic trappings that Hoffmann had given to the Fifth Symphony, the piano trios, Op. 70, and other purely instrumental works. Together, they emphasize only that it was the personality of the critic, rather than his philosophical stance or nationality, that determined which music he preferred and why: a fact that makes it all the more regrettable that neither of them reviewed the Ninth Symphony.

Perhaps, though, the work could be understood only by someone who, like Fröhlich or Berlioz, valued both music and poetry, but valued music more. Only then was it possible to suggest that specific musical techniques could incorporate poetic ideas, without either losing its individual character. This is what Urhan plainly believed, and the pragmatic Berlioz seems to have believed it too, making him, if not an idealist *malgré lui*, at the very least a critic whose priorities were essentially those of his German contemporaries, despite the differences in their understanding of the nature of vocal music.

That understanding, then, had ultimately very little significance for the Romantic generation in France. However much it may have preconditioned their views of musical aesthetics, the conclusions which they reached when confronted with a work like the Ninth Symphony were essentially the same as those of their fellow Romantics in Germany. A reconciliation of metaphysics with more accessible approaches to the same music led in either case to views of the work in which music and poetry were combined to an extent, and in a manner, which the older critics would not have considered possible. This was the one work of Beethoven which conservatives in either country could not begin to understand, because, whether or not the composer had intended it to do so, it played havoc with their sensibilities in a way which they were unable to forgive. For the Romantics, however, the problems raised by the symphony were quite literally irrelevant, whatever they thought of the forms and techniques used by the composer.

This was as true in France as in Germany, and it is difficult not to conclude that the aesthetic reasons for it were the same in both countries. Frenchmen of Grétry's generation may have genuinely misunderstood instrumental music, seeking to clarify it by the use of words. By the time of Fétis, though, the differences between vocal and instrumental music were well established, and both genres were appreciated in their own right. Only the metaphysical Germans insisted on confusing the two. The similarity of opinions in both countries, however, given the unprecedented nature of the Ninth Symphony, could only stem from a truly common view of the nature of musical Romanticism. This view was shared unwittingly by critics whose backgrounds and philosophical positions are as different as possible, but who are united by a common belief in that uniquely Romantic idealism which springs from the world of common experience.

Thus far, I have tried not only to survey the reception of Beethoven's works in Germany and France, but to outline what I believe to be the principles of criticism followed by progressives and conservatives in both countries. I have given disproportionate attention to the progressives, since their reviews tend to be both longer and more controversial philosophically than those of the earlier critics. With their interpretive, analytical bias, they also seem to enter more deeply into the secrets of the music. Furthermore, as I have constantly suggested, they try to synthesize metaphysical and technical interpretations to an extent rarely found in later writings on Beethoven. For these critics, analysis and interpretation were not irreconcilable extremes – they were part and parcel of the same approach to the music.

In the next chapter I will look in detail at three reviews of the Fifth Symphony: those by Hoffmann, Marx and Berlioz, each of which puts such an approach into practice – and meets with a different type and degree of success. Hoffmann's analysis, contained in the review discussed in Chapter 1, is analytical only at the level of the individual phrase or section, with no attempt at discussing overall form, but its entire plan is subjugated to an interpretive purpose whose implications are just as far-reaching and all-encompassing as any formal model, and which entirely disposes with the vocabulary of the affections. Marx, by contrast, writing in his biography in 1859, was preoccupied with form, and his emotional interpretation, though cut out of the same fabric, is always subject to formal laws. Berlioz, in the version of his review printed in *A travers chants*, and first written in 1838, is, as one might expect, less purposeful and systematic than either of the German critics, but he too yields some interesting hints, this time in discussing a purely instrumental work, at the compatibility of seemingly diverse elements of interpretation and structure, whose integrity he carefully maintains. If Berlioz is the least successful of the three, it is only because he frequently seems to be fighting against his own inclinations.

Nevertheless, these reviews, written at widely different times and places, show a unity of purpose – and accomplishment – which only reinforces the conclusions of this and the previous chapter. Romantic critics, they reveal, tried to show not only the what of music, but the why, and they did so with a single-minded regularity which leaves no doubt that they believed these complex questions to be interdependent. That is what Romantic music criticism is about, whether in Germany or in France, and that is why it can seem as baffling today as it once was clear and logical. Let us see if some of that original logic cannot be restored.

5

The Fifth Symphony

Introduction

Beethoven's Fifth Symphony is probably the composer's best-known work, and from the first it attracted more than its share of attention. Hoffmann's enormous review, and the fact that it was printed in its entirety by Europe's most prestigious musical journal, provide the most conspicuous testimony to the esteem in which it was originally held. Fétis wrote an ecstatic review following the first French performance, seconded by Berlioz in the *Revue et gazette musicale*, and Marx devoted an entire chapter of his biography to the Fifth Symphony. There is thus an extraordinary wealth of critical material pertaining to this work, much of it of high literary quality.

In the previous chapters I have dealt with these essays as criticism. In the present chapter I will treat them primarily as analytical documents, and will try to determine what a modern musician can learn from studying them as such.

In our own century, analysis has become a fine art, and today's student can choose from conflicting schools of thought those methods of de- and reconstruction that he finds most beneficial, ignoring others which he considers outmoded or misleading. The overthrow of traditional Marxian 'textbook' analysis which has taken place over the last quarter of a century, and its replacement by more flexible models of form, is a prime example of the change in musical thinking. Is there any reason, then, to return to these outdated concepts, when more immediately compelling alternatives are available? The answer, I believe, is yes, provided that we know what to look for. Reduced to a theoretical skeleton, as in his own *Compositionslehre*, Marx's system symbolizes the textbook approach to analysis, while the technical portions of Hoffmann, as already intimated, would be superfluous were it not for his use of extra-musical, non-analytical associations. In both cases, it is these associations which flesh out the analysis, making it intellectually stimulating and not simply routine.

In his article 'Analysis' in the *New Grove Dictionary*, Ian D. Bent makes a distinction between two types of analysis, which he calls 'descriptive' and 'judicial'; these are also the two primary types of criticism.[1] It is clear that the reviews under consideration fall into the former category; they do not

126

presume to judge the Fifth Symphony, whose worth is taken for granted by the authors. Instead, they provide an account of something of supreme importance in those authors' experience of music, and they do so by describing that music in both technical and non-technical terms. As such they differ categorically from many more recent methodologies of analysis. For the most part, those methodologies are based on certain assumptions; as Leo Treitler has recently written, 'the analytical perspective tends to be from the inside out, or from back to front, rather than from beginning to end. Music is apprehended as synchronic structure ... Analysis whose center of gravity is a synchronic conception of pitch structure is little interested in the phenomenology of music.'[2] It is this phenomenology – what Treitler calls 'the point of view of the auditor', manifested in the perception of music as a sequence of events in time – that early nineteenth-century criticism makes a serious attempt to address. Its analysis, in other words, 'does not draw the blinds before music's expressive force',[3] and for this reason it is still of interest today.

Hoffmann and Marx were not simply Beethoven's critics; they were his contemporaries, and their interpretations of music spring from the same background as the composer's own. One reason Marxian analysis has been largely supplanted is that theoretical descriptions of form from the eighteenth century, for example those by Koch and Galeazzi, have been found to be more accurate reflections of contemporary trends, most notably in the music of Haydn, Mozart and their forerunners. As already shown in Chapter 2, however, Marx's ideas for interpreting music were already formulated during Beethoven's lifetime, and it was from these ideas that his system of analysis grew. To point this out is not necessarily to advocate a re-institution of Marxian sonata form. My contention is simply that Marx's use of that form can be instructive today. Studying nineteenth-century analysis can be informative about how the nineteenth century thought about its own music. Primarily, it demonstrates that for many critics, analysis was not an end in itself; it was intimately connected with an extra-musical interpretation that was part and parcel of the Romantic approach to the most metaphysical of all the arts. The relationship of this approach to technical analysis will be the subject of the present chapter.

It is not my intention, in this chapter, to provide an analysis of the Fifth Symphony in nineteenth-century terms. Anyone wishing to read such an analysis may turn to Hoffmann's review, which is reasonably complete in and of itself, and has been translated into English for the Norton critical edition of Beethoven's score. I am interested only in making conjectures along the lines discussed above, and consequently I will concern myself only with those sections of analysis that can be directly linked to the other aspects of the review under consideration.

Hoffmann, Marx and Berlioz each have their own extra-musical approach to the work. There is, for example, a striking contrast between Hoffmann's primarily negative interpretation and the more positive one of Marx. The negative aspects of Hoffmann's review have already been pointed out in Chapter 1; the music is conceived almost entirely in terms of an imaginary world which is unthinkable and unknowable: which inspires reactions of pain, longing and fear. Concrete associations are eliminated entirely, as is any sense of victory or rest; all is part of an endless process of cataclysmic change. Hoffmann forced even the last movement of the Fifth Symphony into this pattern, disregarding its triumphant, affirmative aspects in his view of the symphony's conclusion.

Marx, however, makes the triumph of the last movement the keynote of his interpretation. The theme of the symphony becomes 'Durch Nacht zum Licht! Durch Kampf zum Sieg!'[4] In other words, the fateful storms of the first movement are resolved as the symphony progresses. The contrast with Hoffmann could not be more complete: Hoffmann is concerned with the world of spirits, Marx with that of humanity; for Hoffmann, the music evokes longing for something extra-terrestrial, while for Marx it suggests a quasi-military struggle in the here and now. This worldliness may seem to defeat the purpose of the present comparison, which depends on the existence of something metaphysical in the contrast between interpretation and analysis. Marx is still an idealist, however, because he perceives music in the Hegelian sense as struggling to transcend itself through the incorporation of these very worldly associations.

The background which he shares with Hoffmann is evident in his belief that music could suggest a higher level of existence without sacrificing the everyday principles which made it comprehensible within an older theoretical tradition. Hoffmann chose to develop the transcendental aspects of his analysis, while Marx tried instead to give music a grammatical framework through which this higher reality could be expressed. The result is that his visual images are more specific and less evocative than Hoffmann's. Ultimately, though, it is the very insufficiency of Marxian 'Tonmalerei' as an interpretive tool – its dependence on an analytical system without concrete meaning – that illustrates the paradoxical nature of Marx's system. By comparison, Hoffmann's analysis was old-fashioned and, as already suggested, limited in its potential. The true novelty of Marxian analysis is that it is analogous to language but without any meaning outside itself; it is as autonomous as even Hanslick could have wished. The specific images furnished by Marx are paradoxical for what they imply about musical form: that it is both meaningful and abstract.

Clearly, then, it is an oversimplification to say, in discussing the unique synthesis found in all the Romantic critics discussed thus far, that analysis occupies the position of worldly restraint, and interpretation that of metaphysical excess. The nature of the combination is different for each critic; they are bound together only by the common assumption that two seemingly different ways of thinking about music can exist side by side.

The first movement

It would be instructive to begin by comparing each author's treatment of the first movement of the Fifth Symphony, since all agree that in this movement the basic themes of the work as a whole are set forth. Hoffmann summarizes his analytical insights into this movement as follows:

There is no simpler motive than that on which the master based the entire Allegro. With great admiration, one becomes aware that Beethoven knew how to relate all secondary ideas and all transition passages through the rhythm of that simple motive so as gradually to unfold the character of the whole work − a character which the principal motive could only suggest. All phrases are short, consisting of only two or three measures, and are distributed to the strings and winds in constant alternation. One would think that something only fragmentary and difficult to grasp could arise from such elements. Instead, it is precisely the ordering of the whole and the constant succession of the repetitions of short phrases and individual chords that holds the heart firmly in unspeakable longing. Completely apart from the fact that the contrapuntal treatment evidences deep study of the art, one can see from the transition passages and the constant allusion to the principal theme that the whole work with all its salient features did not simply flow freely from the master's mind, but was carefully thought through.[5]

One of the most characteristic traits of Hoffmann's analysis, then, is his concern for unity. Once this is recognized, an obvious but highly significant corollary must be stated as well: the same concern for unity is the keynote of Hoffmann's extra-musical interpretation. Nothing could make this more apparent than his surprising treatment of the finale, which he forces into the same emotional world occupied by its predecessors, or the relative neglect which the gentler, less cataclysmic second movement suffers under his pen. Unlike Marx, whose overall approach was evolutionary, Hoffmann believed that nothing really changed as the symphony progressed; that the unity of the first movement was the unity of the whole.

Marx's comments on the first movement are, at first glance, similar to Hoffmann's:

129

The great task which the artist assumes is to include a broad picture of life within this single basic thought; in fact, by adding to this basic thought, to make visible a new side of this picture, in which all the forms imagined until now are raised to new meanings.[6]

Like Hoffmann, Marx conceives of a unity based on a single fundamental idea; unlike Hoffmann, he believes that this unity involved a dynamic process. Hoffmann speaks of a continual unfolding: Marx of new and unimagined meanings which transcend the original conception, much as, in his idea of the symphony as a whole, the finale transcends the other movements by showing the way through struggle to victory.

If Marx seems less technical, more abstract than Hoffmann, Berlioz goes even further, summarizing the first movement entirely in emotional terms:

The first movement is dedicated to the portrayal of disordered sentiments which agitate a great soul in despairing prayer. This is not that concentrated, calm despair which gives the appearance of resignation, not the somber, speechless sorrow of Romeo learning of Juliet's death, but rather the terrible fury of Othello receiving from Iago's mouth the poisoned calumnies which persuade him of Desdemona's crime.[7]

This is followed by more specific comments, also of an emotional nature, and then by some technical observations which seem, at first glance, entirely unrelated. These will be discussed in more detail at a later point in this chapter. For now, let it simply be observed that the first impression given by Berlioz' reviews as a whole is one of complete separation between the analytical and emotional spheres.

This is the case in brief; it remains to be seen whether a more detailed treatment of these reviews will reveal the same priorities throughout. Hoffmann's is once again a good starting point, since it is a 'complete' analysis, leaving nothing to the imagination. As already seen, however, a good deal is left out, particularly in the second movement and the more placid parts of the other movements. Furthermore, Hoffmann chose to emphasize particular points in his analysis by connecting them with his extra-musical interpretations. Thus he apparently found the threefold repetition and crescendo of mm. 14−21 (a) to be more impressive than the unison opening. Other passages in the first movement which he chose to emphasize through extra-musical references include (b) the transition in mm. 33−44, (c) the second theme beginning at m. 59, (d) the chords for full orchestra at mm. 168−79, (e) the D 6/3 chords played by woodwinds and strings in mm. 221−7 and (f) the passage which immediately precedes the repetition of the opening at mm. 476−82.

Schnaus has pointed out that Hoffmann calls attention to certain prominent features of the music, including pauses on the dominant, changes in volume, and gradual rises in pitch, as being particularly Romantic in their effect.[8] Two characteristics of these passages, however, are so outstanding that they deserve special consideration. At no point does Hoffmann distinguish an actual thematic statement; these are all what is normally called connecting material, separating and developing the important thematic events of the movement, and, except for (e), they are all crescendos, or they belong to passages growing in intensity. Even (c) may be included in both these categories, since when Hoffmann says that this remains true to the character of restless longing which marks the movement as a whole, he is surely thinking not so much of the beginning of the theme, whose only connection to the opening is a motivic one, but of mm. 75ff., with their minor inflections and gradual increase in dynamic intensity. However, Hoffmann identifies the important thematic statement beginning at m. 179 as a 'freundlicher Gestalt', associating it with the clouds that light up the night of the mysterious spirit-kingdom. (D) is evidently the most intense passage of all, since Hoffmann assigns it a cathartic function; it serves to purge the listener's breast of the forebodings which weigh it down.

In this manner, Hoffmann makes it clear that transition and growth are the musical embodiment of the longing ('Sehnsucht') which is so essential to his Romantic vision. Just as longing represents a foreboding of the infinite, so these finite crescendos suggest to the sensitive listener an endless drive toward greater and greater intensity of feeling. The thematic material itself cannot accomplish this, since it is static, a mere form ('Gestalt') which literally allows one to see what would otherwise be inaccessible to the true Romantic spirit. So much Hoffmann conveys through his curiously inverted priorities.

Hoffmann does in fact use these extra-musical allusions to emphasize his most important analytical point: the unity of the movement. Listening to the music with Hoffmann's ears, one hears a series of highly charged passages separated by more neutral material which serves as punctuation. No further distinctions are made, nor are they necessary, since the concept thus set forth is both sufficiently complete and completely to the point. Contrast is ignored (the second theme, though melodious, remains true to the character of the movement as a whole), and in its place is postulated a reciprocal relationship in which one type of music evokes the unthinkable, while the other type brings it down to earth, though both are based on the same motivic material. This concept of the unity of apparent opposites was, as already observed, crucial to the philosophical thought of the early nineteenth century, especially Hegel. For Hoffmann, Beethoven's

131

monumental unity could only be expressed by some such combination of traditional analysis with non-musical allusions.

Marx's analysis is less complete; it is also less technical, tending merely to describe the music with the aid of examples rather than analyzing individual chords, as Hoffmann does. For Marx, only central tonalities and pivotal chords are sufficiently important to be listed in this manner. Marx begins squarely with the opening motive, deliberately reminding his readers of Beethoven's familiar comment, 'thus Fate knocks at the door'. Like Hoffmann, he gives a good deal of weight to the transitions which follow, though he is more impressed with mm. 44–56 than with mm. 14–21; that is, with the passage immediately preceding the second theme.

This theme itself is viewed by Marx much as it was by Hoffmann, as a melodious interlude which is nevertheless related to the basic mood of the piece. Marx's priorities are different, however; Hoffmann, as already seen, was determined almost to deny that any contrast existed, but Marx dwells on the contrast, describing it as 'longing for rest'. He uses the word 'Verlangen' rather than Hoffmann's 'Sehnsucht', but the feeling is the same, and Marx links it with exactly the kind of thematic material that Hoffmann apparently considered to be mere punctuation.

Between the second theme and the end of the exposition, Marx finds two more distinct moods. The first, anxious ('ängstlich') and tormenting ('quälerisch'), is obviously associated with the minor key inflections of mm. 75–93, while the second, the confidence ('Zuversicht') of eventual victory, takes in mm. 94–122. Marx is careful to point out that this is only a hint; victory is yet a long way off. He then deliberately indicates, in a separate paragraph, the fact that this is the end of the first part of the movement (what we would now call the exposition), as though this technical distinction were also too important to escape the reader's notice.

The second part (the development) then begins, according to Marx, 'mitten im Ringen' – in the midst of the strife. Apparently, however, he considered the essence of strife to be represented by mm. 195–239; the motive is tossed back and forth between strings and winds, finally dissolving into note-by-note alternation, and Marx points out the severity which this effect lends to the transition between development and recapitulation.

The recapitulation is of course seen as a continuation of the struggle, although Marx gives very few details. The only passage on which he comments extensively is the oboe solo in m. 268, which he sees as a witness to Beethoven's humanity and poetic depth, even if it is a momentary distraction from the 'Streit und Widerstreit' which otherwise makes up the fabric of the work.

In general, Marx takes a more formalistic approach than Hoffmann, because, unlike Hoffmann, he is concerned to show how the musical representation progresses in the course of the piece, not just how the listener's perception of it changes. Hoffmann's spirit-kingdom had been a constant, suggestions of it occurring at fairly regular intervals as the movement progressed. Marx, however, introduces two more or less opposing ideas, that of struggle and that of victory. In Marx, in other words, contrast is already present in the extra-musical sphere, and does not need to emerge in the course of the analysis, as it does with Hoffmann.

Furthermore, the aspects of this contrast change as the movement, and the symphony, progresses. The three sections of the movement, which we would now call exposition, development and recapitulation, represent the stages by which the conflict resolves itself. In the first, the conflict begins, and it is confidently concluded by a prediction of eventual victory; in the second, it continues, reaching an inexorable climax just before the recapitulation; while in the third, with its extended coda, the conflict goes doggedly forward with scarcely a moment's respite. Of course, the suggestion of victory is repeated in the recapitulation, but Marx fails to call attention to this, as though, this time, it were superseded by its context. Marx thus sees the lines of the struggle as determined by the form; it is inconceivable, in his terms, for a musical struggle to be presented at all unless it can resolve itself around clearly determined formal lines.

To a modern reader, Marx's view of the retransition is somewhat difficult to grasp. How can a quiet passage, consisting of slow reiterations of a few basic chords, convey the sort of dynamic tension which Marx attributes, inclusively, to mm. 196–252, in which this passage occupies a central place? The answer is clearly one of formal necessity, which here imposes itself on Marx's extra-musical interpretation. Given that the plan of the piece is one of mounting struggle, tension, of a dramatic if not a tonal variety, must increase constantly as the movement goes on; and, given that it is a piece in sonata form, both types of tension must reach a momentary climax just before the return of the principal theme. Thus, somewhat irrationally, music which is clearly anticipatory in nature is made to bear the burden of carrying the struggle forward. Marx analyzed the way he did because his entire musical thought depended upon this type of analysis.

At the same time, however, it is clear that Marx's emphasis on form in this movement is not merely an imposition. It provides a perfectly logical framework for his extra-musical thought, the nature of which is evolutionary and dynamic rather than static. Hoffmann had no use for form, and his analysis was consequently non-directional and diffuse, just as his extra-musical interpretation was entirely independent of large-scale musical structure, centering instead on individual phrases and short-range contrast. For Marx, form is of the essence of musical thought; nothing can be accomplished without it, either in the musical or the extra-musical sphere.

Berlioz' article contains less of an analysis than either of those just discussed, and for a good reason; it was written, as has just been seen, for the public at large rather than for a musical journal or biography. Berlioz chose to comment on two specific technical aspects of the movement. The first, which he characterizes by the French word 'hoquet' and compares to the painful breathing of a dying man, is found in the passage beginning at m. 197: the same alternations between strings and winds that Marx had found to represent the essence of struggle. For Berlioz they suggest hesitation, punctuated and finally overcome by orchestral violence (mm. 228–32, 240ff.). The second concerns the use of the dominant in second inversion − in other words, an unprepared 6/4, which, Berlioz asserts, occurs numerous times during the movement. There are, in fact, only three such instances; the first, in the midst of the development section at mm. 175–6, can also be analyzed as a passing dissonance, while the second and third, occurring respectively at the beginning of the recapitulation (mm. 251–2) and the end of the coda (mm. 481–2), are correctly described by Berlioz as dissonant open fourths missing the 'note sensible'.

What is the connection of these passages with Berlioz' description of the movement quoted above? Why, out of the entire movement, should he have chosen only these two analytical examples? The answer probably lies in Berlioz' description of the quality of despair presented by the first movement. These are instances of brute musical force: Berlioz refers to 'l'aspect sauvage' of the unprepared 6/4, and the 'violence' of the orchestra just before the recapitulation is all the more striking because it follows a pianissimo passage with a distinctly static character; the contrast might well be taken to represent the fury of Othello set next to the helplessness of Desdemona. Marx, of course, had a very different interpretation of this passage, but the one suggested here is likely to strike modern readers, at least, as more plausible, less dependent upon the imposed necessities of form. Berlioz, though less dogmatic than Marx, seems to take the music at face value, and to have chosen his examples, after all, to support his own extra-musical interpretation of the movement.

All three writers, then, follow the same principle of combining analysis and interpretation. Hoffmann and Berlioz analyze only after having determined on what extra-musical ground the analysis is to rest, while

Marx seems to let the nature of the analysis determine the way in which his extra-musical interpretation is applied to the music. The difference is one of priorities, not of fundamental approach.

The second movement

This same approach is evident in the three writers' descriptions of the Fifth Symphony's second movement. Hoffmann 'analyzes' the movement by pointing out its formal resemblance to some of Haydn's slow movements in which a series of variations is separated by transitions. He then singles out several passages which he considers particularly effective: namely, the chromatic modulations, those which lead to and from the second theme (e.g. mm. 26–31, 37–49), and those which are implied by the chromaticism of the opening theme itself. Hoffmann writes: 'It is as if the frightful spirit which seized and tormented our hearts during the Allegro, threatening every moment from the thunderclouds into which it disappeared, were to step forward, and the friendly spirits which, surrounding us, gave comfort were to flee in haste from its sight.'[9] It could not be more evident from the passages he chooses to observe, and from this comment upon them, that Hoffmann is interested in the second movement only insofar as it reflects the power and transcendence of the first. His analysis reveals this bias beyond all doubt.

Marx, too, finds it unnecessary to comment on the second movement in as much detail as the first. Unlike Hoffmann, however, he finds this movement to be a logical outgrowth of its predecessor, a sort of prayer offered from the depths of a spiritual struggle. Marx also singles out the new theme beginning at m. 31 for specific comment; apart from the opening, this is the only passage in the movement he describes at all, and, like mm. 94ff. in the first movement, he considers this a premonition of eventual victory.

Berlioz treats the second movement at greater length, pointing out three passages that he finds to be of particularly daring effect: mm. 98–101, with the upper pedal E-flat in the woodwinds, mm. 133–43, in which the thirds in contrary motion produce some striking dissonances, and the canonic treatment of the main theme beginning at m. 185. Here there is no apparent extra-musical justification; there is, however, a concern, characteristic of Berlioz, for the effect of these passages upon the audience: he notes that the second example cited above, although forbidden by the theorists, produces 'un effet délicieux', while in the third, the wind parts, which carry the imitation, are difficult to hear above the fortissimo of the full orchestra.

The analyses of the second movement, then, are universally less interesting, for the purpose of the present study, than those of the first. All three writers seem to have felt that this movement was of less inherent value than the first. Hoffmann and Berlioz saw little in common between the two movements, while Marx saw the second as a mere anticipation of what was to come later.

The scherzo

With the third movement, the original fascination returns. Hoffmann calls this movement a 'Menuett', and he expects it, accordingly, after the Haydnesque tradition, to be the most provocative of the symphony. It is not merely cleverness that Hoffmann is interested in, however. As he quickly makes clear, what attracts him about this movement is its ability to 'arouse anew that alarm, those premonitions of the realm of the spirits, with which the passages of the Allegro [i.e. the first movement] assailed the listener's heart'.[10] Hoffmann singles out three recurrent devices which Beethoven uses to achieve this effect: unusual modulations, cadences on the major dominant which are succeeded by a theme in the minor, and the continual extensions which are applied to the principal theme. There follows an extensive analysis of the sort already given to the first movement, with the difference that, while in the former case extra-musical allusions were quite common, here they are few and far between. When, in the second half of the trio, the basses begin the theme and come to a halt two times before finally continuing (mm. 161–4), Hoffmann senses a sinister feeling, though recognizing that to many the effect will seem playful. The shortening of the original note values which occurs in most phrases of the repeat of the 'minuet' heightens the original restless yearning 'to a fear which tightly constricts the breast permitting only fragmentary, disconnected sounds to escape'.[11] Here Hoffmann seems to confuse listener and orchestra, but perhaps this was not an intentional oversight. Finally, the C pedal played by the timpani in the transition to the finale (mm. 324–73) 'arouses the terror of the extraordinary, of the fear of spirits'.[12]

Once again, then, Hoffmann concentrates not on the main thematic events, but on transitions and, in this case, on seemingly fortuitous alterations of the original thematic material. Although he calls the movement a minuet, he seems to understand it quite literally as a scherzo: a movement in which the composer plays with the listener's expectations, producing, in this case, not humor but fear. Its task is to plunge the listener back into the spirit-world of the first movement, from the impositions of which the second movement had temporarily relieved him.

For Marx, by contrast, the third movement points forward. The second movement had left the listener with a suggestion of victory — nothing more. The task of the third is to prepare for the more conclusive victory of the finale.

Marx describes the first part of the movement in almost Hoffmannesque detail, but his description, this time, is loaded with suggestive adjectives and verbs: the opening theme is brooding ('grüblerisch'); it burrows ('gräbt') in the deep; the second theme (mm. 19ff.) consists of hornstrokes ('Hornstösse') which call and impel ('rufen und treiben'); the key of B-flat minor (mm. 45ff.) is gloomy ('trüb') and stifling ('dumpf').

The trio, meanwhile, is 'a new attempt to find the way to the goal'. That goal, of course, is victory, and presumably its imminence is symbolized by the return to the C major tonality which had already played such a significant role in the previous movement. Marx treats this as a simple song form (his own term), pointing accurately to the written-out repetition of the second half. The entire section is 'a fleeting thought', without the power to comfort. In other words, the suggestion of victory in the trio has not been realized; in its place we find a kind of superficial good humor, manifesting itself in such momentary inspirations as the final statement of the theme in the flutes, harmonized by the other winds (mm. 217ff.) and the twice-interrupted beginning of the second half — that Marx does not see Hoffmann's sinister side to this passages goes without saying.

Marx does, however, share Hoffmann's apprehension of the broken staccato restatement of the main section; it is 'in the tone of an old, half-forgotten ballad, which hardly dares to come forth, as though there were no longer any future, hardly even any present'.

Another difference between Marx and Hoffmann thus emerges; while Hoffmann was able to see fear and foreboding at any point during the movement, Marx clearly divided it according to its nature — scherzo with trio — reading the main section as a continuation of the symphony proper, the alternative as yet another glance forward, thus fulfilling the function which Marx has assigned to the movement as a whole. Nothing could show Marx's formalist approach more clearly than his inability to find any connecting bond between the two sections.

At the same time, however, it is clear that Marx the analyst was interested in making such formal distinctions only if and when they help to delineate the emotional structure of the work. His vocabulary and procedure are not those of the modern analyst; they point at all times toward the emotional sphere, so that it is impossible to doubt that, in his less technical writings at least, Marx took emotional interpretation as the essential background for analysis, rather than vice versa. In the *Compositionslehre* this sense of priorities may seem to be disturbed in favor of formal analysis, but as already pointed out, this was only one limited aspect of Marx's personality, and a strictly pedagogical one at that. The biography, as his final major work and his last analytical treatment of Beethoven, presenting systematically each of the major works for emotional interpretation, and corresponding, furthermore, to the techniques he practiced in the earliest years of his career, may be taken as his definitive statement on the subject. The scherzo, then, with its fundamental simplicity of structure, shows clearly how even the most rudimentary of formal analyses (which is all that Marx provides) can be brought to life through a significant placement within an emotional 'analysis' that applies not only to this movement but to the symphony as a whole, thus giving the movement an important sense of context as well as the more obvious one of form.

Marx's analysis, in other words, is not to be understood merely as an abstraction, to be contemplated without reference to an actual sequence of events in time. It is fundamentally a part of a larger progression, and can only be properly understood if the (extra-musical) nature of that progression is taken into account.

Berlioz treats most of the scherzo in even less detail than he did the two preceding movements. Like Marx, he preserves a distinction between the two parts; the first he sees as a somber fantasy recalling the Blocksberg scene from Goethe's *Faust*, the second (the trio) as a kind of grotesque comedy. Berlioz gives virtually no attention to the changes which take place in the repeat of the 'Blocksberg' section, but when the transition to the finale is reached, he suddenly goes into considerable analytical detail. Two things strike him as particularly significant: like Hoffmann, he emphasizes the effect created by the tonic pedal in the timpani throughout this passage; unlike either of the other writers, he also points out the peculiar tension created at the beginning of the transition (mm. 324–41) by the contrast between the C in the timpani and the A-flat harmonies in the orchestra. In other words, he sees this passage not merely as one of tension, but of outright ambiguity as well, only gradually resolved as the finale approaches and the orchestra ranges itself on the dominant seventh chord.

Once again, then, in dealing with this movement, Berlioz confronts us with two seemingly irreconcilable elements, dealing, furthermore, with different sections of the music. Describing the movement proper, he relies only on extra-musical associations, whereas in describing the transition, he falls back upon a detailed technical analysis totally devoid of any outside connection. If there is any sort of link between the two, it lies in the idea of duality; the movement itself is divided into two sections with vastly different characteristics, and the transition is made into a play of opposing tonalities, similarly juxtaposed. As with Hoffmann, such a distinction between minuet and trio, at least, was not necessary. It is possible to see the movement as essentially homogeneous, despite the obvious formal division that was so important to Marx. Hoffmann, in fact, saw a gradual increase in tension as the movement progressed, thus discounting the rounded binary aspect of the form entirely. The formal division was played down by Beethoven as well, who chose not to label the movement as a traditional minuet (or scherzo) and trio.

Berlioz was of course unfamiliar with Marx's interpretation, although he might have known Hoffmann's. In any case, the division of the movement into two contrasting halves would not have been, for him, a foregone conclusion; he could have chosen to take the composer's hint and treat the movement as through-composed. His decision not only to emphasize the minuet–trio division, but virtually to ignore the recomposition of the main section on its return, constitutes a deliberate choice. That Berlioz should then convey the same sense of duality in a technical analysis of the conclusion of the movement is perhaps more than coincidence. Both instances, at least, are characteristic of him alone.

The finale

The finale of the Fifth Symphony, differing so extensively from the earlier movements, is naturally crucial to any interpretation of the work as a whole. Hoffmann's view of this movement is, as already noted (see Chapter 1), his most idiosyncratic. It also provides some surprising clues, through the few carefully selected links that Hoffmann establishes with his spirit-world, to the precise fashion in which this extra-musical phenomenon applies to the music of the symphony as a whole. On the one hand, Hoffmann clearly recognizes the jubilant, triumphant nature of much of the finale; the opening, he says, 'is like radiant, blinding sunlight which suddenly illuminates the dark night'.[13] On the other hand, he makes it clear that he still senses in this movement the longing and anxiety which had marked the rest of the symphony as well. Thus he states that the theme beginning on the upbeat to m. 45 contrasts with those that had come before; banishing the feelings of joy which the listener had 'momentarily' experienced, it leads the heart to experience foreboding once again. Hoffmann seems to associate the foreboding specially with the passage through A minor which takes place in mm. 52–4, as though the mere presence of a minor key were enough to summon up the emotional world of the earlier movements.

It is clear, however, that he felt the nature of the theme itself to be significantly different from that of its predecessors, and that the specific quality which distinguishes it is the great force with which it presses forward.

Schnaus points out that this theme also contains the characteristic rhythm of the opening movement,[14] but if Hoffmann was aware of this, he chose not to call attention to it, whereas he does emphasize the reappearance of that rhythm in the bass during the final Prestissimo. Quite apart from any question of key inflections or motivic structure, then, it is sheer drive and impetuosity that impresses Hoffmann and calls forth other-worldly connotations. What his view of the finale shows conclusively is that with Hoffmann we are not dealing, as with Marx and Berlioz, with a primarily emotional form of extra-musical interpretation. Like those other writers, Hoffmann sees the finale as jubilant and triumphant, but unlike them, he feels that this is of only secondary importance. What counts is an aspect of the music that has nothing to do with tragedy or triumph, sadness or exultation, but which inheres instead in its immediate visceral effect upon the listener. Those passages which are impulsive and dynamic, which seem to strain at the boundaries of the phrases which rein them in, are more impressive to Hoffmann than those that are merely forceful without pointing in any particular direction. Thus it is that the first movement, with its convulsive stops and starts, its yearning fermatas and its preternaturally compelling forward drive provides the key to the mystery, while the mere resolution with which the finale begins remains, despite its power, of only secondary importance.

For Hoffmann, the most impressive passage in the finale is the conclusion: the final chords.

The perfect calmness which the heart feels as a result of the several closing figures that are linked together is destroyed by these single struck chords and pauses. These last chords make the listener anxious once again and remind him of the striking single chords in the Allegro of the symphony. They have the effect of a fire which flames after one had believed it extinguished ... The heart of every sensitive listener, however, will certainly be deeply and intuitively moved by an enduring feeling – precisely that feeling of foreboding, indescribable longing – which remains until the final chord. Indeed, many moments will pass before he will be able to step out of the wonderful realm of the spirits where pain and bliss, taking tonal form, surrounded him.[15]

The essence of the symphony as a whole, then, is that it reaches outside itself, forward to the end of the finale and beyond. With perfect fidelity and consistency, the test of impetuousness is applied by Hoffmann to each movement in turn, and each is judged according to how well it fulfills these expectations. Seen in this perspective, it is not surprising that, for Hoffmann, the finale was not a complete contrast. What impressed him about this movement was not its conclusiveness but its lack of it; its apparent ability to go on forever in the same vein, symbolized by the seemingly interminable fanfare of the final chords.

Marx, after a lengthy digression in which he takes Alexander Oulibicheff to task for his interpretation of the finale, begins his analysis by refuting Berlioz, who had, he believed, found this movement to be too long, so that the triumphant effect of the beginning is not preserved until the end. Marx argues that a lengthy conclusion is needed to balance the weight of the other movements; that triumph must not simply be stated; it must be developed as well, through expansion and the inclusion of additional themes. This explains the weighty tonic section with which the movement begins, including the new theme at m. 26. Marx goes so far as to count the number of pages in each section of the finale, comparing them both to each other and to the earlier movements. The entire movement, he finds, occupies 62 pages in the Breitkopf und Härtel score as opposed to 120 for the three previous movements. In other words, the result occupies half as long as the cause, surely not an inappropriate proportion. (Marx neglects to mention that the fuller scoring of the finale makes it occupy more pages for the same number of measures.)

This peculiar kind of 'analysis' makes up Marx's treatment of the finale: having begun by interpreting the work in terms of a grandiose struggle and victory, he ends by counting pages − an anticlimax and a disappointment from any point of view. By way of conclusion, then, let us once again compare Marx's approach to the symphony with that of Hoffmann, as summarized above. Having followed each writer step by step through the entire symphony, we can appreciate the extent to which Marx concentrates on precisely that juxtaposition of emotional worlds which Hoffmann chose to ignore. For Marx, it is not transition and stability which stand as pole and counterpole, but rather conflict (i.e. tribulation) and victory (i.e. jubilation). Because of this sense of priorities, it is possible for the symphony, in Marx's view, to grow and develop. More importantly, it is possible to analyze individual phrases and themes (for example the C major theme in the second movement) according to their emotional essence. This, then, is the nature of the link established by Marx between musical and extra-musical interpretation − at the same time the simplest and the most easily comprehensible such link, less metaphysical but more direct than Hoffmann's.

Berlioz, as already seen, also adopts this emotional approach. Thus, it is not surprising that, like Marx, he sees the finale as a 'gigantesque chant de victoire' following upon the obscurity and confusion of the preceding transition. Berlioz does not provide any analysis of the finale, preferring instead to defend it from various charges that had been brought against it, among them the accusation, ascribed by Marx to Berlioz himself, that it is too long. In refuting this, Berlioz takes a very different line from

Marx, and a considerably weaker one; he simply states that nothing could equal the effect created by the beginning of the movement, so that it is impossible for the listener's interest not to diminish as the music progresses.

Berlioz, then, grows less analytical as he moves through the four movements of the symphony: he gives the most technical examples for the second movement and the least for the finale. It is interesting to note that it is in precisely these two movements that emotional description is reduced to a minimum. Apart from the rather vague example cited above, Berlioz provides no extra-musical description of the finale, and there is likewise none of the second movement. Once again, this may be mere coincidence, but it is tempting to speculate that Berlioz envisioned a kind of reciprocal relationship between these two aspects of his interpretation: when one dominates, as in the second movement, the other is forgotten, but normally they co-exist in approximately equal proportions. When, as in the finale, Berlioz abandons technical description, he abandons emotional description as well. Only in the second movement is this equilibrium disturbed. If the connection between the two spheres is less explicit than in Marx and Hoffmann, therefore, it seems at least to have had some significance for the author.

Summary

In conclusion, then, a survey of these three approaches to the Fifth Symphony shows fairly definitively that early nineteenth-century analysts as a group were sensitive to, and indeed motivated by, the extra-musical implications of their analyses. The nature of this sensitivity, as has already been observed, varies from one analyst to the next, as do its very implications, and in some cases, as with Berlioz, it is obscure. The fact of its existence, however, is beyond all reasonable doubt, and whenever it is found it reveals something paradoxical in its very nature, which points once again to the true nature of Romantic musical thought. Before proceeding, therefore, it would be worthwhile to return to the question of priorities. What, in other words, did analysis mean to the writers we have been discussing?

I have already pointed out that the science of musical analysis has advanced considerably since the early nineteenth century. We must remind ourselves that, although the goal of analysis has always been to instruct, the nature of that instruction has changed as its audience has become more and more specialized. Nowadays an analysis like the technical portions of Hoffmann's review would never be published in a serious musical journal, not because it is inaccurate but because, as stated in Chapter 1, it is of the sort now considered to be self-explanatory. To provide such an analysis, a specialist is not required. If this is true of Hoffmann, it is considerably more true of Marx and Berlioz, neither of whom went into anything like the same detail in analyzing the Fifth Symphony. If Hoffmann's critique belongs in a textbook on theory, those by Marx and Berlioz would not be out of place in one on music appreciation; their mixture of extra-musical interpretation with the highlighting of passages seen by the authors as significant is a familiar one in today's books written for the general public. Marx's approach to the study of form is also so thoroughly ingrained in the minds of most modern musicians that, on the few occasions when he goes into Hoffmann-like detail, as in his treatment of the beginning of the finale of the Fifth Symphony, the resemblance to current pedagogical technique is only too clear. We must first admit, then, that in speaking of analysis *per se* in the criticism of the early nineteenth century, we are dealing with techniques and methods of the schoolboy variety – nothing more. Such analysis, for those writers, can only have had a strictly utilitarian purpose; it is any technique which the author uses to illustrate points of interest in the work at hand, or to suggest something of fundamental importance about its nature.

Thus defined, analysis becomes self-evidently the tool of the author: one which he uses to back up his own view of a work which he has already expounded. The difference between this and the modern approach needs to be underscored once more: today analysis is frequently an end in itself; in the early nineteenth century it was manifestly a means to an end, that end being most accurately defined as the explanation of a philosophical position whose paradoxical nature makes it incomprehensible in any other terms. If the most sophisticated analyses of 150 years ago have been reduced to the level of textbook fodder, it is surely not because our understanding of music has advanced momentously in the interval. The age that produced Beethoven's Fifth Symphony was also capable of doing it justice; to deny this is to deny the appropriateness of the nineteenth century's musical culture to the era of Romanticism in the arts. What has changed is the sense of priorities with which a writer approaches his task.

The goal of this chapter has been to restore the original sense of priorities, and to show that the way a nineteenth-century writer analyzes a work reflects his deepest convictions regarding its nature and purpose. We must not expect that studying nineteenth-century analysis will provide any new insights of a technical nature. What it will provide is insights into the nineteenth century's view of music, which in turn can help us to understand how Romantic music, and Beethoven's in particular, was understood by its creators.

Conclusion

I have maintained throughout this book that the first critical writings are in agreement about certain fundamental aspects of Beethoven's music — specifically, that they all seek to find a link between analysis and extra-musical interpretation. This is, I believe, not simply coincidence; it shows that Romantic thought about music, despite its diversity, is unified by certain common assumptions, which, to paraphrase Alfred North White-head, are never called into question because they are taken for granted by the authors. Almost all of these authors found Beethoven to be the composer most suited to the type of criticism they brought to bear. In short, they provide a meaningful definition of what it means to call Beethoven a Romantic composer: the most representative musician of his age.

Another, and greater, problem confronts the modern reader of this criticism. If Beethoven was the composer ideally suited to Romanticism, why does our anti-Romantic age still consider him to be among the greatest composers of all time? Perhaps this is only a problem outside the German-speaking world, since German scholars continue to draw on the critical writings of Wilhelm Dilthey, Karl Marx, Theodor Adorno, and other thinkers in the idealistic tradition who have never been in vogue among musicians in England and America. It is doubtful, however, whether philosophers have ever determined what makes one composer more popular or enduring than another. Most writers on Beethoven for the public at large, while doing lip service to the *Zeitgeist* theory, tend to imply that his music is somehow greater than the culture that gave it birth: that Beethoven reconciled timeless forces and that this explains his widespread and enduring appeal.

Perhaps it is for this very reason that practicing musicians tend to be impatient with aesthetic theories which try to limit the appeal of music to one or the other of Beethoven's self-evident strengths. Beethoven was the master of form, so Hanslick and others have proclaimed that form is the essence of music, and expression is somehow beside the point. Nobody I have ever talked to who is in any way involved with the making of music subscribes to this point of view, despite its philosophical prestige. At the same time, however, many musicians are equally dissatisfied with the

144

apparent alternative: the theory that music consists solely in the communication of emotions. That there exists a 'musical' dimension to art which is not adequately defined by either form or expression *per se* seems self-evident to anyone who has actively performed.

It is this musical dimension which I believe is addressed by Beethoven's first critics in their unique synthesis of opposing viewpoints. Rather than using their writings to define Beethoven as a Romantic composer, perhaps it is more meaningful to 'demythologize' them: to purge them of assumptions which are meaningless to the modern world and use them, in this revised form, to resolve some of the dilemmas of contemporary aesthetics.

Perhaps the most prestigious philosophical approach to music in our century has been that first advanced by Susanne Langer in *Philosophy in a New Key*. Langer defined music as the creation of 'forms symbolic of human emotion', and claims to have resolved in this manner the conflict between form and expression.[1] Two recent books by Peter Kivy, however, dealing respectively with musical expression and musical representation, show that even Langer has not put to rest the old Aristotelian doctrines of art as imitation. Indeed, the contrast between Langer's description of music as a symbolic language and Kivy's attempts to vindicate its representational properties recalls nothing so much as the idealist—realist conflict faced and resolved by the writers discussed in the previous chapter.

That this should be so is extremely important, since it is essential to the theories both of Langer and of the German idealists that human consciousness progresses from one era to the next, finding not only new answers to old questions but new questions to formulate. In Langer's view, one such step is defined by twentieth-century man's preoccupation with symbols — non-denotative, metaphorical linguistic formulations — and the mode of thinking which they represent. Music, if it is truly a metaphorical language, should thus have a unique appeal to modern man, just as the Romantic aestheticians considered it the most advanced form of artistic expression.

Why, then, has Beethoven not been succeeded by a host of composers with even more lasting and universal appeal? One possible answer is that the unique synthesis that he achieved was not determined by philosophical trends, but by purely musical ones, which Romantic aestheticians exploited to support their views of art, without ever understanding precisely what it was that Beethoven accomplished. If this is correct, then it is the critics we have studied, practicing musicians all, who really came to terms with the dilemma and adequately resolved it. What they did is extremely significant. They rejected — explicitly, in the case of A. B. Marx — the Romantic theories about music in favor of a view which was more in line with Romantic epistemology: with the theory of knowledge as it then existed, rather than as it might exist in some future, ideal world.

Does this mean that in order to understand Beethoven properly we must also accept the theories of expression and tone-painting advanced by his first critics? Arnold Schering believed so, and made a lengthy case in favor of poetic interpretation in his much-criticized book *Beethoven und die Dichtung*. Another possibility, which seems at first glance to hold more promise, is to suppose that Beethoven expressed his personality directly in his music, giving each work an autobiographical significance. Among recent Beethoven scholars, Maynard Solomon is most notable for explaining the evolution of the composer's style on the basis of influences from his life. More recently, the programmatic view of Beethoven's music has found an articulate exponent in Owen Jander, who claims to have found the original program of the second movement of the Fourth Piano Concerto in versions of the Orpheus story current in Beethoven's Vienna.[2]

The critics we have studied, however, were mostly reluctant to make either literary or autobiographical generalizations about Beethoven's work; Fröhlich was among the first to do so consistently, and he did not write until after Beethoven's death. This reluctance is easily explained. A host of writers from Rochlitz in 1798 to Eduard Hanslick 60 years later recognized the existence of extra-musical associations, but despaired of representing them precisely in words. A.B. Marx offers perhaps the most familiar solution to this problem in his Beethoven biography. After giving his own emotional interpretation of the Piano Sonata, Op. 2, no. 1, he claims that it is unimportant whether Beethoven himself thought of the music in precisely those terms – the technical resemblances between the themes, at least, are beyond dispute. Marx, though, unlike Hanslick, was not suggesting that we should dispense with extra-musical reference as a guide to analysis; as we have seen, he believed passionately in this kind of interpretation. How did he reconcile this belief with the apparently opposite conviction of the unimportance of Beethoven's intent?

For an answer to this question we must turn once again, but with a newfound skepticism, to a study of the philosophical context in which Marx's ideas originated. One writer has claimed that the primary goal of German philosophy at the turn of the nineteenth century was to reconcile Kantian moral freedom, with its severe restrictions on metaphysical perception, with the intuitive emotionalism of the so-called *Sturm und Drang*.[3] Kant's moral laws were subjective, in the sense that they originated with the individual, but they were also 'inter-subjective', since Kant believed them, paradoxically, to be common to all people. Likewise, for Kant, perception still had an object, despite the fact that the very laws

146

by which perception operated were the product of the individual mind. Thus Kant preserved one essential aspect of Cartesian epistemology: the belief in the possibility of a subject−object relationship in cognition. It was precisely this relationship that Hegel attempted to undermine in the *Phenomenology of Spirit*. To simplify and clarify Hegel's reasoning: each object in his system strove to become a subject, and, this accomplished, the entire relationship was raised to a new level of significance, as the distinction between the individual and the outside world became increasingly unimportant. Fichte, too, in abolishing the Kantian 'Ding an Sich', attempted to give further weight to subjective perception and undermine the significance of the subject−object relationship. What these thinkers show us is that no monumental change can take place overnight, and that the obsession of the later Hegelians with the operation of a 'subject' in human history − Hegel's 'Weltgeist' or Schopenhauer's 'will' − began by taking for granted that there was a perceived dichotomy between the individual and the object of contemplation.

In music, this dichotomy had led to the belief that composers represented objective affections, which, like Kant's moral laws, were universally comprehensible. A Kantian aesthetic of music, then, would be one which placed the responsibility for creating these affections in the personality of the composer, but nevertheless asserted their universal validity. That Kant did not express himself in precisely these terms in the *Critique of Judgement* is unimportant, since, as has often been recognized, Kant knew little either about music or about the theories of musical aesthetics which were current at the time he wrote; A. B. Marx, as we have seen, rejected even Hegel's views on musical aesthetics, and apparently dismissed out of hand the pure formalism which later writers have found foreshadowed in Kant's third critique.

Unfortunately, a disproportionate amount of attention has been given to other idealists, like Tieck and Wackenroder, who were also not professional musicians, and who claimed that musical emotion was too complex to be described in objective terms. Marx, who certainly knew more about music than any of these philosophers, seems to have believed that Beethoven's personality was relatively unimportant precisely because the emotions he represented in music were universal ones, originating in each person's experience but nevertheless common to all people. Fröhlich, likewise, seems to have found the expression of Beethoven's personality in the Ninth Symphony valid only insofar as it dealt with universal feelings and experiences.

These writers, then, unlike Tieck and Wackenroder, believed that the experience of Beethoven's music could be described in words precisely because Beethoven had made himself a metaphor for the 'subject' which moves music history, while at the same time referring to experiences that everyone could recognize. The problem of the vagueness of musical emotion, then, was solved by these writers through the belief that Beethoven's music was rooted in the old affections, but at the same time transfigured them, making them representative of the universality of individual experience.

If other composers were less readily understood, this was perhaps because their music referred to experiences more individual in nature, or, conversely, failed to transcend the objective vocabulary of the old affections. To make his music completely successful, a composer must not simply create a symbolic language, but must make the emotions and experiences which that language symbolized clear to at least the majority of a sympathetic audience, who would recognize in them one individual's expression of common human experience. The position of Beethoven's first critics can thus be seen to have links to both the ideas first advanced by Langer in *Philosophy in a New Key* and the more recent apologies for Aristotelian emotional theories offered by Kivy in *The Corded Shell*. I do not mean to reject either Langer or Kivy out of hand, but simply to suggest that neither individually offers an adequate explanation for Beethoven's greatness — of why this particular composer has been judged both by his contemporaries and by posterity to have succeeded where others failed. In this respect, then, neither writer provides a complete explanation for the 'musical' dimension of art mentioned above.

How, then, are the insights of Beethoven's first critics to be explained in terms relevant to the modern world? First, we must recognize that Langer and Kivy, with their divergent views of musical expression, stand as part of a tradition of 'hermeneutic' interpretation which can be traced back to the enormous influence of Dilthey's thoughts about art on late nineteenth-century German musicians. In *Beiträge zur musikalischen Hermeneutik*, a series of essays ably edited by Carl Dahlhaus, various writers explain how Dilthey's ambiguous comments on musical expression and meaning led to theories as diverse as those of Schering, Hermann Kretzschmar, and the later hermeneutic writers.[4] Schering, as already seen, recommended interpreting each work of Beethoven according to a literary model, while Kretzschmar endorsed a full-scale return to the *Affektenlehre* of the eighteenth century.

The distinction between these two theories may be blurred, since both authors believed that they were reformulating musical aesthetics in 'symbolic' terms. Nevertheless, Kretzschmar, who emphasized the vague and indeterminate nature of eighteenth-century affections, stands at the opposite pole from Schering, who apparently believed that Beethoven's musical language had to be clarified programmatically in order to be understood. Both approaches are described by Dahlhaus as outdated on the first page of the volume just cited, but many later writers in this tradition have either sought a precise, 'literary' interpretation of music or have preferred a symbolist approach, while leaving the task of precise definition to purely musical analysis.[5]

It is thus doubly important that the first critics of Beethoven tried to link what would now be called symbolist and descriptive approaches to his music, both in the interpretive and in the analytical sections of their reviews. Thus Marx, despite the sectionalized, somewhat static view of musical form which he set forth in his theoretical writings, is able in the biography to link form effortlessly with the dynamic, psychological processes which he finds in the Fifth Symphony. Likewise, Hoffmann links his metaphysical fantasies to explicit details of the musical structure. The almost total failure of modern writers to recognize this aspect of Hoffmann's review is a result of our changing priorities, which lead us today to place as much emphasis on symbolism *per se* as the Romantic writers placed on the synthesis of opposing ideas.

Modern theorists, as well as historians and aestheticians, thus have much to learn from these reviews. It has been claimed that the complex relationships between surface details and structure in tonal works revealed by modern analysis make the expressive approach to performing and understanding music obsolete.[6] If the critics studied above were correct, a similar correspondence between foreground and background (to use the Schenkerian terms) can be found in musical expression. Far from presenting an either−or choice, descriptions of music as 'expressive of' (Kivy) particular emotions may be made to complement those which see emotion in general as symbolized by the coherence and unity of an entire composition. Something which complements in reverse the modern 'organicist' approach to analysis is thus implicit in the writings of these critics: a linguistic process which begins with a series of interconnected images and proceeds to a metaphorical whole, largely through the process known as 'thematic transformation'.

The importance of this process is perhaps obscured by the modern prejudice against purely thematic analysis in the music of this period. Descriptions of it, however, are by no means unique to music criticism in the first decades of the nineteenth century. In an illuminating essay, M. H. Abrams defines what he terms the 'greater Romantic lyric': a pattern of composition which ends 'where it began, at the outer scene, but with an altered mood and deepened understanding which is the result of the intervening meditation'.[7] As an example of this type of poem we might take Keats' *Ode on a Grecian Urn*, which begins by defining its subject and proceeds to raise that subject to a new level of symbolic meaning before its reappearance in the finale stanza. When Hoffmann suggests that the experience of listening to Beethoven's Fifth Symphony is a constant experience of growth, he might be implying a similar transformation in our understanding of the thematic material. This speculation is rendered more plausible by the fact that he defines the theme of the Fifth Symphony both as neutral punctuation and as the key to the deepest unity of the work; the latter understanding, he implies, will emerge only after repeated hearings.

This resemblance between poetic and musical procedures is not simply a manifestation of *Zeitgeist*. Although the Beethoven symphonies were written at about the same time as the Romantic lyrics to which Abrams refers, similar examples of thematic transformation incorporated into sonata form can be found as early as Haydn's Symphony no. 44 of 1772 or as late as Schoenberg's fourth String Quartet of 1936, to name only two particularly striking examples. Both of these works depend, for their full emotional import, on the opening motive being not only reheard, but also reinterpreted, when it reappears later in the first movement. Clearly, then, this is not just a case of tracing extra-musical influences on Beethoven's style; if anything, the chronological scope of the examples just cited would show that the process described by Abrams not only began as a purely musical phenomenon, but also was far more important to the history of music than to that of any literary genre. Perhaps the eagerness of early Romantic poet–philosophers to impose their interpretations upon music simply shows a recognition on their part that musical processes – particularly music's ability to transform neutral or stereotyped material, like the themes of the Beethoven symphonies, into metaphorical symbols – were tending more quickly than those of the other arts toward an exemplification of the goals of post-Kantian thought.

The Romantic aestheticians' insistence on the symbolic value of music, in other words, can only be explained if it be realized that Hegel and his followers anticipated an advanced state of consciousness in which the work of art was transcended by other means of representing concrete reality. It is no wonder that practicing music critics did not embrace this view, tending instead to the contrary assertion that the language of music became more concrete with the passage of time. This was simply a recognition of fact – namely that as music 'progressed' into the nineteenth century the complex system of expressive figures inherited from the baroque gave way to a preference for a type of thematic material which was at once simpler, more striking, and more popular in its appeal.

Conclusion

Thematic and emotional analysis, in other words, may still be able to convey as much of a composer's intent as do the purely structural analyses common to much current music theory. They may also, in the long run, be necessary to define that 'musical' element in Beethoven which stems neither from expression nor from structure but from the mysterious combination of the two. In other words, analysis along the lines studied in this book provides a foundation from which constructive criticism of Beethoven's music, and of other works of the classic and Romantic periods, is possible. Such criticism need not reject the insights of more recent analytical techniques, but can actually reinforce them.

For example, in the first 'Razumovsky' Quartet, Op. 59, no.1, no thematically sensitive analyst can deny that the main themes of the first movement bear a motivic resemblance to one another, or that the 'distillations' of the thematic material which occur toward the end of the first and fourth movements provide a psychological link which unifies the entire work. The transformation of the quartet's opening statement by the cello to the triumphant proclamation of the same theme in full harmony fully three octaves higher in the coda (m.348) may sound in technical terms like rather a crude trick, but there can be no denying that it works emotionally, providing the unity which a critic like Hoffmann would seek in the otherwise uniquely gigantic structure of the first movement.

At the same time, the barest reduction will reveal that this statement is the key to the structure not only of the movement, but of the quartet as a whole. It is a singular feature of the first movement that at no point does it contain a harmonically supported resolution of B-flat to A. This same lack of resolution of the dominant seventh is projected at the background level, where an octave rise in the uppermost register which begins at m.16 is completed with the C at m.386, while the dissonant seventh is never adequately resolved in this register before the conclusion of the movement.

The second movement is a 'composing out' of this unresolved B-flat: a fact which explains the importance played by B-flat to A as a tonal relationship in this highly rhythmic scherzo. At m.213 the resolution arrives in the correct register, but it does not receive the proper harmonic support, being the tonic of an A minor triad which is entirely placed in the highest register of the quartet. At the climax of the slow movement, which also arrives on a high-register A, the violin and cello are correctly spaced for a resolution, but the implicit tonic at this point is C, so the instruments form a diminished seventh chord which can only be read as a collection of appoggiaturas to V/V in F minor (m.109). Only at the conclusion of the finale, which presents a similar dramatization of the main theme of that movement to that which was heard in the first, is the B-flat resolved in a manner which is both harmonically and registrally correct (mm. 313–15). These transformations of the main themes of the two outer movements, both of which have an audible expressive effect on the short range, thus provide the key to the background structure, and hence the unity, of the entire four-movement cycle.

Here, then, is an illustration on the broadest scale of the sort of correspondence which our critics constantly tried to trace. The restatement of the theme in the first movement is a moment of key expressive significance – the off-beat accents, double stops, and extreme registral spacing would make this clear even if it were heard in isolation. At the same time, it provides the consummation of the process of motivic transformation which takes place throughout the movement, and thus gives this process a symbolic significance. Conversely, however, it makes audible one crucial phase of the background structure of the entire work, thus justifying our critics' belief that otherwise abstract structure could be resolved into thematic details which invite description in emotional terms.

Ultimately, then, what may be learned from studying the first critics of Beethoven is extremely important to the dilemma of contemporary musicology. Joseph Kerman has frequently pointed out that criticism, analysis, and the documentary study of music history seem to be at loggerheads more often than not. In Beethoven's time, the first two approaches, at least, stood in a complementary relationship which clearly shows that neither was conceivable without the other to support it.

An important reminder which comes from Beethoven's first critics is the relative humility with which they approached Beethoven's music: they did not call attention to their own achievement, and it has consequently been underestimated by most contemporary scholars. Perhaps the bare hints found in the above discussion are more than speculation, and reveal in terms appreciable to those same scholars the unique understanding of Beethoven's music achieved by those who shared his musical culture, its precepts, and its unique insights.

Index of reviews cited

Op. 10: Three sonatas for piano
AMZ II, no. 21 (Oct. 19, 1799), col. 25.

Op. 11: Trio for piano, clarinet and cello in B-flat
AMZ I, no. 33 (May 15, 1799), col. 541.

Op. 12: Three sonatas for violin and piano
AMZ I, no. 36 (June 5, 1799), col. 570.

Op. 13: Sonata for piano in C minor ('Pathétique')
AMZ II, no. 21 (Feb. 19, 1800), col. 373.

Op. 21: Symphony no. 1 in C
Berlioz, *A travers chants*.
Revue musicale, April 16, 1831, p. 84.

Op. 23: Sonata in A major for violin and piano
AMZ IV, no. 35 (May 26, 1802), col. 569.

Op. 24: Sonata in F major for violin and piano ('Spring')
Ibid.

Op. 26: Sonata in A-flat major for piano
AMZ IV, no. 40 (June 30, 1802), col. 650.

Op. 27: Two sonatas 'quasi una fantasia' for piano
Ibid.

Op. 28: Sonata in D major for piano ('Pastoral')
AMZ V, no. 11 (Dec. 18, 1802), col. 188.

Op. 29: Quintet in C major for strings
BAMZ V, no. 47 (Nov. 13, 1828), p. 445.

Op. 30, no. 1: Sonata for violin and piano in A major
AMZ VI, no. 5 (Nov. 2, 1803), col. 77.

Op. 35: Variations and Fugue for piano ('Eroica')
AMZ VI, no. 21 (Feb. 22, 1804), col. 388.

Op. 36: Symphony no. 2 in D major
Berlioz, *A travers chants*.
Journal des débats, June 1, 1827.

Op. 37: Concerto no. 3 in C minor for piano
AMZ VII, no. 28 (April 10, 1805), col. 445.

Op. 48: Six songs on texts by Gellert
AMZ VI, no. 36 (June 6, 1804), col. 608.

Op. 55: Symphony no. 3 in E-flat major ('Eroica')
AMZ IX, no. 21 (Feb. 18, 1807), col. 321.
Berlioz, *A travers chants.*
Journal des débats, Mar. 19, 1828.
Revue musicale III (1828), pp. 145–9.

Op. 57: Sonata in F minor for piano ('Appassionata')
AMZ IX, no. 27 (April 1, 1807), col. 433.

Op. 60: Symphony no. 4 in B-flat major
Berlioz, *A travers chants.*
Journal des débats, Mar. 11, 1830.
Revue musicale VII (1830), pp. 116–18.

Op. 62: Overture to Collin's *Coriolan*
AMZ XIV, no. 32 (Aug. 5, 1812), col. 519.

Op. 66: Variations for cello and piano on 'Ein Mädchen oder Weibchen' from
Mozart's *Die Zauberflöte*
AMZ I, no. 23 (Mar. 6, 1798), col. 366.

Op. 67: Symphony no. 5 in C minor
AMZ XII, nos. 40 and 41 (July 4 and 11, 1810), cols. 630, 652.
Revue musicale, 1828, pp. 274, 313, 343.
Berlioz, *A travers chants.*

Op. 68: Symphony no. 6 in F major ('Pastoral')
AMZ XII, no. 16 (Jan. 17, 1810), col. 241.
Journal des débats, Mar. 24, 1829; Mar. 30, 1830.
Revue musicale, Mar., 1829, p. 173.
Berlioz, *A travers chants.*

Op. 70: Two trios for piano, violin, and cello
AMZ XV, no. 9 (Mar. 3, 1813), col. 141.

Op. 72: *Fidelio*
AMZ XVII, nos. 21, 22, 23, 24 and 25 (May 24, May 31, June 7, June 14 and
June 28, 1815).

Op. 74: Quartet in E-flat major for strings ('Harp')
AMZ XIII, no. 21 (May 22, 1811), col. 349.

Op. 84: Incidental music to Goethe's *Egmont*
AMZ XV, no. 29 (July 21, 1813), col. 473.

Op. 86: Mass in C major
AMZ XV, nos. 24 and 25 (July 16 and 23, 1813), cols. 389, 409.

Op. 91: *Wellington's Sieg bei Vittoria*
AMZ XVIII, no. 15 (April 10, 1816), col. 241.

Op. 92: Symphony no. 7 in A major
AMZ XVIII, no. 48 (Nov. 27, 1816), col. 817.

WAMZ I, no.4 (Jan. 23, 1817), p.25.
Journal des débats, Mar. 9, 1829.
Revue musicale, 1829, pp.131, 235, 326.
Berlioz, *A travers chants*.

Op. 93: Symphony no.8 in F major
AMZ XX, no.9 (Mar. 4, 1818), col. 161.
WAMZ II, no.3 (Jan. 17, 1818), p.17.
Revue musicale, Feb. 25, 1832, p.28; Mar. 10, 1832, p.45.
Berlioz, *A travers chants*.

Op. 96: Sonata in G major for violin and piano
AMZ XIX, no.13 (Mar. 26, 1817), col. 228.
WAMZ III, no.79 (Oct. 2, 1819), p.633.

Op. 97: Piano Trio in B-flat major ('Archduke')
WAMZ I, nos.16 and 17 (April 17 and 24, 1817), pp.125, 139.

Op. 101: Sonata in A major for piano
AMZ XIX, no.40 (Oct. 1, 1817), col. 686.

Op. 102: Two sonatas for cello and piano
AMZ XX, no.45 (Nov. 11, 1818), col. 792.
BAMZ I, no.48, p.409.

Op. 108: 25 Scottish songs
BAMZ I, no.18, p.159.

Op. 109: Sonata in E major for piano
AMZ XXVI, no.14 (April 1, 1824), col. 213.

Op. 110: Sonata in A-flat major for piano
Ibid.
BAMZ I, no.10 (Mar. 10, 1824), p.87.

Op. 111: Sonata in C minor for piano.
Ibid.
BAMZ I, no.11 (Mar. 17, 1824), p.95.

Op. 112: Choral setting for Goethe's *Meeresstille und glückliche Fahrt*
AMZ XXIV, no.41 (Oct. 9, 1822), col. 674.
BAMZ I, no.46 (Nov. 17, 1824), p.391.

Op. 118: Trio 'Tremate empi, tremate'
AMZ XXVIII, no.30 (July 26, 1826), col. 494.

Op. 119: 11 bagatelles for piano
BAMZ I, no.14, p.128.

Op. 121: *Opferlied*
AMZ XXVII, no.44 (Nov. 2, 1825), col. 740.

Op. 122: *Bundeslied*
Ibid.
BAMZ III, no.5, p.34.

Op. 123: Mass in D (*Missa Solemnis*)
  Caecilia IX (1828), pp. 22, 27, 217.

Op. 125: Symphony no. 9 in D minor ('Choral')
  BAMZ III, no. 47 (Nov. 22, 1826), p. 375.
  Caecilia VIII (1828), pp. 231, 256; IX (1828), p. 217.
  Revue musicale, April 2, 1831, p. 69.
  Berlioz, *A travers chants.*

Op. 127: Quartet in E-flat major for strings
  BAMZ IV, no. 4, p. 25.

Op. 131: Quartet in C-sharp minor for strings
  AMZ XXX, no. 30 (July 23, 1828), col. 485.
  Caecilia IX (1828), p. 45.

Op. 132: Quartet in A minor for strings
  Ibid.

Op. 135: Quartet in F major for strings
  Ibid.

WoO 46: Variations for cello and piano on 'Bei Männern welche Liebe fühlen' from Mozart's *Die Zauberflöte*
  AMZ V, no. 11 (Dec. 18, 1802), col. 188.

WoO 72: Variations for piano on 'Une fièvre brûlante' from Grétry's *Richard Coeur de Lion*
  AMZ I, no. 23 (Mar. 6, 1798), col. 366.

WoO 73: Variations for piano on 'La stessa, la stessissima' from Salieri's *Falstaff*
  AMZ I, no. 38 (June 19, 1799), col. 607.

WoO 80: Variations for piano on an original theme in C minor
  AMZ X, no. 6 (Nov. 4, 1807), col. 94.

APPENDIX B

Originals of quotes given in translation

p. 7   Dass Herr van Beethoven ein sehr fertiger Klavierspieler ist, ist bekannt, und wenn es nicht bekannt wäre, konnte mann es aus diesen Veränderungen vermuten. Ob er aber ein eben so glücklicher Tonsetzer sey, ist eine Frage, die, nach vorliegenden Proben zu urtheilen, schwerer bejahet werden dürfet.

Nein, es ist wahr, Hr. v. B. mag phantasieren können, aber gut zu variien versteht er nicht.

p. 8   Seine Fülle von Ideen ... veranlasst ihn aber noch zu oft, Gedanken wild aufeinander zu häufen und sie mitunter vermittelst einer etwas bizarren Manier dergestalt zu gruppiren, dass dadurch nicht selten eine dunkle Künstlichkeit oder eine künstliche Dunkelheit hervorgebracht wird.

p. 10   Der originelle, feurige und kühne Geist dieses Komponisten, der schon in seinen frühern Werken dem aufmerksamern nicht entgehen konnte, der aber wahrscheinlich darum nicht überall die freundlichste Aufnahme fand, weil er zuweilen selbst unfreundlich, wild, düster und trübe daherstürmte, wird sich jetzt immer mehr klar, fängt immer mehr an, alles Uebermaas zu verschmähen, und tritt, ohne von seinem Charakter zu verlieren, immer wohlgefälliger hervor.

p. 10   Weniger Gebildeten, oder auch denen, die an Musik nichts, als ein leichtes Amusement haben wollen, werden auch diese Werke vergebens angepriesen werden.

p. 12   Wenn dem vorletzten Sechszehntheile im zweiten Takte des Largo in dieser langsamen Bewegung der F moll-Akkord zum Grunde läge, wäre es richtiger und zuverlässig besser. Die strenge Analogie zwischen diesem und den vierten Takte, wo die Oberstimme mit jener ähnlich in Terzen fortschreitet, kann das Herbe unmöglich versüssen, was in dem angeführten Takttheile so fühlbar wird.

p. 13   Dies Konzert ist in Absicht auf Geist und Effekt eins der vorzüglichsten unter allen, die nur jemals geschrieben worden sind, und (ich) versuche nun aus dem Werke selbst zu erklären, woher dieser Effekt komme, in wiefern derselbe durch die Materie und deren Konstruction erreicht wird.

p. 13   Jetzt scheint es dies Eigenheit und der reiche Gehalt des Werkes zu verlangen, dass man auch einmall zunächst seinen technischen Theil ernsthaft und fest ins Auge fasse, und von dieser, so wie von der angrenzenden mechanischen Seite her, dem Verf. genau, Schritt vor Schritt folge – ein Verfahren, zu welchem der Gründlichkeit der Ausarbeitung dieser Komposition selbst auffordert, und welches, wenn

157

es einer Rechtfertigung bedürfte, diese in dem Nützen finden würde, den junge Künstler an solchen Analysen ziehen, und in dem erhöheten Vergnügen, das gebildete Liebhaber hernach bey dem Anhören des Werks selbst empfinden können. Vielleicht fasset dann einmal jemand alles das zusammen und führet es auf den Mittelpunkt; geschähe das aber auch nicht mehr unbestimmte, zweifelhafte Gefühl ein genügendes Urtheil ab, das sodann allmählich in die allgemeine Meinung übergehet und so den Stand der Kunstwerks, seinen Einfluss in das Ganze, sein Schicksaal bestimmt.

p. 14   Den ersten Satz, ein Allegro con brio in C moll, fangen die Saiteninstrumente mit diesem Gedanken in Unisono an, welcher dann von Hoboen, Fagotten und Hörnern auf der zum Grunde liegende Dominante wiederhollt wird: so wie denn im Verfolg des Ganzen dieser Gedanke und dies Rhythmus, bald ganz, bald Theilweise, den Figuren u. dgl. zum Grunde liegt und ausgeführt wird. Besonders glücklich hat B. die wenigen Noten des dritten Takts fast durch den ganzen Satz, oft sehr unerwartet, angebracht, und dadurch die heterogenste einander genähert, zusammengehalten und verschmolzen.

p. 14   Ganz überraschend, durchaus neu u. schön ist es z. B., dass im Verfolg des 2ten Theils, wo des Ausführens der frühern Ideen fast zu viel zu werden anfängt, plötzlich ein ganz neuer, nicht gehörter Gesang von den Blasinstrumenten aufgefasst und episodisch behandelt wird – wodurch denn nicht nur die Summe des Angenehmen und seine Mannigfaltigkeit vermehrt, sondern der Zuhörer auch erfrischt wird, dem Verf. wieder gern zu folgen, wenn er zu den verlassenen Heimath zurückkehrt, und mit noch reicherer Kunst die Hauptgedanken einkleidet und durchführt ... Schon aus diesem Wenigen wird man abnehmen, dass dieses Allegro, ohngeachtet seiner Lange, mit einer Sorgsamkeit zur Einheit zusammengehalten ist, die Bewunderung abnöthigt.

p. 15   Die Aufhaltung des ersten volligen Schlusses in die Tonika durch zwey und dreyssig Takte reizt und spannet immer höher, und fesselt den Zuhörer unwiderstehlich. Ein gleiches bewirkt B. ganz vollkommen, unter andern, auch in den Stellen, wo er wieder in das Thema einleitet, und dann gewöhnlich durch die chromatische Tonleiter eine oder mehrere Oktaven hindurch bis zur kleinen 7 oder 9 aufsteigt, den Zuhörer aber noch nicht zur Beruhigung kommen lässt, sondern ihn in Spannung erhält, bis das Thema völlig zu Ende ist.

p. 15   Kraftvoll und prächtig schliesst dies Allegro, und nun folgt ein grosser Trauermarsch, aus C moll, im Zweyvierteltakt, den Rec. ohne Bedenklichkeit, wenigstens von Seiten der Erfindung und des Entwurfs, für B.s Triumph erklären möchte. Es lässt sich vielleicht denken, dass Komponisten von Talent, vielen Studium und unermüdlichem Fleiss, etwas hervor brachten, das Arbeiten, wie jener erste Satz, an die Seite gesetzt werden könnte: Stücke, wie dies zweyte aber, empfängt, gebiert, und erziehet kein Mensch in solche Vollkommenheit, ohne wahres Genie.

p. 20   Aber alles das wird durch den gewaltigen Feuergeist, der in diesem Kolossalen Produkt wehet, durch den Reichthum an neuen Ideen und die fast durchaus originelle Behandlung derselben, so wie auch durch die

Appendix B

Tiefe der Kunstgelehrsamkeit, so weit überwogen, dass man dem Werke das Horoskop stellen kann, es werde bleiben und mit immer neuem vergnügen gehört werden, wenn tausend eben jetzt gefeyerte Modesachen längst zu Grabe getragen sind.

p. 21
So öffnet uns auch Beethovens Instrumentalmusik das Reich des Ungeheueren und Unermesslichen. Glühende Strahlen schiessen durch dieses Reiches tiefe Nacht, und wir werden Riesenschatten gewahr, die auf- und abwogen, enger und enger uns einschliessen, und alles in uns vernichten, nur nicht den Schmerz der unendlichen Sehnsucht, in welcher jede Lust, die, schnell in jauchzenden Tönen emporgestiegen, hinsinkt und untergeht, und nur in diesem Schmerz, der, Liebe, Hoffnung, Freude in sich verzehrend, aber nicht zerstörend, unsre Brust mit einem vollstimmigen Zusammenklänge aller Leidenschaften zersprengen will, leben wir fort und sind entzückte Geisterseher.

p. 23
Das erste Allegro, 2/4 Takt C moll, fängt mit dem nur aus zwei Takten bestehenden Hauptgedanken, der in der Folge, mannigfach gestaltet, immer wieder durchblickt, an. Im zweiten Takt eine Fermate; dann eine Wiederholung jenes Gedankens einen Ton tiefer, und wieder eine Fermate; beide Male nur Saiteninstrumente und Klarinetten. Noch ist nicht einmal die Tonart entschieden; der Zuhörer vermutet Es dur. Die zweite Violine fängt wieder den Hauptgedanken an, im zweiten Takt entscheidet nun der Grundton C, den Violoncelle und Fagotte anschlagen, die Tonart C moll, indem Bratsche und erste Violine in Nachahmungen eintreten, bis diese endlich dem Hauptgedanken zwei Takte anreihet, die dreimal wiederholt (zum letztenmal mit einfallendem ganzen Orchester) und in eine Fermate auf der Dominante ausgehend, des Zuhörers Gemüte das Unbekannte, Geheimnisvolle ahnen lassen.

p. 23
Nach dieser Fermate imitieren, in der Tonika verweilend, den Hauptgedanken Violinen und Bratsche, während der Bass dann und wann eine Figur, die jenen Gedanken nachahmt, anschlägt, bis ein immer steigender Zwischensatz, der aufs neue jene Ahnung stärker und dringender aufregt, zu einem Tutti leitet, dessen Thema wieder den rhythmischen Verhalt des Hauptgedankens hat und ihm innig verwandt ist. Der Sexten-Akkord auf dem Grundton D, bereitet die verwandte Dur-Tonart Es vor, in welcher das Horn wieder den Hauptgedanken nachahmt. Die erste Violine greift nun ein zweites Thema auf, welches zwar melodiös ist, aber doch dem Charakter ängstlicher, unruhvoller Sehnsucht, den der ganze Satz ausspricht, getreu bleibt.

p. 24
Das nun eintretende Hauptthema des Allegro trägt den Charakter einer nicht zu stillenden Unruhe, einer nicht zu befriedigenden Sehnsucht in sich ... Die Transposition dieses Themas einen Ton tiefer (Bmoll), gleich nach der Taktpause, ist auch unerwartet und steigert die Spannung, in die man durch die ersten Takte versetzt wurde ... alles ist mit tiefem Sinn zur höchsten tragischen Wirkung, und zur höchsten spannenden Erwartung dessen, was uns der Aufflug des geheimnisvollen Vorhangs enthüllen wird, vereinigt.

159

p. 25   So wie der Sturmwind die Wolken verjagt, mit im Augenblick wechseln-den Lichtern und Schatten − wie sich dann im rastlosen Jagen und Treiben Gestalten bilden, verfliessen und wieder bilden, so eilt nach der zweiten Fermate der Satz unaufhaltsam fort.

p. 28   Sie sind die Erzeugnisse eines tiefsinnigen Geistes; und doch verräth nichts ihr Entstehen: man lebt, denselben hingegeben, in einer eignen unsichtbarne Welt, und nur das Wiedereintreten der Gedanken in die Wirklichkeit nach dem Verschwinden seiner Töne, erinnert an den Künstler und die Kunst. Scheint uns in Haydn's Werken die Phantasie dem regelnden Verstande oft noch unterworfen, so stehen beyde in Mozarts Tonstücken in so unauflöslicher Verbindung, dass sie fast nirgends einzeln und getrennt erscheinen.

p. 30   Auch wollen wir eingestehen, dass die Musik dieser Oper für viele weiche Naturen nervenangreifend sey. Doch hörten wir dies auch von einigen, die einen Shakespeare und seine gigantischen Werke herrlich nennen, der die herbsten Dissonanzen des Lebens in den vielstimmigen Chor seiner grossen Dramen gefügt hat.

p. 39   Anwendung der vollständigsten Kenntniss aller Muskeln und Körper-theile, der Luftperspective, der Farbenmischung u. s. w. machen das Bild noch nicht zum Kunstwerk, und eben so wenig wird ein Tonstück ein solches, weil es vielleicht alle denkbaren contrapunk-tischen und technischen Seltenheiten in sich schliesst ... So wie selbst dem geübtesten Partiturenleser das blosse Lesen der Noten ... den vollständigen Genuss eines Tonstückes nicht gewähren, zu einem treffenden Finalurtheil über dasselbe nicht genügen kann, so reicht das schriftliche Citiren einzelner Stellen durch notenbeyspiele, zur Ueberzeugung der Andern, denen das Werk fremd ist, auch gewiss nicht hin. Man muss schlechterdings das Ganze im Zusammenhang und geistvoll ausgeführt hören. − Ein gewisses unerklärbares Etwas reisst uns alsdann vielleicht hin, sogar schwere Sünden gegen die musikalischen Gesetze nicht zu beachten oder zu verzeihen; so wie hinwiederum die grösste Regelrechtigkeit und technische Kunst, die beym Lesen, hochlich erfreuten, beym Hören, bisweilen allen Werth einbüssen.

p. 41   Jeder, der den schweren Weg vom ersten Versuche bis zu einer nur leidlichen Geburt gemacht hat, wird wissen, dass es eine Augen − und eine Ohren-Musik giebt; dass oft, was in der Partitur sich ganz herrlich ausnimmt, in der Ausführung gar keinen Effect macht, und so umgekehrt. Nach und nach nun wurde Beethoven und musste den umständen nach werden − ein Augencomponist.

p. 42   Der letzte Satz ... spielt völlig in den unglückseligen Wohnungen derer, die vom Himmel gestürzt sind. Es ist als ob die Geister der Tiefe ein Fest des Hohnes über Alles, was Menschenfreude heisst, feyerten. Riesenstark tritt die gefährliche Schaar auf und zerreist das menschliche Herz und zergraust den Götterfunken mit wildärmendem ungeheuerm Spott.

p. 47   Was wollte Beethoven? was konnte er geben? Irgend eine Komposition von grosser, grossartiger Gestaltung? So wurden ihm unsere Aesthetiker gerathen haben, nämlich die jenigen alten und neuen Datums, die der Musik nichts als Formenspiel, oder nichts als höchst allgemeine Anregung unbestimmtbarer Stimmungen als Aufgabe beimessen, weil sie unfähig sei, 'das Konkrete auszusprechen'. Beethoven war anderer ansicht. Als Künstler hatte er mit lebensleeren Abstraktionen nichts zu schaffen; Leben zu schaffen, Leben aus seinem Leben, war sein Beruf, wie aller Künstler. Der Künstler weiss, was seine Kunst vermag, er vor allen, er allein.

pp. 47–8   Ich habe mich versprochen; nur auf die Benützung einer Figur aus dem ersten Thema wollte ich Sie Seite 17 aufmerksam machen, unter der die Triolenfigur der Violen und Violoncelle in Oktaven voll in die weiche Klarinetten-Fagottlage hineinbraust, die Bässe den Grundton in ruhigen Pulsen wiederholen, und in der weiten Quinte, aber tief drunten, die Hörner dröhnen, bis es heller, wie goldenes Sonnenlicht auf Felshöh'n, hineinbricht, und alles jauchzet, alles, alles jauchzet, und in der Lebensluft des Seins die Hügel zu beben scheinen – und nun alles still wird in schöner Ebbe und Flut der Rührung und Freude.
'Aber woher deuten Sie das Alles?'
Ich besitze Salomo's Geheimniss der Vogelsprache.

p. 52   Unsre, unsre subjektive Einbildungskraft? – Man erwäge wohl, wen dies 'Eure' umfasst! nicht weniger, als alle grossen, von Euch selber dafür anerkannten Tonkünstler, von Bach und Händel ... bis auf unsre Tage. Sie Alle haben in ihrer Kunst jene Fähigkeit zu finden gewusst und darauf ihres Lebens Beruf gebaut. Oder – wenn Ihr es zu sagen wägt – sie Alle sind Thoren gewesen, Irrsinnige in ihrem eignen Berufsfelde.

p. 56   Unendlich, wie in der landschaftlichen und sonst aussermesslichen Natur, sind in der Instrumentenwelt die Gestaltungen und Kombinationen. Jetzt streift das Naturleben an menschlichen Ausdruck und Gesang und man ist versucht, menschliche Bedeutung und Gesangsprache herauszuhören, jetzt löset sich das Gestaltete in sein Element, den einfachen Klang auf; und die einfachste, verlorne Form bildet sich daran wieder in vielfacher Zusammenstellung zu einem grossen bedeutsamen Ganzen, wie Blatt an Blatt uns den Baum darstellt.

p. 57   Das er sein Werk nicht in diesem Sinne gefasst beweisen schon die Ansätze zur zehnten Symphonie. Ob ihn nicht demungeachtet dunkle Ahnungen vom Ende der Laufbahn angeweht, – wer kann es wissen? nur das ist sicher, das ein eigenthümlicher Grundklang aus dem Werk' uns anweht.

p. 57   Aus Beethovens letzten Tongedichten spricht bisweilen eine so zarte, innige, verklärende Rührung, dass man versucht ist, ein Vorgefühl baldiger Abberufung daraus zu vernehmen; es sind Träume und Ahnungen, die über die Saiten, wie bald über die Erde hinschweben, mit leisem Hauch – ob er Sehnsucht oder des Scheidens Seufzer? – ihnen Klang weckend und mit ihm dahin verschieden! – Kein Tonkünstler hat dergleichen gegeben; denn keiner wurde so von der Welt immer mehr losgebunden, von Liebe und Hass, Bewunderung und Kälte der Gesellschaft so mehr und mehr geschieden und in sich verschlossen, als Er, der gottbeseligte Einsiedler.

Appendix B

In diese Region seines Schaffens und Lebens (was desselbe ist) gehört auch der oben angekündigte Gesang, den sich doch ja kein fühlender Freund der Tonkunst länger vorenthalte. Man muss sich in den träumerischen Dehnungen der Klänge selbst mit verlieren, um die Seelensprache des Sängers zu verstehen.

p. 62   Das Allegretto ist die Klage eines Jünglings, der die Geliebte verloren hat. Die Zeit übte bereits ihr Recht; Verzweiflung ist gewichen und Resignation will walten. Man vernimmt den Ausdruck eines sanften Schmerzes. Gern ruft der Jüngling dann die Erinnerung an das genossene Glück zurück. Er schwelgt in ihr, aber sie erhöht seinen Schmerz; wilder Unmuth führt zur Abspannung, der sanftere Schmerz kehrt zurück, und verloren in ihn, sinkt er allmählig in Schlummer.

p. 72   Die Musik trägt das menschliche Herz auf ihren Ätherschwingen durch alle Wonnen und Schmerzen der Erde, – und durch alle Morgenröthen in den blauen Äther der Himmel – und zeigt ihm Wetterwolken von ferne, die heranzurücken drohen, – und lässt es die Tiefen der Unterwelt ahnen, ohne es in Schauder zu erdrücken, sondern trägt es wieder empor, sanft auf lieblichen Wolken in den Hain der Ruhe.

p. 72   Es gehört also wohl etwas anderes, Höheres und etwas Tieferes dazu, um ein anschauendes Subject für das Object der Kunst zu finden, nämlich die Höhe der Bildung und die Tiefe des Gemüths. Sind diese vorhanden, dann wird's auch keine Noth haben mit dem verstanden der musikalischen Mahlerey.

pp. 75–6   Desshalb tragen ... alle Tonstücke dieses Werks in ihrer ganzen Öconomie den Stempel des Riesenhaften, des Ungeheuern, desshalb reissen ferner seine gewaltsamen Tempo's den Hörenden wie in einem Stürme von einer Empfindung mit sich fort, und lassen ihn kaum zu sich selber kommen.

p. 76   Beethoven fühlte, dass bei einem solchen Aufwande verschiedenartiger Kräfte, bei einer solchen Anhäufung vieler, dem Anscheine nach heterogener Massen, noch eine grössere Gradation aller Potenzen herbeigeführt werden musste. – Er liess desshalb mitten in seinem Chor die turkische Musik eintreten.

p. 81   Die Musik an alles mahnend kommt, was gerade in uns verschlossen, starr, zweifelhaft, verworren, lastend liegt und auf Lösung und Versöhnung wartet, welche andere Sprachen, Kunstmittle und Lebens-Einflüsse vergebens versuchen. Jemehr ein Mensch sein Leben mit freywahltenden Gefühlen vor Starrheit bewahrt, je mehr er allem Daseyn durch Lebens-Poesie sich verwandt füllt, desto besser wird er Musik hören.

Gefühlen lassen sich aber als Text nicht denken, sie sollen von uns weder beim Künstler gesucht, noch uns selbst abgefragt werden, weil man ohne das Mittel der Reflexion fühlt.

p. 82   Zugleich wäre keine Zwitter-Art der Sinfonie, sondern jene gesteigerte hergestellt, wie wir sie in dem entwickelten Tonstücke Beethovens Genie's verdanken: – das feste rednerische Kunstgebilde, das wir in Haydns und Mozarts trefflichen Sinfonieen finden, würde zugleich Träger und Verkünder einer hohen poetischen Anschauung, in welcher sich das Wesen der Redekunst der Wortsprache mit jedem der Tonsprache verschmolzen hatte.

p. 89 Ob nun unser Meister gerade das dachte, gerade das wollte, lässt sich freylich nicht wohl bestimmt ausmitteln; dass aber, als er im Moment der Weihe die Ideen dazu von oben empfing, und mit voller Seele daran ging, weil eben der Drang von Innen ihn dazu bemüssigte, doch solche, oder doch gewiss ähnliche Gefühle in ihm aufdämmerten, könnte, bey genauer Kenntnis seines tiefen Gemuths, seines von reiner Religiösität erfüllten Herzens, fast unbedingt behauptet, ja mit beynahe logischer Evidenz erwiesen werden.

p. 96 Er lässt die beiden Chöre, sowohl den des Gesanges als jenen der Instrumente, wenn es nur thunlich ist, als selbständig auftreten, aufhebend durch seine Genialität die durch hundertjährige Praxis geheiligte Bestimmung: das die Instrumentation dem Gesange untergeordnet sein müsse. – Jedes Werk des grossen Schöpfers ist seiner Hände Preis; alles Geschaffene stimmt ein in den heiligen Jubel; warum soll dieser nicht von den einzelnen Instrumenten, so wie von dem ganzen Chöre dieser, unabhängig von Worten, ertönen können? ... Nicht allein bilden hier die Instrumente den Uebergang zu den folgenden Äusserungen frommen Dankes, ... sondern diese Gefühle sind auch vor dem Eintritte der Singstimmen von den Instrumenten so wahr entwickelt, dass der Hörer beim ausgesprochenen Wort nur die Bestärkung der in seiner Seele gebildeter Erregung und Anschauung erhält.

p. 97 Bei dem *Domine Deus* tritt der erste Gedanke mit seinem lebensvollen Schwung wieder ein. Und auch hier spricht sich eine Eigenthümlichkeit in der Behandlung des *Gloria* aus. So wie nämlich ein Hauptgefühl in allen einzelnen Stücken herrscht, zu welchem sich die, in den Nebenpartieen entwickelten Empfindungen, als untergeordnete Theile verhalten; so ist auch ein Hauptthema da, auf welches immer wieder zurückgeleitet wird, das also gleichsam der Lichtpunkt des Ganzen ist.

p. 100 Was übrigens die wunderliche Trompeten-Fanfarre, das eingemengte Rezitativ, der fugirte, den Ideen fluss nur störende Instrumental-Satz, ... was die dumpfen, unrhythmischen, bizarren Paukenschläge im Grunde bedeuten sollen, mag der liebe Himmel wissen. Keiner fühlte sich berufen, den Meister diessfalls zu befragen; er selbst erklärte sich niemals bestimmt darüber, und nahm somit das Mysterium mit ins Grab.

p. 107 Il serait difficile de trouver une composition musicale plus grandiose, plus pittoresque, plus riche en développements neufs et savants, que cette symphonie. Le troisième morceau surtout est un admirable chef-d'oeuvre. L'instrumentation en est indéfinissable tant elle est semée d'effets nouveaus: le rhythme, le chant, l'harmonie, tout est original, tout est jeté dans un moule qui n'appartient qu'au génie métaphysique et mystérieux de Beethoven. On retrouve bien de temps en temps les défauts de l'école allemande, plus de bizarrerie que de charme, plus de calcul que de vraie inspiration, et une décomposition trop subtile, trop analytique des phrases, même les moins chantantes; mais on est subjugé par la vigueur et l'enchaînement des pensées, par des contrastes aussi ingénieux qu'innatendus, par la grandeur vraiment imposante des masses harmoniques.

pp. 118–19 Si l'on fait attention au sens des vers de Schiller, on ne trouve rien dans l'expression musicale qui s'y rapporte; Beethoven en a même bouleversé l'ordre. Mais l'étonnement s'accroît encore lorsqu'après les premiers développements du choeur dans un mouvement grave, on rentre dans le domaine de l'instrumentation pour passer par tous les degrés de la fantaisie la plus bizarre jusqu'à la caricature de la thème principale en mouvement rapide, dont la célerité s'accroît d'un moment à l'autre.

p. 119 Beethoven était concentré dans ses idées musicales; il avait grandi, il avait vieilli s'occupant exclusivement de son art. Il ne connaissait que son dieu, la nature et la musique; aussi quand il avait saisi l'idée fondamentale d'un morceau, s'embarrassait-il peu du reste. Dans cet hymne sublime de Schiller, Beethoven est à la hauteur du poète tant qu'il est question de l'amitié et du divin créateur; mais du reste aucune trace de facture musicale en rapport avec les paroles, aucun égard à la prosodie, pas plus qu'aux allégories poétiques. C'est, à notre avis, sous ce point de vue seulement qu'on doit essayer d'analyser ce sublime ouvrage; il faut le juger uniquement comme oeuvre musicale, et comme tel il mérite l'admiration qu'il a excitée.

p. 121 Jamais personne n'avait eu l'idée de faire *parler* les basses et les contrebasses, ... Beethoven seul, dans sa symphonie en *ut mineur*, avait tenté cette innovation, mais ce n'était qu'un essai: tandis qu'ici le récitatif est largement établi; il a son rôle, c'est réellement une voix qui parle.

p. 122 Sans chercher ce que le compositeur a pu vouloir exprimer d'idées à lui personnelles, dans ce vaste poème musical, étude pour laquelle le champ des conjectures est ouvert a chacun, ... voyons si la nouveauté de la forme ne serait pas ici justifiée par une intention indépendante de toute pensée philosophique ou religieuse, ... par une intention, enfin, purement musicale et poétique.

p. 129 Es gibt keinen einfacheren Gedanken, als den, welchen der Meister dem ganzen Allegro zum Grunde legte und mit Bewunderung wird man gewahr, wie er alle Nebengedanken, alle Zwischensätze durch rhythmischen Verhalt jenem einfachen Thema so anzureihen wusste, dass sie nur dazu dienten, den Charakter des Ganzen, den jenes Thema nur andeuten könnte, immer mehr und mehr zu entfalten. Alle Sätze sind kurz, nur aus zwei, drei Takten bestehend, und noch dazu verteilt im beständigen Wechsel der Saiteninstrumente und der Blasinstrumente. Man sollte glauben, dass aus solchen Elementen nur etwas Zerstückeltes, schwer zu Fassendes entstehen könnte: aber statt dessen ist es eben jene Einrichtung des Ganzen, so wie auch die beständig aufeinander folgende Wiederholung der kurzen Sätze und einzelner Akkorde, welche das Gemut festhält in einer unnennbaren Sehnsucht. – Ganz davon abgesehen, dass die kontrapunktische Behandlung von tiefem Studium der Kunst zeugt, so sind es auch die Zwischensätze und die beständigen Anspielungen auf das Hauptthema, welche dartun, wie der Meister das Ganze mit allen den charaktervollen Zügen nicht allein im Geist auffasste, sondern auch durchdachte.

p. 130   Es ist die hohe Energie des Künstlers, mit dem einen Grundgedanken ein weites Lebensbild durchdrungen zu haben, und, wenn alles gesagt scheint, im Anhang aus demselben Grundmotiv eine neue Seite des grossen Lebensbildes, in der alle bisher vorgeführten Gestalten zu neuer Bedeutung sich aufrichten, zur Anschauung zu bringen.

p. 130   Le premier morceau est consacré à la peinture des sentiments désordonnés qui bouleversent une grande âme en proie au désespoir; non ce désespoir concentré, calme, qui emprunte les apparences de la résignation; non pas cette douleur sombre et muette de Roméo apprenant la mort de Juliette, mais bien la fureur terrible d'Othello recevant de la bouche d'Iago les calomnies empoisonnées qui le persuadent du crime de Desdemona.

p. 140   Die vollkommene Beruhigung des Gemüts, durch mehrere aneinander gereihte Schlussfiguren herbeigeführt, wird durch diese einzeln in Pausen angeschlagenen Akkorde, welche an die einzelnen Schläge in dem Allegro der Symphonie erinnern, wieder aufgehoben und der Zuhörer noch durch die letzten Akkorde aufs neue gespannt. Sie wirken, wie ein Feuer, das man gedämpft glaubte und das immer wieder in hell auflodernden Flammen in die Höhe schlägt ... aber das Gemüt jedes sinnigen Zuhörers wird gewiss von einem fortdauernden Gefühl, das eben jene unnennbare, ahnungsvolle Sehnsucht ist, tief und innig ergriffen und bis zum Schlussakkord darin erhalten; ja noch manchen Moment nach demselben wird er nicht aus dem wundervollen Geisterreiche, wo Schmerz und Lust in Tönen gestaltet ihn umfingen, hinaustreten können.

Notes

Introduction

1 Nicholas Slonimsky, *Lexicon of Musical Invective: Critical Assaults on Composers since Beethoven's Time* (New York, 1953), p. 42.
2 *Ibid.*, p. 47.
3 *Music in the Romantic Era* (New York, 1947), p. 340.
4 *Romanic Review* XXXV (1944), p. 75.
5 *Die Idee der Absoluten Musik* (Kassel, 1978).
6 For a discussion of various 'hermeneutic' approaches which attempt to reconcile analysis and interpretation in music in general, and often in Beethoven in particular, see Carl Dahlhaus, ed., *Beiträge zur musikalischen Hermeneutik* (Regensburg, 1975). Some of these writers and their approaches will be discussed in the conclusion to this book. See also Thrasybulos Georgiades, *Music and Language* (Cambridge, 1982), and, for an analysis of thematic transformation which lends added support to some of my later conjectures, Rudolf Steglich, 'Das melodische Hauptmotiv in Beethovens "Fidelio"', in *Archiv für Musikwissenschaft* IX (1952), pp. 51–67.
7 James Engell, *The Creative Imagination: Enlightenment to Romanticism* (Cambridge, MA, 1981), p. 303.

1: The Leipzig *Allgemeine musikalische Zeitung*

1 Horst Leuchtmann, 'Rochlitz, Friedrich', in *The New Grove Dictionary of Music and Musicians* (London, 1980), 16, pp. 83–4.
2 For details on Rochlitz' co-workers, see Marthe Bigenwald, *Die Anfänge der Leipziger Allgemeinen Musikalischen Zeitung* (Sibiu-Hermannstadt, 1938).
3 Ölten and Cologne, 1954.
4 Munich and Salzburg, 1977.
5 Several other sources are listed in the bibliography; these are generally less important, but readers who would like the essential data in concise form might also consult *Die Bedeutung der Allgemeinen Musikalischen Zeitung* by Clemens Christoph von Gleich (Amsterdam, n.d.). This is an advertising pamphlet issued by a Dutch reprint company, with a history of the *AMZ* in German and a brief description in English at the end, notable for stating ingenuously that the journal was designed 'for the mediocre mind' – a clumsy attempt to render the German 'Mittelmässigkeit' into English. What was meant, of course, was that the *AMZ* was not written only for professional musicians but for amateurs as well: the 'middle class' of German musical culture.
6 The review is translated in Elliott Forbes, ed., *Thayer's Life of Beethoven* (Princeton, 1967), pp. 277–8.

7 Both Thayer and Max Graf, in quoting this review, state that Mozart did not write these variations, and it is not clear whether either author is aware of their existence. The work in question, however, is undoubtedly K. Anh. 285: Seven Variations on 'Une fièvre brûlante' from Grétry's *Richard Coeur de Lion*. Mozart's widow cast doubt on the authenticity of this set, and it is not likely that such a citation proves her wrong. The anonymous critic also claims that the piece was written by Mozart in his early youth, when in reality Grétry's opera was not performed until 1784, in Paris, and did not reach Vienna until 1788. His source seems, therefore, not to have been very reliable.

8 Emily Anderson, ed., *The Letters of Beethoven* (New York, 1961), 1, pp. 51–2.

9 The review of the concerto testifies that it had already been heard many times in Leipzig, while the concert reports in the *AMZ* (see pp. 19–20) give evidence of the widespread dissemination of both works.

10 This and other quotations from the 'Eroica' review are taken from an unpublished translation by Harold Serwer and Kerala J. Snyder.

11 See, for example, the correspondence report from Prague in *AMZ* IX, col. 610.

12 The nearest competitor is Rochlitz himself, but his correspondence report on this symphony (*AMZ* IX, col. 497) is more an account of the audience reaction than of the piece itself.

13 Schnaus, *E. T. A. Hoffmann als Beethoven-Resenzent*, pp. 25–9.

14 *Ibid.*, p. 26.

15 *Ibid.*, pp. 56–62, 80–3.

16 Peter Branscombe, 'Kanne, Friedrich August', in *The New Grove Dictionary*, 9, p. 794.

17 Robert Haas, 'Beethoven in der zeitgenössischen Kritik', in *Beethoven-Almanach der Deutschen Musikbücherei auf des Jahr 1927*, ed. Gustav Bosse (Regensburg, 1927).

18 In a letter to Breitkopf und Härtel dated Oct. 9, 1811, Beethoven once again lashed out against critics in general. Kalischer, in his edition of the letters, states his opinion that this attack, as well as Beethoven's reference to 'the wretched review', are a reaction to this article, printed May 22, 1811. Since this was the only substantially negative review of Beethoven to appear in the *AMZ* that year, there is no reason to doubt that it is the one referred to. See A. C. Kalischer, *Beethoven's Letters* (New York, 1909), 1, pp. 231–2.

19 See Graf, *Composer and Critic* (New York, 1946), pp. 147–55, and Olin Downes, *Symphonic Masterpieces* (New York, 1935), pp. 47–9.

20 A few weeks after the review of the 'Eroica' was published, the Viennese correspondent, reporting on a new performance, failed to repeat his harsh opinion, apparently in deference to the critic (*AMZ* IX, no. 25, Mar. 18, 1807, col. 400). Later, however, he reasserted himself (*AMZ* X, no. 15, Jan. 6, 1808, col. 239).

21 Up to and including the seventh volume of the *AMZ*, these are catalogued in Schnaus, *E. T. A. Hoffmann als Beethoven-Resenzent*, pp. 17–18.

22 The well-known comment about the First Symphony sounding more like a wind-band than a full orchestra (*AMZ* III, no. 3, Oct. 15, 1800, col. 48 – in a report from Vienna) is overshadowed by the generally enthusiastic reception of the work by correspondent and public alike. See also the reports from Leipzig (*AMZ* IV, no. 15, Jan. 6, 1802, col. 234) and Berlin (*AMZ* VII, no. 10, Dec. 5, 1804, col. 157).

23 *The Classical Style* (New York, 1972), p. 19.
24 Gerhard Allroggen, 'Hoffmann, Ernst Theodor Amadeus', in *The New Grove Dictionary*, 8, p. 622.
25 E. T. A. Hoffmann, *Schriften zur Musik* (Munich, 1963).
26 See Oliver Strunk, *Source Readings in Music History* (New York, 1950), pp. 775–81.
27 In the Norton Critical Score of the Fifth Symphony, ed. Elliott Forbes (New York, 1971).
28 For a more accurate picture of Hoffmann, see Harvey Waterman Hewett-Thayer, *E. T. A. Hoffmann: Author of the Tales* (Princeton, 1948).
29 R. Murray Schafer, *E. T. A. Hoffmann and Music* (Toronto and Buffalo, 1975), p. 84.
30 Allroggen, 'Hoffmann, Ernst Theodor Amadeus'.
31 See Schnaus, *E. T. A. Hoffmann als Beethoven-Resenzent*, pp. 47–8.
32 *Ibid.*, pp. 56–88.
33 *Ibid.*, pp. 64–71.
34 *Ibid.*, pp. 89–103.
35 In the introduction to the Fifth Symphony review. *Ibid.*, pp. 111–17.
36 *Ibid.*, pp. 126–31.
37 *Ibid.*, pp. 103–7.
38 The first performance of the revised version took place on May 23, 1814.
39 Anderson, *The Letters of Beethoven*, 2, p. 517.
40 For details on Wendt's later contributions to the *AMZ*, see Ludwig Finscher, 'Zum Begriff der Klassik in der Musik', in *Deutsches Jahrbuch für Musikwissenschaft* XI (1966), pp. 21–3.
41 *Ibid.*
42 Most notably in the *Génie du Chrétianisme* (1802).
43 A. W. Schlegel, *A Course of Lectures on Dramatic Art and Literature*, translated by John Black, Esq. (London, 1846), pp. 26–7.
44 F. W. J. von Schelling, *Schriften zur Philosophie der Kunst und zur Freiheitslehre* (Leipzig, 1907; lectures delivered at Jena, 1802–3), p. 139, my translation.
45 An earlier revision, made in 1806, had been less successful.
46 A report on this performance appears in *AMZ* XVII, no. 14 (April 15, 1815), col. 242. The precise date of performance is not mentioned. The version performed at Leipzig seems to have been the original (1805) three-act opera. The number of acts was reduced to two in the first revision. It is now fashionable to call the original *Leonore*, the composer's preferred title, but at the time it was also known as *Fidelio*.
47 Johann Mattheson, *Der Vollkommene Capellmeister* (Kassel, 1954), p. 2.
48 Bellamy Hosler, *Changing Aesthetic Views of Instrumental Music in 18th-Century Germany* (Ann Arbor, 1981), p. 75.
49 *Ibid.*, p. 69.
50 *Ibid.*, p. 73.
51 Schelling, *Sämtliche Werke*, 7, p. 202. Quoted and translated in James Engell's *The Creative Imagination*, p. 304.
52 *AMZ* XVI, no. 4 (Jan. 1814), cols. 70–1.
53 O. G. Sonneck, ed., *Beethoven: Impressions by his Contemporaries* (New York, 1967), pp. 116–20.

54 *Ibid.*, p.125.
55 Leon Plantinga, *Schumann as Critic* (New Haven, 1976), p.39.
56 See p.42.
57 This article is so reminiscent of Wendt's treatment of *Fidelio* that, in the absence of documentary evidence, it may tentatively be ascribed to him. The author's idolization of Mozart, his treatment of the histories of form and expression, and his skepticism about Beethoven's form of progress, which he sees as culminating in the last works with unfortunate effect, are particularly revealing.
58 For further information on Woldemar, see Helmut Kirchmeyer, 'Der Fall Woldemar: Materialen zur Geschichte der Beethovenpolemik seit 1827', in Heinz Becker, ed., *Beiträge zur Geschichte der Musikkritik* (Regensburg, 1965), pp.19–25, and below, Chapter 3.
59 In an introductory paragraph, the 'Redaktion' of the *AMZ* qualified somewhat the opinions expressed in the article – an unusual step under any circumstances.
60 See, for example, *AMZ* XVIII, no.8 (Feb. 21, 1816), col. 121, and *AMZ* XXIX, no.13 (Mar. 28, 1827), col. 228.
61 Hector Berlioz, *A travers chants: études musicales, adorations, boutades et critiques*, 4th edn (Paris, 1886), p.49. My translation.
62 Robert Haas observed that it is virtually impossible to find negative criticism of Beethoven in the Viennese press after around 1810. See 'Beethoven in der zeitgenössischen Kritik'.
63 Maynard Solomon, 'On Beethoven's Creative Process: a Two-Part Invention', in *Music and Letters* LXI (1980), pp.272–83. Cf. *AMZ* XXX, no.1 (Jan. 2, 1828), pp.10–16.

2: Berlin and A.B. Marx

1 See Helmut Kirchmeyer, 'Ein Kapitel Adolf Bernhard Marx: über Sendungs- bewusstsein und Bildungsstand der Berliner Musikkritik zwischen 1824 und 1830', in Walter Salmen, ed., *Beiträge zur Geschichte der Musikanschauung im 19. Jahrhundert* (Regensburg, 1965), pp.73–101.
2 W.T. Jones, *A History of Western Philosophy* (New York, 1952), p.872.
3 *Ueber Malerei in der Tonkunst* (Berlin, 1828).
4 A.B. Marx, *Ludwig van Beethoven: Leben und Schaffen* (Berlin, 1859; repr. 1863–4), 1, pp.236–7.
5 Marx, *Ueber Malerei*, p.21.
6 Marx, *Beethoven*, 1, p.169.
7 See Arnfried Edler, 'Zur Musikanschauung von Adolf Bernhard Marx', in Salmen, *Beiträge zur Geschichte der Musikanschauung*, p.107.
8 Marx, *Beethoven*, 1, p.237.
9 *Ibid.*, p.236.
10 *Ibid.*, pp.238–9.
11 *Ibid.*, p.251.
12 *Ibid.*, pp.99–104.
13 *Ibid.*, p.86.
14 *Ibid.*, p.80.
15 *Ibid.*, pp.82–3.
16 See Edler, 'Zur Musikanschauung', pp.103–7.

17 *Ibid.*, p. 103.
18 Marx, *Beethoven*, 1, p. 253.
19 *Ibid.*, pp. 254–6.
20 *Ibid.*, p. 252.
21 It should be noted, however, that Hegel shunned the concept of synthesis, and used it only derogatorily. See Walter Kaufmann, *Hegel: Reinterpretation, Texts and Commentary* (Garden City, New York, 1965), p. 168n.
22 Marx, *Beethoven*, 1, p. 257.
23 Kirchmeyer, 'Ein Kapitel Adolf Bernhard Marx', pp. 78–84.
24 In a postscript to the first volume, Marx made it clear that he was referring specifically to the Leipzig *AMZ* (*ibid.*, p. 80).
25 *Ibid.*, pp. 77–80.
26 Marx, *Beethoven*, 2, pp. 302–3.
27 *Ibid.*, pp. 143–7.
28 See Rochlitz' (?) comments quoted in Chapter 1, and Louis Spohr's in his *Selbstbiographie* (Kassell and Göttingen, 1860–1).
29 Marx, *Beethoven*, 2, p. 270.
30 Quartet no. 5 in E-flat, published Vienna 1788.
31 'Ein Kapitel Adolf Bernhard Marx', p. 76.
32 Leon Plantinga, *Schumann as Critic*, p. 32.

3: Other German sources

1 *Beethoven im Spiegel der zeitgenössischen rheinischen Presse* (Würzburg, 1933).
2 Georg Kaiser, *Beiträge zu einer Charakteristik Carl Maria von Webers als Musikschriftsteller* (Leipzig, 1910).
3 David Benjamin Levy, for example, in his dissertation 'Early Performances of Beethoven's Ninth Symphony: a Comparative Study of Five Major Cities' (Univ. of Rochester, 1979), pp. 65–6, states that an account of the first performance of the Ninth Symphony appeared in *Caecilia*, promising an independent report to follow, but that none appeared. Actually, no fewer than three extensive reviews of the symphony appeared a few years later. Gudrun Henneberg, in *Idee und Begriff des musikalischen Kunstwerks im Spiegel des deutschsprachigen Schrifttums der ersten Hälfte des 19. Jahrhunderts* (Tutzing, 1983), covers *Caecilia* more thoroughly than any other modern writer, but from a different perspective than that used in this book.
4 See Helmut Kirchmeyer, 'Der Fall Woldemar', pp. 19–25.
5 Robert Haas, 'Beethoven in der zeitgenössischen Kritik'.
6 'Der Fall Woldemar'.
7 *Ibid.*, p. 20.
8 Imogen Fellinger, *Verzeichnis der Musikzeitschriften des 19. Jahrhunderts* (Regensburg, 1968), p. 53.
9 'Der Fall Woldemar', p. 23.
10 Ludwig Rellstab, *Gesammelte Schriften* (Leipzig, 1843–8).
11 In this respect, it is important to note that the favorable article on the 'Pastoral' Symphony in the *AMZ* once attributed to Hoffmann was found by Bigenwald to have been written by Rochlitz, no enemy to tone-painting.
12 See Carl Dahlhaus, *Aesthetics of Music*, trans. William Austin (Cambridge, 1982), pp. 24–31.

13 Paul Henry Lang, Review of Leo Schrade's *Beethoven in France*, in *Romanic Review* XXXV (1944), pp. 73–82.

14 See, for example, Heinrich Christoph Koch, *Versuch einer Anleitung zur Composition*, 1 (Leipzig, 1782), p. 3, and Wilhelm Friedrich Marpurg, *Historisch-Kritische Beiträge zur Aufnahme der Musik*, 1 (Berlin, 1755), p. 521.

15 Einstein, *Music in the Romantic Era*, p. 340.

16 'Early Performances'.

17 See, for example, Louis Spohr, *Lebenserinnerungen* (Tutzing, 1968).

18 Levy, 'Early Performances', p. 89. The entire review is translated by Levy.

19 *Ibid.*, p. 91.

20 *Ibid.*

21 John Warrack, 'Fröhlich, (Franz) Joseph', in *The New Grove Dictionary*, 6, p. 864.

22 Occasionally the Second Symphony, too, because of the adverse circumstances in which it was written, is given a psychological interpretation, albeit an 'escapist' one which denies the influence of Beethoven's life upon his art.

23 M. Grétry, *Mémoires ou essais sur la musique* (Paris, 1789), p. 414.

24 *Ibid.*, p. 287.

25 Karl Spazier, trans., *Grétrys Versuche über Musik* (Leipzig, 1800). Quoted in *AMZ* XIX (1827), col. 536.

26 Immanuel Kant, *Critique of Judgement*, trans. James Creed Meredith (Oxford, 1952), p. 194.

27 Quoted in Dahlhaus, *Aesthetics of Music*, p. 25.

28 Friedrich Rochlitz, *Für Freunde der Tonkunst*, 2 (Leipzig, 1825), pp. 398–427.

29 Arthur Schopenhauer, *The World as Will and Idea*, trans. R. B. Haldane and J. Kemp (London, n.d.), p. 333. Henneberg (*Idee und Begriff des musikalischen Kunstwerks*, p. 312), apparently following an old German tradition, attributes this article to Fröhlich himself, but this attribution seems highly doubtful on purely empirical grounds.

30 Rosen, *The Classical Style*, pp. 405–33, and Leo Treitler, 'To Worship That Celestial Sound: Motives for Analysis', in *Journal of Musicology* I (1982), pp. 161–70.

31 William Weber, 'The Classical Repertory of Nineteenth Century Orchestras', in *The Orchestra: a Reference History*, ed. Joan Peyser (forthcoming: New York, 1986(?)).

32 Carl Maria von Weber, *Writings on Music*, ed. John Warrack (Cambridge, 1981).

33 John Warrack, *Carl Maria von Weber* (Cambridge, 1976), p. 99.

34 *Ibid.*, pp. 99–100.

35 *Ibid.*, p. 100.

36 Anton Schindler, *Biographie von Ludwig van Beethoven* (Münster, 1840), p. 99.

37 Kaiser, *Beiträge zu einer Charakteristik Carl Maria von Webers*, p. 54.

38 *Neue Zeitschrift für Musik*, 1840, no. 48 (Dec. 12), p. 189.

39 *Blätter für Literarische Unterhaltung*, 1840, no. 319 (Nov. 14), p. 1287.

40 *Ibid.*, 1840, no. 366 (Dec. 31), p. 1480.

41 Anton Schindler, *Beethoven in Paris* (Münster, 1842), p. 114.

42 Kaiser, *Beiträge zu einer Charakteristik Carl Maria von Webers*, p. 55.

43 *Ibid.*, p. 56.

44 *Ibid.*, p. 53.
45 *Ibid.*, pp. 56−7.
46 Warrack, *Carl Maria von Weber*, p. 100.

4: French Beethoven criticism

1 Leo Schrade, *Beethoven in France: the Growth of an Idea* (New Haven, 1942), p. ix.
2 *Romanic Review* XXXV (1944), pp. 73−82.
3 Göttingen, 1950.
4 Ph.D. diss., University of Pennsylvania, 1972.
5 See also J. G. Prod'homme, 'Beethoven en France', in *Mercure de France* 194 (March 15, 1927), p. 592.
6 Bloom, 'François-Joseph Fétis', pp. 110−11.
7 Schindler, *Beethoven in Paris*.
8 Cited in Schrade, *Beethoven in France*, p. 3.
9 March, 1810, p. 9. Cited in J. G. Prod'homme, *Les Symphonies de Beethoven* (Paris, 1906), p. 20.
10 *Beethoven in France*, p. 28.
11 Hector Berlioz, *A travers chants* (Paris, 1971) pp. 36−7.
12 The sources for Berlioz' reviews are listed in Bloom, 'François-Joseph Fétis', p. 167n. Many reviews, like those in the *Débats*, are short and superficial, mentioning Beethoven only briefly in the context of other music; these will not be considered here. The reviews of the symphonies first appeared in the *Revue et gazette musicale*; it is these which were reprinted, with minor modifications, in *A travers chants*. For my present purposes, I will consider the final versions to be definitive.
13 Schrade, *Beethoven in France*, p. 28.
14 Berlioz, *A travers chants*, p. 46.
15 Letter to the Princess Sayn-Wittgenstein, May 17, 1856. See Humphrey Searle, ed., *Hector Berlioz: a Selection from his Letters* (London, 1966), p. 145.
16 Berlioz, *A travers chants*, p. 109.
17 *Ibid.*, pp. 61−6.
18 Review of Leo Schrade's *Beethoven in France*, pp. 78−80.
19 *Revue et gazette musicale*, Feb. 4, 1838, p. 49. Cited in Prod'homme, *Les Symphonies de Beethoven*, pp. 47−8, and translated in Bloom, 'François-Joseph Fétis', p. 169. This passage was eliminated from the version of the review printed in *A travers chants*.
20 *Revue musicale* (1829), pp. 129−32. Part of this review is quoted and translated in Bloom, 'François-Joseph Fétis', pp. 177−80; part of the remainder appears in Prod'homme, *Les Symphonies de Beethoven*, pp. 325−6.
21 Bloom, 'François-Joseph Fétis', pp. 175−6.
22 *Revue musicale* (1829), pp. 325−6. This later review is quoted in Prod'homme, *Les Symphonies de Beethoven*, pp. 326−7. Fétis' opinion on the second movement was also repeated on this occasion; it is from this review that the above quote is taken.
23 Bloom, 'François-Joseph Fétis', p. 179.
24 David Cairns, ed., *The Memoirs of Hector Berlioz* (London, 1969), pp. 217−18.
25 Bloom, 'François-Joseph Fétis', pp. 179−80.

26 Lang, Review of Leo Schrade's *Beethoven in France*, p. 75.
27 *Revue musicale* (1829), pp. 326–7. Quoted in Bloom, 'François-Joseph Fétis', pp. 182–3.
28 *Journal des débats*, Mar. 9, 1839. Quoted in Prod'homme, *Les Symphonies de Beethoven*, pp. 324–5.
29 E.g. Rochlitz in the *AMZ* (see Chapter 1). The symphony also received a lengthy and laudatory review in the Leipzig *Zeitung für die Elegante Welt*, X, no. 133 (July 5, 1810), p. 133.
30 *Journals des débats*, Mar. 24, 1820. Quoted in Prod'homme, *Les Symphonies de Beethoven*, pp. 269–70.
31 *Revue musicale* (1829), pp. 173–6. Quoted and translated in Bloom, 'François-Joseph Fétis', pp. 160–4.
32 Berlioz, *A travers chants*, pp. 55–60.
33 See *Three Classics in the Aesthetics of Music* (New York, 1962), pp. 38–9.
34 This theory was explored most specifically in Charles Batteux, *Les beaus arts reduits a un même principe* (Paris, 1747).
35 Bloom, 'François-Joseph Fétis', pp. 157–9.
36 David Benjamin Levy, 'Early Performances', p. 289.
37 *Ibid.*, p. 290.
38 Louis Spohr, *Lebenserinnerungen*.
39 Levy, 'Early Performances', pp. 292–301.
40 *Revue musicale* (1834), p. 90.
41 Levy, 'Early Performances', p. 299.
42 *Gazette musicale* I (1834), pp. 41–2. Quoted and translated in Levy, 'Early Performances', p. 301.
43 Levy, 'Early Performances'.
44 Barry Brook, *La Symphonie française dans la seconde moitié du XVIIIème siècle* (Paris, 1962).
45 Levy, 'Early Performances', p. 333.
46 Berlioz' review appears in *A travers chants*, pp. 70–9. The translation quoted here is from Levy, 'Early Performances', p. 313.
47 Levy, 'Early Performances', p. 318.
48 Nicholas Temperley has pointed out ('The *Symphonie Fantastique* and its Program', in *Musical Quarterly* LVII (1971), pp. 593–608) that, strictly speaking, Berlioz wrote only one program, that for the *Symphonie Fantastique*. Temperley argues against the well-known position of Barzun and others with regard to this program – that it was not intended to be taken quite seriously by the composer. Lest I should seem, from the above arguments, to reject Temperley's position, it is important to note that if Berlioz was in earnest about his program, this would be perfectly consistent with his general distrust of programs by others, at least within the framework of the common assumptions which have been discussed. Berlioz' rejection of Beethoven's programs, which are never so specific or so systematic as his own, and his concomitant vindication of 'absolute' music represent simply the other extreme, showing that reconciliation of opposites which has already been noted elsewhere, and which seems to have imposed itself effortlessly upon the Romantic imagination.

5: The Fifth Symphony

1 Ian D. Bent, 'Analysis', in *The New Grove Dictionary of Music and Musicians*, ed. Stanley Sadie (London, 1980), 1, p. 342.
2 Leo Treitler, 'To Worship That Celestial Sound', p. 158.
3 *Ibid.*, p. 153.
4 Marx, *Beethoven*, 2, p. 58.
5 E. T. A. Hoffmann, 'Review of the Fifth Symphony', trans. F. John Adams, Jr., in Elliott Forbes, ed., *Ludwig van Beethoven: Symphony no. 5 in C minor* (New York, 1971), p. 156.
6 Marx, *Beethoven*, 2, p. 62.
7 Hector Berlioz, *A travers chants* (Paris, 1971), p. 51.
8 Schnaus, *E. T. A. Hoffmann als Beethoven-Resenzent*, pp. 89−95.
9 Hoffmann, 'Review of the Fifth Symphony', p. 158.
10 *Ibid.*
11 *Ibid.*, p. 159.
12 *Ibid.*, p. 160.
13 *Ibid.*, p. 161.
14 Schnaus, *E. T. A. Hoffmann als Beethoven-Resenzent*, p. 91.
15 Hoffmann, 'Review of the Fifth Symphony', pp. 162−3.

Conclusion

1 Susanne Langer, *Philosophy in a New Key* (Cambridge, 1951), pp. 204−45.
2 Owen Jander, 'Beethoven's "Orpheus in Hades": The *Andante con moto* of the Fourth Piano Concerto', in *19th Century Music* VIII (1984−5), pp. 195−212.
3 Charles Taylor, *Hegel* (Cambridge, 1975), pp. 51−75.
4 Carl Dahlhaus, ed., *Beiträge zur musikalischen Hermeneutik* (Regensburg, 1975).
5 Cf. Harry Goldschmidt, *Die Erscheinung Beethoven: Beethoven-Studien I* (Leipzig, 1974), pp. 25−88 and Steglich, 'Das melodische Hauptmotiv in Beethovens "Fidelio"'.
6 Jonathan Dunsby, in an unpublished paper delivered at Yale in 1982.
7 M. H. Abrams, 'Structure and Style in the Greater Romantic Lyric', in *Romanticism and Consciousness*, ed. Harold Bloom (New York, 1970).

Bibliography

Abrams, M. H. 'Structure and Style in the Greater Romantic Lyric', in *Romanticism and Consciousness*, ed. Harold Bloom. New York: W. W. Norton, 1970.

Allgemeine Musikalische Zeitung. Leipzig: Breitkopf und Härtel, 1798–1848.

Allgemeine Musikalische Zeitung mit Besonderer Rücksicht auf den Österreichischen Kaiserstaat. Vienna: A. Strauss, 1817–24.

Allroggen, Gerhard. 'Hoffmann, Ernst Theodor Amadeus', in *The New Grove Dictionary of Music and Musicians*, ed. Stanley Sadie. London: Macmillan, 1980. 8, pp. 618–26.

Anderson, Emily. *The Letters of Beethoven*. New York: St. Martin's Press, 1961.

Andres, Helmut. *Beiträge zur Geschichte der Musikkritik*. Greifswals: Buchdruckerei Julius Abel, 1938.

Barbour, John Murray. 'Allgemeine Musikalische Zeitung, Prototype of Contemporary Music Journalism', in *Notes* V (1948), pp. 325–7.

Barzun, Jacques. *Berlioz and the Romantic Century*. Boston: Little, Brown, 1950. 2 vols.

Beardsley, Monroe Curtis. *Aesthetics from Classical Greece to the Present: a Short History*. New York: Macmillan, 1966.

Becking, Gustav. *Studien zu Beethovens Personalstil: das Scherzothema*. Leipzig: Breitkopf und Härtel, 1921.

Bent, Ian D. 'Analysis', in *The New Grove Dictionary of Music and Musicians*, ed. Stanley Sadie. London: Macmillan, 1980. 1, p. 342.

Berliner Allgemeine Musikalische Zeitung. Berlin: Schlesinger, 1824–30.

Berlioz, Hector. *A travers chants: études musicales, adorations, boutades et critiques*. Paris: M. Lévy Frères, 1862.

Berlioz, Hector. *The Memoirs of Hector Berlioz, Member of the French Institute, Including his Travels in Italy, Germany, Russia and England, 1803–1865*, trans. and ed. David Cairns. London: Gollancz, 1969.

Bigenwald, Marthe. *Die Anfänge der Leipziger Allgemeinen Musikalischen Zeitung*. Sibiu-Hermannstadt, 1938.

Bloom, Peter Anthony. 'François-Joseph Fétis and the Revue Musicale'. Ph.D. diss., University of Pennsylvania, 1972.

Blume, Friedrich. *Classic and Romantic Music*, trans. M. D. Herder Norton. New York: W. W. Norton, 1970.

Bosanquet, Bernard. *A History of Aesthetic*, second edition. London: George Allen and Unwin, 1904.

Branscombe, Peter. 'Kanne, Friedrich August', in *The New Grove Dictionary of Music and Musicians*, ed. Stanley Sadie. London: Macmillan, 1980. 9, p. 794.

Brook, Barry. *La Symphonie française dans la seconde moitié du XVIIIème siècle*. Paris: Institut de musicologie de l'Université de Paris, 1962.

175

Bibliography

Brümmer, Eugen, *Beethoven im Spiegel der zeitgenössischen rheinischen Presse*. Würzburg: Verlag Konrad Triltsch, 1933.

Caecilia: eine Zeitschrift für die Musikalische Welt. Mainz: B. Schott's Söhne, 1824–48.

Dahlhaus, Carl. *Aesthetics of Music*, trans. William Austin. Cambridge: Cambridge University Press, 1982.

Dahlhaus, Carl. *Foundations of Music History*, trans. J. B. Robinson. Cambridge: Cambridge University Press, 1983.

Dahlhaus Carl. *Die Idee der Absoluten Musik*. Kassel: Bärenreiter-Verlag, 1978.

Dahlhaus Carl, ed. *Beiträge zur musikalischen Hermeneutik*. Regensburg: Gustav Bosse Verlag, 1975.

Dahlhaus, Carl. 'Romantische Musikästhetik und Wiener Klassik', in *Archiv fur Musikwissenschaft* XXIX (1972), pp. 167–81.

Dean, Winton. 'Criticism', in *The New Grove Dictionary of Music and Musicians*, ed. Stanley Sadie. London: Macmillan, 1980. 5, pp. 36–50.

Dolinski, Kurt. *Die Anfänge der musikalischen Fachpresse in Deutschland*. Berlin: Hermann Schmidt, 1940.

Downes, Olin. *Symphonic Masterpieces*. New York, 1935.

Edler, Arnfried. 'Zur Musikanschauung von Adolf Bernhard Marx', in Walter Salmen, ed., *Beiträge zur Geschichte der Musikanschauung im 19. Jahrhundert*. Regensburg: Gustav Bosse Verlag, 1965. (Studien der Musikgeschichte des 19. Jahrhunderts, 1).

Eggebrecht, Hans Heinrich. 'Zur Geschichte der Beethoven-Rezeption', in *Abhandlungen der geistes- und sozialwissenschaftlichen Klasse der Akademie der Wissenschaften und der Literatur*. Mainz: Verlag der Akademie der Wissenschaften und der Literatur, in Kommission bei Franz Steiner Verlag, Wiesbaden, Jahrgang 1972, no. 3.

Ehinger, H. *E. T. A. Hoffmann als Musiker und Musikschriftsteller*. Ölten and Cologne: Walter Verlag, 1954.

Ehinger, H. *Friedrich Rochlitz als Musikschriftsteller*. Leipzig: Breitkopf und Härtel, 1929.

Einstein, Alfred. *Music in the Romantic Era*. New York: W. W. Norton, 1947.

Engell, James. *The Creative Imagination: Enlightenment to Romanticism*. Cambridge: Harvard University Press, 1981.

Fellinger, Imogen. *Verzeichnis der Musikzeitschriften des 19. Jahrhunderts*. Regensburg: Gustav Bosse Verlag, 1968. (Studien der Musikgeschichte des 19. Jahrhunderts, 10).

Finscher, Ludwig. 'Zum Begriff der Klassik in der Musik', in *Deutsches Jahrbuch für Musikwissenschaft* XI (1966), pp. 21–3.

Forchert, Arno. 'Adolf Bernhard Marx und seine Berliner Allgemeine Musikalische Zeitung', in *Studien zur Muikgeschichte Berlins im frühen 19. Jahrhundert*, ed. Carl Dalhaus. Regensburg: Gustav Bosse Verlag, 1980, pp. 381–404.

Georgiades, Thrasybulos. *Music and Language*, trans. Marie Louise Göllner. Cambridge: Cambridge University Press, 1982.

Gleich, Clemens Christoph Johannes von. *Die Bedeutung der Allgemeinen Musikalischen Zeitung*. Amsterdam: Fritz Knuf, n.d.

Goldschmidt, Harry. *Die Erscheinung Beethoven: Beethoven-Studien I*. Leipzig: VEB Deutscher Verlag für Musik, 1974.

Bibliography

Gordon, Philip. 'Franz Grillparzer: Critic of Music', in *Musical Quarterly* II (1916), pp. 552–61.

Graf, Max. *Composer and Critic*. New York: W.W. Norton, 1946.

Grétry, M. *Mémoires ou essais sur la musique*. Paris: chez l'auteur, 1789.

Grove, Sir George. *Beethoven and his Nine Symphonies*, second edition. London: Novello, 1896.

Haas, Robert. 'Beethoven in der zeitgenössischen Kritik', in *Beethoven-Almanach der Deutschen Musikbücherei auf das Jahr 1927*, ed. Gustav Bosse. Regensburg: Gustav Bosse Verlag, 1927.

Hagan, Dorothy. 'French Musical Criticism between the Revolutions (1830–1848)'. Ph.D. diss., University of Illinois, 1965.

Hanslick, Eduard. *The Beautiful in Music*, trans. Gustav Cohen, ed. Morris Weitz. New York: Liberal Arts Press, 1957.

Hegel, G.F. *Phenomenology of Spirit*, trans. A.V. Miller. London: Oxford University Press, 1977.

Hegel, G.F. *The Philosophy of Fine Art*, trans. F.P.B. Osmaston. London: G. Bell and Sons, 1920. 4 vols.

Henneberg, Gudrun. *Idee und Begriff des musikalischen Kunstwerks im Spiegel des deutschsprachigen Schrifttums der ersten Hälfte des 19. Jahrhunderts*. Tutzing: Hans Schneider, 1983.

Hewett-Thayer, Harvey Waterman. *E.T.A. Hoffmann: Author of the Tales*. Princeton: Princeton University Press, 1948.

Hirschfeld, Robert. 'Musikalische Kritik in der Wiener Zeitung', in *Zur Geschichte der Kaiserlichen Wiener Zeitung*. Vienna: 1903, pp. 197–235.

Hoffmann, Ernst Theodor Amadeus. *Schriften zur Musik, Nachlese*, ed. Friedrich Schnapp. Munich: Winkler-Verlag, 1963.

Hosler, Bellamy. *Changing Aesthetic Views of Instrumental Music in 18th-Century Germany*. Ann Arbor: UMI Research Press, 1981.

Jander, Owen. 'Beethoven's "Orpheus in Hades": The *Andante con moto* of the Fourth Piano Concerto', in *19th Century Music* VIII (1984–5), pp. 195–212.

Jones, W.T. *A History of Western Philosophy*. New York: Harcourt, Brace and World, 1952.

Kaiser, Georg. *Beiträge zu einer Charakteristik Carl Maria von Webers als Musikschriftsteller*. Diss., Leipzig, 1910.

Kalischer, Alfred. *Beethoven und seine Zeitgenössen*. Berlin: Schuster und Loeffler, n.d. 4 vols.

Kalischer, Alfred. *Beethoven's Letters: a Critical Edition with Explanatory Notes*, trans. J.S. Shedlock. London: J.M. Dent, 1909.

Kant, Immanuel. *Critique of Judgement*, trans. James Creed Meredith. London: Oxford University Press, 1952.

Kaufmann, Walter. *Hegel: Reinterpretation, Texts and Commentary*. Garden City, New York: Doubleday, 1965.

Kerst, Friedrich. 'Karl Maria von Weber als Schriftsteller', in *Die Musik* V (1906), iii, pp. 324–30.

Kindermann, Jurgen. 'Romantische Aspekte in E.T.A. Hoffmanns Musikanschauung', in *Beiträge zur Geschichte der Musikanschauung im 19. Jahrhundert*. Regensburg: Gustav Bosse Verlag, 1965.

Kirchmeyer, Helmut. 'Der Fall Woldemar: Materialen zur Geschichte der

Bibliography

Beethovenpolemik seit 1827', in Heinz Becker, ed., *Beiträge zur Geschichte der Musikkritik*. Regensburg: Gustav Bosse Verlag, 1965, pp. 19–25. (Studien der Musikgeschichte des 19. Jahrhunderts, 5).

Kirchmeyer, Helmut. 'Ein Kapitel Adolf Bernhard Marx: über Sendungsbewusstsein und Bildungsstand der Berliner Musikkritik zwischen 1824 und 1830', in Walter Salmen, ed., *Beiträge zur Geschichte der Musikanschauung im 19. Jahrhundert*. Regensburg: Gustav Bosse Verlag, 1965, pp. 73–101.

Kivy, Peter. *The Corded Shell: Reflections on Musical Expression*. Princeton: Princeton University Press, 1980.

Kivy, Peter. *Sound and Semblance*. Princeton: Princeton University Press, 1984.

Koch, Heinrich Christoph. *Versuch einer Anleitung zur Composition*. Leipzig, 1782.

Kroll, Erwin, 'E. T. A. Hoffmann und Beethoven', in *Beethoven-Zentenarfeier, Internationaler musikhistorischer Kongress*. Vienna: 1927.

Kroll, Erwin. *E. T. A. Hoffmanns musikalische Anschauungen*. Königsberg: Emil Rautenberg, 1909.

Kropfinger, Klaus. 'Klassik-Rezeption in Berlin (1800–1830)', in *Studien der Musikgeschichte Berlins im frühen 19. Jahrhundert*. Regensburg: Gustav Bosse Verlag, 1980, pp. 301–80.

Lang, Paul Henry. Review of Leo Schrade's *Beethoven in France*, in *Romanic Review* XXXV (1944), pp. 73–82.

Langer, Susanne. *Feeling and Form*. New York: Scribner, 1953.

Langer, Susanne. *Philosophy in a New Key*. Cambridge, MA: Harvard University Press, 1951.

Leuchtmann, Horst. 'Rochlitz, Friedrich', in *The New Grove Dictionary of Music and Musicians*, ed. Stanley Sadie. London: Macmillan, 1980. 16, pp. 83–4.

Levy, David Benjamin. 'Early Performances of Beethoven's Ninth Symphony: a Comparative Study of Five Major Cities'. Ph.D. Diss., Eastman, 1979.

Longyear, R. M. Review of Murray Schafer's *E. T. A. Hoffmann and Music*, in *Musical Quarterly* LXII (1976), p. 282.

MacDonald, Hugh. 'Berlioz, Hector', in *The New Grove Dictionary of Music and Musicians*, ed. Stanley Sadie. London: Macmillan, 1980. 2, pp. 579–610.

Magani, L. 'Beethoven and the Aesthetic Thought of his Time', in *International Review of Music Aesthetics and Sociology* I (1970), pp. 125–36.

Marpurg, Wilhelm Friedrich. *Historisch-Kritische Beiträge zur Aufnahme der Musik*. Berlin, 1755. 4 vols.

Marx, Adolf Bernhard. *Die Lehre von der musikalischen Komposition, praktisch-theoretisch*. Leipzig, 1837–47. 4 vols.

Marx, Adolf Bernhard. *Ludwig van Beethoven: Leben und Schaffen*. Berlin: Verlag von Otto Janke, 1863–4. 2 vols.

Marx, Adolf Bernhard. *Ueber Malerei in der Tonkunst: ein Maigruss an die Kunstphilosophen*. Berlin: G. Finck, 1828.

Mattheson, Johann. *Der Vollkommene Capellmeister*. Reprinted by Bärenreiter-Verlag, Kassel, 1954.

Meyer, Leonard. *Emotion and Meaning in Music*. Chicago: University of Chicago Press, 1956.

Moyer, Brigitte. 'Marx, Adolf Bernhard', in *The New Grove Dictionary of Music and Musicians*, ed. Stanley Sadie. London: Macmillan, 1980. 11, pp. 739–41.

Bibliography

Müller, Hans von. 'Hoffmann und Härtel', in *Süddeutsche Monatshefte*, Jahrgang 5, Dec. 1907 and March 1908.

Oulibicheff, Aleksandr. *Beethoven: ses critiques, ses glossateurs*. Leipzig: F. A. Brockhaus, 1857.

Plantinga, Leon. *Schumann as Critic*. New Haven: Yale University Press, 1967.

Prod'homme, J. G. 'The Baron de Trémont: Souvenirs of Beethoven and other Contemporaries', in *Musical Quarterly* VI (1920), pp. 366–91.

Prod'homme, J. G. 'Beethoven en France', in *Mercure de France* 194 (March 15, 1927), p. 592.

Prod'homme, J. G. *Les Symphonies de Beethoven*. New York: Da Capo Press, 1977.

Rellstab, Ludwig. *Gesammelte Schriften*. Leipzig: F. A. Brockhaus, 1843–8.

Revue musicale. Paris: 1827–35.

Rochlitz, Friedrich. *Für Freunde der Tonkunst*. Leipzig: C. Cnobloch, 1825.

Rosen, Charles. *The Classical Style*. New York: W. W. Norton, 1972.

Schafer, R. Murray. *E. T. A. Hoffmann and Music*. Toronto and Buffalo: University of Toronto Press, 1975.

Schelling, F. W. J. von. *Schriften zur Philosophie der Kunst und zur Freiheitslehre*. Leipzig, 1907.

Schering, Arnold. *Beethoven und die Dichtung*. New York: Georg Olms Verlag, 1973.

Schindler, Anton. *Beethoven in Paris*. Münster: Aschendorff, 1842.

Schindler, Anton. *Biographie von Ludwig von Beethoven*. Münster: Aschendorff, 1840.

Schlegel, August Wilhelm. *A Course of Lectures on Dramatic Art and Literature*, trans. John Black, Esq. London: H. G. Bonn, 1846.

Schmitt-Thomas, Reinhold. 'Die Entwicklung der deutschen Konzertkritik im Spiegel der Leipziger Allgemeinen Musikalischen Zeitung'. Diss., Frankfurt, 1968.

Schnaus, Peter. *E. T. A. Hoffmann als Beethoven-Resenzent der Allgemeinen Musikalischen Zeitung*. Munich and Salzburg: Musikverlag Emil Katzbichler, 1977. (Freiburger Schriften zur Musikwissenschaft, ed. Hans Heinrich Eggebrecht, 8).

Schopenhauer, Arthur. *The World as Will and Idea*, trans. R. B. Haldane and J. Kemp, 7th edn. London: Kegan Paul, Trench, Trubner & Co., Ltd., n.d.

Schrade, Leo. *Beethoven in France: the Growth of an Idea*. New Haven: Yale University Press, 1942.

Searle, Humphrey, ed. *Hector Berlioz: a Selection from his Letters*. London, 1966.

Slonimsky, Nicolas. *Lexicon of Musical Invective: Critical Assaults on Composers since Beethoven's Time*. New York: Coleman–Ross, 1953.

Solomon, Maynard. 'On Beethoven's Creative Process: a Two-Part Invention', in *Music and Letters* LXI (1980), pp. 272–83.

Sonneck, O. G. *Beethoven: Impressions by his Contemporaries*. New York: Dover Publications, 1967.

Spohr, Louis. *Selbstbiographie*. Kassell and Göttingen: G. H. Wigand, 1860–1. 2 vols.

Springer, Hermann. 'Beethoven und die Musikkritik', in *Beethoven-Zentenarfeier: internationaler musikhistorischer Kongress*. Vienna: Universal-Edition, 1927, pp. 32–4.

Bibliography

Steglich, Rudolf. 'Das melodische Hauptmotiv in Beethovens "Fidelio"', in *Archiv für Musikwissenschaft* IX (1952), pp. 51–67.

Strunk, Oliver. *Source Readings in Music History*. New York, 1950.

Temperley, Nicholas. 'The *Symphonie Fantastique* and its Program', in *Musical Quarterly* LVII (1971), pp. 593–608.

Thayer, Alexander Wheelock. *Thayer's Life of Beethoven*, rev. and ed. Elliott Forbes. Princeton: Princeton University Press, 1967.

Three Classics in the Aesthetics of Music. New York: Dover, 1962.

Treitler, Leo. 'History, Criticism, and Beethoven's Ninth Symphony', in *19th Century Music* IV (1980), pp. 193–210.

Treitler, Leo. 'To Worship That Celestial Sound: Motives for Analysis', in *Journal of Musicology* I (1982), pp. 153–70.

Wackenroder, Wilhelm Heinrich and Tieck, Ludwig. *Outpourings of an Art-Loving Friar*, trans. Edward Mornin. New York: Frederick Ungar Publishing Co., 1975.

Warrack, John. *Carl Maria von Weber*. Cambridge: Cambridge University Press, 1976.

Warrack, John. 'Weber, Carl Maria von: 6. The Critic', in *The New Grove Dictionary of Music and Musicians*, ed. Stanley Sadie. London: Macmillan, 1980. 20, pp. 249–50.

Warrack, John. 'Fröhlich, (Franz) Joseph', in *The New Grove Dictionary of Music and Musicians*, ed. Stanley Sadie. London: Macmillan, 1980. 6, p. 864.

Weber, Carl Maria von. *Hinterlassene Schriften*. Dresden and Leipzig, 1828.

Weber, Carl Maria von. *Writings on Music*, ed. John Warrack. Cambridge: Cambridge University Press, 1981.

Whitehead, Alfred North. *Science and the Modern World*. New York: Free Press, 1950.

Zeitung für die Elegante Welt. Leipzig: L. Voss, 1801–32.

Index

Note: unless otherwise noted in parenthesis, all musical pieces referred to are Beethoven's.

Abrams, M. H., 149–50
absolutism, 2, 32, 119; form, 82; Marx,
  33; Schelling, 3; Schopenhauer, 91,
  104; Tieck, 91; Wackenroder, 91;
  Weber, 71
abstraction, 2; French reaction, 120;
  Hoffmann, 70; symphonies, 74, 82
Affektenlehre, 39, 48, 78, 114, 116, 124;
  Kretzschmar, 148; Mattheson, 91;
  Romanticism, 72
AMZ, *see* appropriate editors, critics and
  contributors
Apel, A., 80–1
Aristotelianism, 2; Fétis, 116; Kivy, 148;
  Wendt, 32; *see also* Enlightenment

Bach, Johann Sebastian, 38
BAMZ, *see* appropriate critics and
  contributors
Baumgarten, Alexander Gottlieb, 51
Beethoven, L. van: attitude toward
  Freischütz, 42; deafness, 37, 41–2, 52,
  69, 77–8; reaction to reviews, 9–10,
  18, 27, 37–8, 167n18; as a Romantic,
  39; *see also* Romanticism
Beethoven, L. van: works, **Chamber
  Music with Piano**, op. 11 (Piano Trio,
  B-flat), 7, 8, 21, Hoffmann, 24–5;
  op. 12 (Three Violin Sonatas, D, A,
  E-flat), 7, 8, 12; French reaction, 107;
  op. 17 (Horn Sonata, F), 19; op. 23
  (Violin Sonata, a), 10, 78; op. 24
  (Violin Sonata ['Spring'], F), 10; WoO
  46 (Variations, E-flat, on 'Bei
  Männern, welche Liebe fühlen') 11;
  op. 30 (Three Violin Sonatas, A, c, G),
  11; op. 66 (Variations, F, on 'Ein
  Mädchen oder Weibchen'), 7; op. 70
  (Two Piano Trios, D ['Ghost'], E-flat),
  21, 25; op. 96 (Violin Sonata, G), 41,
  93; op. 97 (Piano Trio ['Archduke'],
  B-flat), 93; op. 102 (Two Cello
  Sonatas, C, D), 38, 39, 58, 60–1, 92;
  Chamber Music for Strings, op. 18

(Six String Quartets, F, G, D, c, A,
  B-flat), 18, 19, 94; op. 29 (String
  Quintet, C), 53, 59; op. 59 (Three
  String Quartets ['Razumovsky'], F, e,
  C), 151–2, op. 74 (String Quartet
  ['Harp'], E-flat), 18, 36; op. 127
  (String Quartet, E-flat), 60–1, 67,
  Weber review, 68, 93–4; op. 130
  (String Quartet, B-flat), 42, 88, 92;
  op. 131 (String Quartet, c-sharp), 92,
  95, Rochlitz' critique 36, 43, Weber
  critique, 68, Seyfried critique, 88; op.
  132 (String Quartet, a), 42, 92, Marx
  critique, 57–8, Weiler, 94; op. 133
  (*Grosse Fuge*, B-flat), 67; op. 135
  (String Quartet, F), 62, 94, 'M.'
  critique, 58, Marx critique, 57–8,
  Weiler critique, 94; **Chamber Music
  for Wind alone and with Strings**, op.
  20 (Septet, D-flat), 19; **Concertos**, op.
  37 (Piano Concerto no. 3, c), 13, 14,
  19–20, 78; op. 58 (Piano Concerto
  no. 4, G), 19, 146; **Choral Works with
  Orchestra**, op. 85 (*Christus am
  Oelberge*), 19–20; op. 112 (Goethe's
  Meeresstille und glückliche Fahrt), 40,
  54–5, 61; op. 121 (*Opferlied*), 40; op.
  122 (*Bundeslied*), 40, 61; **Incidental
  Music**, op. 84 (*Egmont*), Hoffmann
  review 21, 24, 26, images, 72; op. 113
  (von Kotzebue's *The Ruins of Athens*),
  59; op. 117 (von Kotzebue's *King
  Stephen*), 59; **Masses**, op. 86 (Mass, C),
  Hoffmann critique, 21, Marx critique,
  24, 25–6; op. 123 (*Missa Solemnis*),
  40, 42, Fröhlich, 96–9, Seyfried, 88,
  Weber, 68; **Opera**, op. 72 (*Fidelio*), 19,
  168n46, Beethoven on, 38, Marx
  critique, 56, origin, 31, Wendt review,
  26–7, 29–31, 34–5, 169n57;
  Orchestral, op. 21 (Symphony no. 1, C),
  167n22; op. 36 (Symphony no. 2, D),
  19–20, 108; op. 55 (Symphony no. 3
  ['Eroica']), 13–15, 19, 62, funeral march,

Beethoven, L. van: works, (contd)
62, Marx review, 47, 48–9, Schindler,
106, unity, 14, von Weber, 100–1;
op. 56 (['Triple Concerto'], C), 19–20;
op. 62 (Overture to Collin's *Coriolan*,
c), 19, 24, Hoffmann review, 21, 24;
op. 67 (Symphony no. 5, c), 2, 19, 62,
74, 126–43, Berlioz' critique, 78, 125,
134–6, 138–43, Hoffmann critique, 7,
20–6, 31, 34–5, 49, 52, 78, 129–40,
142–3, Marx critique, 128–30, 132–9,
140–2, 143; op. 91 (*Wellington's Sieg
bei Vittoria*, also *Wellington's
Victory*), 35–6, 38, 67, Weber, 65, 69,
71; op. 92 (Symphony no. 7, A), 93,
association with *Wellington's Victory*,
35, 36, Berlioz' critique, 42, 111–13,
Fétis, 113–15, synthesis, 62–3, op. 93
(Symphony no. 8, F), 37, 93,
association with *Wellington's Victory*,
36; op. 125 (Symphony no. 9, d), 37,
42, 68, 71, 73–92, 120, Berlioz' review,
122–3, French reactions, 109–10,
118–19, 121, 122–4, Fröhlich, 77, 121,
Grossheim critique, 119, journal
reactions, 40, 65, 67, 170n3, Kanne,
86, Marx's review, 55–7, 59, *Ode to
Joy*, 56, 74, 87, Fétis, 118–19,
Grossheim, 119, Seyfried, 100, Urhan,
121, *see also* Schiller, union of poetry
and music, 73, 82, Seyfried, 88,
Stoepel, 119, Urhan critique, 121–2;
op. 138 (Overture ['Leonore no. 1'],
C), 19; Tenth Symphony, 57; **Piano
Sonatas**, op. 2 (Sonata no. 1, f, Sonata
no. 2, A, Sonata no. 3, C), 49; op. 10
(Sonata no. 5, c, Sonata no. 6, F,
Sonata no. 7, D), 8–9; op. 13 (Sonata
no. 8 ['Pathétique'], c), 9, 14, 78; op.
26 (Sonata no. 12, A-flat), 10, 80–1;
op. 27/2 (Sonata no. 14 ['Moonlight'],
c-sharp), 10, 18, 78; op. 28 (Sonata no.
15 ['Pastoral'], D), 11, Berlioz, 111,
116, Debussy, 116, Fétis, 115–18,
170n11; op. 57 (Sonata no. 23, f
['Appassionata']), 18, 78; op. 90
(Sonata no. 27, e), 93; op. 101 (Sonata
no. 28, A), 41; op. 106 (Sonata no. 29
['Hammerklavier'], B-flat), 40, 41, 92;
op. 109 (Sonata no. 30, E), 39, 61, 63;
op. 110 (Sonata no. 31, A-flat), 39, 61,
92, Marx, 53–4; op. 111 (Sonata no.
32, c), 39–40, 58; **Piano Variations**,
WoO 72 (Eight Variations on the
Romance 'Une fièvre brûlante'), 7;
WoO 73 (Ten Variations on the Duet
'La stessa, la stessissima'), 7; op. 35

('Eroica Variations'), 11–12, 17; WoO
78 (Seven Variations on 'God Save the
King', C), 19; WoO 79 (Five Variations
on 'Rule Britannia', D), 19; WoO 80
(32 Variations on an Original Theme,
c), 18–19; op. 120 (['Diabelli']
Variations), 40, 92; **Shorter Piano
Pieces**, op. 126 (Six Bagatelles, G, g,
D-flat, b, G, D-flat), 60–2; **Solo
Voices and Orchestra**, op. 65 (['Ah
perfido'] concert aria), 19; op. 116
(Bettoni's 'Tremate, empi, tremati'
Trio), 40; op. 118 (Elegy, 'Sanft wie
du lebtest'), 57; **Songs**, op. 48 (Six
Songs, or *Gellert-Lieder*), 18; op. 98
(cycle of six songs), 41; op. 107
(Scottish Songs), 60; op. 108 (Scottish
Songs), 60
Berlioz, Hector: Fifth Symphony, 78, 125,
134, 135–6, 138–9, 140–3; Seventh
Symphony, 42, 111–13; Ninth
Symphony, 109–10, 122–3, extra-
musical program, 70, 173n48; as
French critic, 108–9, 117–18;
'Pastoral' Symphony, 116; theories,
110–11, 123
Bloom, Peter Anthony, 106
Breitkopf und Härtel, 5, 9, 67, 141,
167n18

Caec., 170n3; *see also* appropriate critics
and contributors
Castile-Blaze: Seventh Symphony, 115;
descriptive metaphors, 117; as French
critic, 108–9; 'Pastoral' Symphony,
115–17
Collin, 24, 26

Dahlhaus, Carl, 2, 148–9
Debussy, Claude, 116
Dilthey, Wilhelm, 144, 148
Dittersdorf, Karl Ditters von, 59

Einstein, Alfred, 1–2, 72
Engell, James, 3
Enlightenment, 32, 33; *see also*
Aristotelianism
expression, aesthetic of, 2, 3, 34, 146
extra-musical interpretations, 3, 62, 144,
146; allusions, 23, 115, 126; approach,
128; associations, 26; Berlioz, 70,
111–12, 128; French reactions, 70,
111–12, 117; Hoffmann, 23, 26, 126,
129–31, 136, 139; ideas, 46, 111–12;
Marx, 128, 133; op. 126, 62; 'Pastoral'
Symphony, program, 70

Index

Fétis, François-Joseph: Seventh
Symphony, 113–15; Ninth Symphony,
109–10; as French critic, 108–9;
'Pastoral' Symphony, 115–18
Fichte, Johann Gottlieb, 67; subjective
idealism, 33, 34
Fink, Christian Gottfried Wilhelm, 36
formalism, 82, 124–5; Hanslick, 144
Fröhlich, Franz Joseph, 78, 81, 82,
171n29; Ninth Symphony, 77, 83–7,
89, 121; *Missa Solemnis*, 96–9; on
music and speech, 82–4, 86, 91

Goethe, Johann Wolfgang von: *Egmont*,
21, 24, 26, 72; *Meeresstille und
glückliche Fahrt*, 40, 54–5, 61 (op.
112)
Grempler, Ingeborg, 106
Grétry, André-Ernest-Modeste, 81; anti-
Romanticism, 82; on music and speech,
78, 80, 120; 'Une fièvre brûlante', 7, 8,
167n7
Grossheim, Dr, 119; Ninth Symphony,
87–8; *Missa Solemnis*, 99
Grundidee, 59, 82

Habeneck, F.A., 108, 115
Hanslick, Eduard, 2, 35, 144; extra-
musical associations, 146; Marx, 51,
128
Haydn, Joseph, 22, 37, 59, 107–8, 136;
Grétry, 79; Marx, 49; on music and
speech, 79, 82; Wendt, 27–8
Hegel, G.W.F., 46, 131; Kant, 147;
Marx, 27, 42, 50, 51, 58, 64,
compared, 147; music aesthetics, 52;
Wendt, 30
hermeneutics, 148, 166n6
Hiller, Adam, 43
Hoffmann, E.T.A., 1–3, 6, 37, 40, 128;
Fifth Symphony, 7, 11, 20–6, 78,
129–40, 142–3; Ninth Symphony, 74;
Fröhlich, 87; general criticism, 123,
124, 126; idealism, 32–5, 50; Kanne,
72–3; 'Pastoral' Symphony, 170n11;
Wendt, 27–35, 72–3; word choice, 15,
16; *see also* spirit-kingdom
Hosler, Bellamy, 33, 34

idealism, 1–3, 70, 71, 144–5; Ninth
Symphony, 118; Fichte, 33, 34; French
reaction, 122, 144–5; Hoffmann, 32,
40, 50; Kanne, 72; Marx, 48, 50;
Schopenhauer, 3; Wendt, 32

Jean Paul: Scheller's Platonism, 95; unity,
27

Jander, Owen, 146

Kaiser, Georg, 65, 103
Kanne, Friedrich August, 17, 18, 42, 65–6,
89; Third Piano Concerto, 78; Ninth
Symphony, 86; Berlioz, 122; on music
and poetry, 86, 91; tone-painting,
72–3, 75–7; Weber, 103; word choice,
23
Kant, Immanuel, 2, 3, 33–5, 80, 106;
Marx, 146–7; on music, 79, 146–7
Kerman, Joseph, 152
Kirchmeyer, Helmut, 63, 66, 67, 68
Kivy, Peter, 145, 148, 149
Koch, Heinrich Christoph, 91, 127
Kretzschmar, Hermann, 148

Lang, Paul Henry, 2, 70, 105, 111, 114,
116
Langer, Susanne, 145, 148
Levy, David Benjamin, 73, 118
literature, 104; French, 2, 70, 115;
interpretation, 146, 148; metaphors in
reviews, 95; Shakespeare, 121; Wendt,
72

'M.', 53, 58, 59
Marx, Adolf Bernhard, 27, 38, 45; Fifth
Symphony, 128–30, 132–43, 146;
aesthetic theories, 33, 35, 47, 69, 85,
88–9, 124–5, extra-musical approach,
146, form, 124–5, tone-painting, 47,
118; Fröhlich, 77, 87; Lang, 70;
Mattheson, 79; method of criticism,
126–7; 'Pastoral' Symphony, 47;
Ueber Malerei in der Tonkunst, 47, 51,
88–9, 118; *see also* Hegel
Mattheson, Johann, 33, 34, 51, 79
Mozart, Wolfgang Amadeus, 22, 62;
Apel, 80; 'Bei Männern, welche Liebe
fühlen', 11; 'Ein Mädchen oder
Weibchen', 7; Rochlitz, 44; spurious
work, 8, 167n7; Wendt, 27–8

N.E., 61
neoclassicism, 117

Platonism, 29; Schelling, 95
program music, 146; Berlioz, 122; French
appreciation, 114; literary metaphors
in reviews, 95; 'Pastoral' Symphony,
48; representation, 2, 104, 105

Rellstab, Ludwig, 53, 61; von Weber,
67–8
representative music, *see* program
music

183

Rochlitz, Friedrich, 5, 8, 27, 37–8, 91, 167n12; aesthetic theory, 79; Apel, 80–2; as editor, 9–10, 16–17; Kirchmeyer, 66–7; late music, 43, 44; 'Pastoral' Symphony, 19, 170n11

Romanticism, 1–3, 16, 73, 80; anti-Romanticism, 82, 144, 146; characteristics, 44, 72; crisis, 39; Engell, 3; Fröhlich, 83; 'greater Romantic lyric', 150; Grétry, 82; harmony, 59; Hoffmann, 22, 26, 72; Kanne, 72; Marx, 51–2, 72; music, 28, 31–2, 124, 125; Schlegel, 43; Schopenhauer, 43; sublime, 2, 32; tone-painting, 71; Weber, 71; Wendt, 33–5

Rossini, Giacomo, 37

Schelling, F. W. J. von: absolutism, 3; aesthetics, 29, 33–4, 72; Hoffmann, 28; Wendt, 28

Schering, Arnold, 146, 148–9

Schiller, Friedrich, 31, 74, 87, 118–19; Apel, 80

Schindler, Anton: von Weber, 102, 106

Schlegel, August Wilhelm: Christian transcendentalism, 28–9; Hoffmann, 28–9, 32; Romanticism, 43; Wendt, 28–9; word choice, 32

Schnaus, Peter: Hoffmann's criticism, 15–16, 21, Fifth Symphony, 130–1; Hoffmann's word choice, 16

Schönberg, Arnold, 38

Schopenhauer, Arthur, 3, 32–3, 51, 81, 171n29; absolutism, 91; *Die Welt als Wille und Vorstellung*, 31, 70; Romanticism, 43

Schrade, Leo, 106–7; Castile-Blaze, 109; Lang, 111

Schumann, Robert, 38, 63, 66

Seyfried, Ignaz von, 93; *Missa Solemnis*, 88–9, 92, 99–100; on music and speech, 91; op. 131, 88–9

Shakespeare, William: characters, 134; comparison to Beethoven, 27, 30, 121; Urhan, 121

Slonimsky, Nicolas, 1, 69

Solomon, Maynard, 146

spirit-kingdom: Fifth Symphony, 139; as a constant, 133; Hoffmann's, 22, 23, 24, 25, 35, 78; Hoffmann and Wendt's,

48, non-objective, 34; supra-sensory word, 49, 50

Stoepel, François: Ninth Symphony, 119–20

Tieck, Ludwig: absolutism, 91; aesthetics, 51; Hoffmann, 32; influence, 147–8

tone-painting, 39, 40, 117, 146; French reaction, 117; Fröhlich, 99; Kanne, 69–73, 75; Marx, 46, 47, 70–1, 118, 128; theory, 48–9, development of music, 50; universal affections, 51; Weber, 69–73

tone-poems, 57

transcendentalism, 22, 80, 122; Fifth Symphony, 2; Christian, 28–9; Hoffmann, 128; world-soul, 96

Treitler, Leo: analysis, 84, 127

unity: Ninth Symphony, 122; Berlioz, 122; 'Eroica' Symphony, 14; Hoffmann, 129, 131–2; Marx, 49, 130; 'Moonlight' Sonata, 10; op. 102, 49; 'Pathétique' Sonata, 9

Urhan, Chrétien: Ninth Symphony, 109, 121–2; Berlioz, 117; on music and speech, 123

v.d.O..r., 53, 60–1

Wackenroder, Wilhelm: absolutism, 91, aesthetics, 51, Hoffmann, 32; influence, 147–8

Wagner, Richard, 2, 57; Ninth Symphony, 67; theories, 35

WAMZ, see appropriate critics and contributors

Warrack, John, 100–3

Weber, Carl Maria von, 65, 67; *Euryanthe*, 102, 103; Nägeli, 101; Warrack, 100, 101, 103

Weber, Gottfried, 38, 42, 65, 68; tone-painting, 69–73, 117

Weiler, von: Seventh Symphony, 112; Woldemar, 94–5

Wendt, Amadeus, 27–35, 66, 67, 69; *Fidelio*, 27–31, 123, 169n57; Hoffmann, 72–3; idealism, 32–3, 70

Woldemar, Ernst, 41; late music, 65, 66–7, 69; Weber, 68

Zeitgeist, 144, 150